The Future Is Degrowth

The Future Is Degrowth

A Guide to a World beyond Capitalism

Matthias Schmelzer
Andrea Vetter
Aaron Vansintjan

VERSO
London • New York

First published by Verso 2022

1 3 5 7 9 10 8 6 4 2

Verso
UK: 6 Meard Street, London W1F 0EG
US: 388 Atlantic Avenue, Brooklyn, NY 11217
versobooks.com

Verso is the imprint of New Left Books

ISBN-13: 978-1-83976-584-1
ISBN-13: 978-1-83976-585-8 (UK EBK)
ISBN-13: 978-1-83976-586-5 (US EBK)

British Library Cataloguing in Publication Data
A catalogue record for this book is available from the British Library

Library of Congress Cataloging-in-Publication Data
Names: Schmelzer, Matthias, author.
Title: The future is degrowth : a guide to a world beyond capitalism /
  Matthias Schmelzer, Aaron Vansintjan, Andrea Vetter.
Description: New York : Verso, 2022. | Includes bibliographical references
  and index.
Identifiers: LCCN 2022005477 (print) | LCCN 2022005478 (ebook) | ISBN
  9781839765841 (Trade Paperback) | ISBN 9781839765865 (eBook)
Subjects: LCSH: Negative growth (Economics) | Economic development. |
  Imperialism. | Exploitation. | Capitalism.
Classification: LCC HD75.6 .S375 2022 (print) | LCC HD75.6 (ebook) | DDC
  330.9--dc23/eng/20220223
LC record available at https://lccn.loc.gov/2022005477
LC ebook record available at https://lccn.loc.gov/2022005478

Typeset in Minion by Hewer Text UK Ltd, Edinburgh
Printed and bound by CPI Group (UK) Ltd, Croydon CR0 4YY

Contents

Preface

Over the last fifteen years, degrowth has made significant contributions: it has helped to politicize the debate on sustainability and development, question green growth and technologically focused futurism, strengthen utopian alternatives, and bring together social movements, academics, and those engaged in the solidarity economy and civil society. During times of intense and continuous crisis, the degrowth community has become a gathering place for people who are seeking answers to how we got in this mess in the first place, and how we can get out of it. This book describes the debates that have happened within this community, and relays them to a wider audience.

This is an expanded version of an original German book, first published in 2019, *Degrowth/Postwachstum zur Einführung*, written by Matthias Schmelzer and Andrea Vetter. For the English version, we worked with Aaron Vansintjan to extend it for an international audience, changing it significantly in terms of structure, argumentation, and content. Many people and organizations have been instrumental in making this book a reality. We would like to thank our publisher, Verso Books, who gave us the opportunity to bring the degrowth debate to the centre of the English-speaking left. The writing of this book was made possible by several institutions: the Konzeptwerk Neue Ökonomie (Laboratory for a New Economy) in Leipzig enabled Andrea and

Matthias to work in a self-organized collective at the interface of NGOs and social movements doing organizing and outreach around social and ecological justice and alternative economics. The 'Post-Growth Societies' research group at the Friedrich-Schiller-University Jena, which played a key role in shaping and advancing the academic debate on capitalist growth drivers and post-growth, as well as the follow-up 'flumen' project, provided an intellectual context for working on and discussing this book. The Barcelona Degrowth Reading Group and the organization Research & Degrowth have also been crucial through providing a supportive and critically engaged environment for learning about degrowth. Also, we are grateful for the financial support of the Rosa Luxemburg Foundation in New York City, who made it possible for Aaron to work on the book. Finally, during the process of writing this book, we were all involved with and learned from various social movements. Without the support of all of these, this book would not exist.

Degrowth thinkers, following feminist theories of science, point out that there can be no 'neutral' science but that the production of knowledge is always bound to a specific location. This introduction has been written by three politically engaged academics who are part of a wider community, the members of which have shaped and transformed our thinking. Even so, in this book, we have sought to balance a thorough and fair representation of degrowth with a critical engagement with those same ideas. We hope that we have succeeded in this effort.

We also want to thank all the individuals who made the creation of this book possible and accompanied it through intensive and often critical discussions. In particular, we want to thank Frank Adler, Max Ajl, Bengi Akbulut, Rut Elliot Blomqvist, Ulrich Brand, Ky Brooks, Hubertus Buchstein, Michaela Christ, Silke van Dyk, Dennis Eversberg, Christoph Gran, Friederike Habermann, Lina Hansen, Giorgos Kallis, Vijay Kolinjivadi, Martin Krobath, Cornelia Kühn, Steffen Lange, Steffen Liebig, Eva Mahnke, Christoph Sanders, Tilman Santarius, Ulrich Schachtschneider, Bernd Sommer, and Nina Treu. We also thank the German publisher Junius for making this English book possible. All errors and inaccuracies are of course the sole responsibility of the authors.

We hope that this book can be an inspiration to think differently about today and tomorrow, to continue researching ways beyond growth, and to strengthen social movements that aim at building a future for all beyond capitalism.

Matthias Schmelzer, Andrea Vetter, and Aaron Vansintjan
Berlin and Montreal, December 2021

1

Introduction

In April 2020, a group of academics in the Netherlands wrote a manifesto for a post-pandemic recovery. This manifesto, with its five demands based on the principles of a little-known 'degrowth' movement, gained widespread attention. In this moment of insecurity and destabilization, it pushed the degrowth agenda into Dutch mainstream media and the traditional corridors of power, and it was discussed on prime-time television and in parliament. The claim that the neoliberal and growth-based model of development underpins many of our current crises – including the coronavirus pandemic – resonated with many, as did the call for a strategy to reorient the conversation away from symptoms and towards underlying causes. The manifesto made five key policy proposals:

1. A move away from development focused on aggregate GDP growth (economic growth is conventionally measured as increasing gross domestic product, or GDP) to differentiate between sectors that can grow and need investment (the so-called critical public sectors, clean energy, education, health, and more) and sectors that must radically degrow due to their fundamental unsustainability or their role in driving continuous and excessive consumption (especially private sector oil, gas, mining, advertising, and so forth);

2. An economic framework focused on redistribution, which estab-
    lishes a universal basic income rooted in a universal social policy
    system, a strong progressive taxation of income, profits, and
    wealth, reduced working hours and job sharing, and which recog-
    nizes care work and essential public services such as health and
    education for their intrinsic value;

3. Agricultural transformation towards regenerative agriculture
    based on biodiversity conservation, sustainable and mostly local
    and vegetarian food production, as well as fair agricultural
    employment conditions and wages;

4. Reduction of consumption and travel, with a drastic shift from
    luxury and wasteful consumption and travel to basic, necessary,
    sustainable, and satisfying consumption and travel;

5. Debt cancellation, especially for workers and small business
    owners and for countries in the Global South (both from richer
    countries and international financial institutions).[1]

Whether these proposals really grasp the core of degrowth will become
clear throughout the rest of this book. We feature them in full here to
highlight how the economic crisis caused by the pandemic has shifted
the conversation around economic growth. On the one hand, as illustrated by the Dutch example (and we will cite several others later on), a
widespread feeling – encapsulated in the slogan that went viral, 'We
don't want to get back to normal, since normalcy was the problem' –
created a window of opportunity for degrowth ideas to become known
and see more widespread support.

On the other hand, and likely as a reaction to the increasing popularity of degrowth ideas, major newspapers from *Forbes* to the *Financial
Times* and *The Spectator* started to publish opinion pieces that frontally
attacked degrowth. These argued that 'the coronavirus crisis reveals the
misery of degrowth', that degrowth would make the recession

---

1 Degrowth.info international editorial team, 'Planning for Post-corona: Five
Proposals to Craft a Radically More Sustainable and Equal World', *Degrowth*
(blog), 11 May 2020, degrowth.info. See also Feminisms and Degrowth Alliance,
'Feminist Degrowth Reflections on COVID-19 and the Politics of Social
Reproduction', *Degrowth* (blog), 20 April 2020, degrowth.info.

permanent, or that it would be a 'recipe for misery and disaster'.[2] And, indeed, this is how many people initially understand degrowth, as a call for economic recession, austere lifestyles, romantic luddism – as a reaction against progress. However, as we will argue throughout the book, recessions and what happened during the pandemic do not represent degrowth, far from it.

So, what is this idea that, at the height of the pandemic, sparked a debate about radical alternatives, as illustrated by the Dutch manifesto, and which also provoked intense reactions from the establishment, as illustrated by the ongoing wave of half-baked opinion pieces lambasting degrowth?

'Degrowth' is a term that is increasingly mobilized by scholars and activists to criticize the hegemony of growth – and a proposal for a radical reorganization of society that leads to a drastic reduction in the use of energy and resources and that is deemed necessary, desirable, and possible. Degrowth starts from the fact – demonstrated by an increasing number of studies – that further economic growth in industrialized countries is unsustainable. Even if that growth is 'green' or 'inclusive', or even as part of a transformative progressive agenda that massively invests in renewable energies and the sustainability transition, industrialized countries cannot reduce their environmental impact (emissions, material throughput, etc.) fast and sufficiently enough while, at the same time, growing their economies. The transformation needed in industrialized countries – if they are to reduce their emissions and environmental impacts fast enough to leave space for the Global South to develop – will also lead to reducing the size of Global North economies.[3] While

---

2 Benedict McAleenan, 'The Coronavirus Crisis Reveals the Misery of Degrowth', Spectator.co.uk, 27 March 2020.

3 For some recent papers linking to more evidence, see Jason Hickel and Giorgos Kallis, 'Is Green Growth Possible?', *New Political Economy* 25, no. 4 (April 2019): 1–18; Timothée Parrique et al., *Decoupling Debunked: Evidence and Arguments against Green Growth as a Sole Strategy for Sustainability* (Brussels: EEB, 2019); Thomas Wiedmann et al., 'Scientists' Warning on Affluence', *Nature Communications* 11, no. 1 (2020): 3107; Helmut Haberl et al., 'A Systematic Review of the Evidence on Decoupling of GDP, Resource Use and GHG Emissions, Part II: Synthesizing the Insights', *Environmental Research Letters* 15, no. 6 (2020): 065003.

this need for sufficiency, a reduction of the material throughput for the most affluent, or an end to overconsumption may sound radical to many, it is increasingly common ground among ecologically oriented progressives. For example, Naomi Klein writes in her recent book that lays out the case for a Green New Deal:

> The bottom line is that an ecological crisis that has its roots in the overconsumption of natural resources must be addressed not just by improving the efficiency of our economies, but also by reducing the amount of material stuff that the wealthiest 20 percent of people on the planet consume.[4]

Degrowth claims that such a transformation in the Global North is not only possible but also desirable: it is feasible to live well without growth and to make society more just, democratic, and truly prosperous on the way. To do this, however, a fundamental political and economic reorganization of society is necessary, which aims at overcoming multiple structural growth dependencies inherent in the capitalist economy – from industrialized infrastructures to social systems to the ideological myths of growth societies. More specifically, degrowth can be defined as the democratic transition to a society that – in order to enable global ecological justice – is based on a much smaller throughput of energy and resources, that deepens democracy and guarantees a good life and social justice for all, and that does not depend on continuous expansion (see chapter 4 for a more thorough exposition of this definition). Before explaining where degrowth comes from and what exactly it proposes, we start by situating ourselves in a particular moment, showing why degrowth has taken such a crucial place in the political landscape today.

Why degrowth and not a Green New Deal?

It has been noted for decades, but by now everybody can see it clearly: we live in a time of many and accelerating crises. Climate breakdown

---

4 Naomi Klein, *On Fire: The Burning Case for a Green New Deal* (London: Penguin, 2019), 100.

is breathing down our neck. Biodiversity is collapsing in ecosystems around the world, and many natural safety nets – water cycles, soil fertility, fish stocks, microbial diversity – are unravelling. Civil war and natural disasters have ripped whole countries apart, sending millions of people to seek safety – only to be blocked by militarized borders. A pandemic has brought the global economy to a shuddering halt. Financial and economic crises roil the world roughly every decade. There is a resurgence of nationalist and racist electoral parties. Meanwhile, mass movements arise every year to demand change, blocking business as usual. While leaders have promised prosperity and a middle-class lifestyle for all decades ago, those standards of living are becoming less and less attainable for most, as high levels of stable employment tilt towards precarity and endemic unemployment.

Which proposals might get us out of this mess? Here, we find it useful to borrow a term from Immanuel Wallerstein, the world-systems theorist. In the 2000s – during what we could now consider the heyday of neoliberalism and the corresponding global movements against it – Wallerstein suggested that there were two main political camps: the 'Spirit of Davos', where the world's economic and political elites meet at the annual World Economic Forum, and the 'Spirit of Porto Alegre', the birthplace of the World Social Forums, where the world's popular social movements come together. Today, these camps have been split into two poles each.[5]

On the Davos side, there are not only the globalists, many of whom are in favour of green capitalism, but also feudal authoritarians and neo-fascists, as represented in particular by Donald Trump in the United States, Jair Bolsonaro in Brazil, and Rodrigo Duterte in the Philippines. The globalists recognize the reality of climate change, and advocate ecological modernization and green growth. They think there is no need to fundamentally change the current system – we just need better technology, more efficiency, and the proper application of science

---

5 Immanuel Wallerstein et al., *Does Capitalism Have a Future?* (New York: Oxford University Press, 2013), 45.

and market mechanisms.[6] Just replace what we have now with electric cars, carbon capture and storage, green appliances, and renewable and nuclear energy – and the problem is solved. Neo-fascists, by contrast, are more explicitly in favour of a kind of eco-apartheid: close the borders to migrants fleeing ecological collapse and the ravages of capitalist globalization, expand military powers to defend the privileges of those who have benefited from economic growth, further entrench the global division of labour, and accelerate the extraction of resources. What drives this reactionary idea is the willingness to change everything *in order to preserve* what is seen as the natural order of things. Ultimately, this proposal will lead to a world more unequal than the one that exists today and will still cause the wide-scale collapse of the present system. Importantly, both camps – the globalists and the neofascists – favour growth; they just support different means to attain it.[7]

On the other side, the Porto Alegre camp also has two poles. On the one hand, there is progressive productivism: those parts of the left that – in the tradition of socialist and social-democratic workers' movements – focus on growth, increases in technical productivity, and redistribution, and that tend to prefer vertical forms of organization. Often, these leftists argue for keeping existing technological infrastructure, but seek to make it more efficient and socially just through centralized and hierarchical state planning. Proposals for utopias based on overcoming work through productivity increases or a 'fully automated

6 John Asafu-Adjaye et al., 'An Ecomodernist Manifesto', ecomodernism.org, 2015; Steven Pinker, *Enlightenment Now: The Case for Reason, Science, Humanism, and Progress* (London: Penguin Books, 2018); Giorgos Kallis and Sam Bliss, 'Post-environmentalism: Origins and Evolution of a Strange Idea', *Journal of Political Ecology* 26, no. 1 (2019): 466–85.

7 Harsha Walia, *Border and Rule: Global Migration, Capitalism, and the Rise of Racist Nationalism* (Haymarket Books, 2021); Andreas Malm and the Zetkin Collective, *White Skin, Black Fuel: On the Danger of Fossil Fascism* (London: Verso, 2021). As we discuss in section 3.8, criticism of growth also exists in the Davos camp, above all in the form of enlightened conservatism and in parts of the ethnic and nationalist right. But, by and large, the dominant project of the right today is that of more growth – and, given that the right fundamentally aims to strengthen social hierarchies, it will likely stay ideologically in the service of economic growth.

luxury communism' also fall in this camp.[8] Let us call this 'left productivism'. On the other hand, there are the libertarian movements and currents that strongly focus on self-organization from below and that fundamentally question growth – we could call this 'left libertarianism'. This pole positions itself against hierarchy and productivism, and seeks to fundamentally alter global relations towards a multi-polar, post-growth internationalism. Today, degrowth has become one of the key reference points within left libertarianism in the Global North – or, as put in a recent volume, within the 'mosaic of alternatives' that fight for a good life beyond growth, industrialism, and domination.[9]

In the last half-decade, one phrase has been at the centre of both controversies and potential alliances between the productivist and libertarian poles: the Green New Deal. Some watered-down versions of a Green New Deal or 'Green Deal' are promoted by governments, international organizations, and the European Commission, which essentially boil down to the ecological modernization of capitalism. These would be considered green growth globalism, firmly placed in the Davos camp.

But we are here only interested in the more transformative leftist variants. Long a set of policies for transition upheld by Green Party candidates, the Green New Deal is increasingly becoming a cornerstone of radical environmental politics and also larger political parties, such as the Labour Party in the UK and parts of the Democratic Party in the United States.[10] The basic proposal seeks – through public investment and regulations – to radically reduce fossil fuel consumption and

---

8 Aaron Bastani, *Fully Automated Luxury Communism. A Manifesto* (London: Verso, 2019); Paul Mason, *PostCapitalism: A Guide to Our Future* (London: Penguin Books, 2015).

9 Corinna Burkhart, Matthias Schmelzer, and Nina Treu, eds., *Degrowth in Movement(s): Exploring Pathways for Transformation* (Winchester: Zer0, 2020). Globally, the situation is of course much more complex. See, for example, Max Ajl, *A People's Green New Deal* (London: Pluto Press, 2021).

10 Similar proposals have been presented in South Korea, New Zealand, and the European Parliament. See, for example, Ann Pettifor, *The Case for the Green New Deal* (London: Verso, 2019); Ajl, *A People's Green New Deal*; Noam Chomsky and Robert Pollin, *Climate Crisis and the Global Green New Deal: The Political Economy of Saving the Planet* (London: Verso, 2020).

transition to a fully renewable economy, while guaranteeing just working conditions and full employment, as well as vastly improved living conditions, for all, and in particular for marginalized communities. Inspired by the New Deal carried out by US president Franklin D. Roosevelt following the Great Depression in the 1930s, the idea is for a large-scale mobilization and public investment programme of green Keynesianism that fundamentally restructures the economy.

While at first sight it appears that there is stark opposition between these more transformative, leftist Green New Deals and degrowth, we argue throughout the book that there are many overlaps and similarities, that there is a wide scope for learning from each other and for collaborations, and that degrowth offers an important corrective for existing Green New Deal proposals. Degrowth's particular strengths include its strong analysis of the biophysical metabolism of capitalism, the global justice and resource implications of ecological modernization, the ideological hegemony perpetuated by growth-based economics, and its advancement of more deeply transformative policy proposals for an economy based on autonomy, care, and sufficiency.[11]

What distinguishes degrowth most clearly from other socio-ecological proposals is the politicization of social metabolism and its ramifications for policy design. Degrowth shares with most programmes of ecological modernization – and with the Green New Deals – the call for massive investments into rapidly building up the material infrastructures for a post-fossil society, from (community-controlled) renewable energy sources to (democratically managed) public transport networks, to retrofitted (social or collective) housing, or to (worker-owned) industrial plants (such as for long-lasting, repairable, and recyclable consumer products). Similar to the outlook of Kate Aronoff, Alyssa Battistoni, Daniel A. Cohen, and Thea Riofrancos in *A*

---

11 Robert Pollin, 'De-growth vs a Green New Deal', *New Left Review* 112 (2018): 5–25. There are, of course, also a number of key lessons for degrowth. See, for example, Riccardo Mastini, Giorgos Kallis, and Jason Hickel, 'A Green New Deal without Growth?', *Ecological Economics* 179 (2021): 106832; Elena Hofferberth and Matthias Schmelzer, 'Degrowth vs Green New Deal: Gekoppelt wird ein Schuh draus', *politische ökologie* 159 (2019): 31–7.

Planet to Win, degrowth also calls for 'a "Last Stimulus" of green economic development in the short term to build landscapes of public affluence, develop new political-economic models, jump off the growth treadmill, break with capital, and settle into a slower groove'.[12] However, the degrowth analysis – which takes into account extensive research on climate injustice and the possibilities of decoupling emissions from economic growth – posits that this needs to be accompanied by an economy-wide transition beyond economic growth. These studies show that a Green New Deal with growth – even if temporary – will likely be not sustainable.

Thus, while Green New Deal proposals tend to emphasize this investment push and the growth of everything sustainable, degrowth *also and at least as rigorously* puts the focus on the many things that will have to go. To bring about a globally just and sustainable economy, large areas of production and consumption will need to be dismantled, while other systems will need to be built in their place. In contrast to most Green New Deals, degrowth formulates active policies to achieve a selective downscaling and de-accumulation of those economic activities that cannot be made sustainable, contribute little use values, or are superfluous consumption – and these include things like advertising, planned obsolescence, 'bullshit jobs', private planes, or fossil fuel and defence industries. Degrowth claims that there is a need to reduce energy and material throughput to avoid ecological overshoot. Furthermore, the necessary policies that put a cap on emissions, rapidly curb fossil production, and end overconsumption will likely lead to a reduction of GDP. While this might not be bad in and of itself (as GDP is a highly problematic indicator), societies need to be prepared by reorganizing institutions so that they are no longer dependent on growth and accumulation.[13]

There is certainly a tension that needs to be addressed here, since

12 Kate Aronoff et al., *A Planet to Win: Why We Need a Green New Deal* (London: Verso, 2019), 35f.

13 For details, see chapters 4 and 5. See also Kai Kuhnhenn et al., *A Societal Transformation Scenario for Staying Below 1.5°C* (Berlin: Konzeptwerk Neue Ökonomie & Heinrich-Böll Stiftung, 2020); Mastini et al., 'A Green New Deal without Growth?'.

Green New Deal platforms are either in favour of economic growth or vague on whether the goal is growth, even as they propose policies that will in fact spur economic expansion.[14] So, how could the 'last stimulus' of the Green New Deal be combined with more transformative policies? These policies should, on the one hand, aim at degrowing those areas of production and consumption that are related to excess energy, mass, and emissions and, on the other hand, ensure that these investments do not merely stabilize an economic system built around growth and accumulation, but initiate its transformation. Furthermore, Green New Deal platforms have been criticized for simply continuing, rather than challenging, uneven neo-colonial relationships between industrialized countries and the rest of the world.[15] For example, by expanding solar power and lithium battery storage technology without taking apart the unequal relationships between rich countries buying lithium and poor countries mining it, the Green New Deal may just create new problems and entrench neo-colonialism.[16]

Degrowth, we argue in this book, offers perspectives that should be productively integrated and critically adapted into progressive politics, including those of what has been proposed as a 'Green New Deal without Growth'. Proponents of degrowth are therefore not only faced with the challenge of organizing social majorities for a political project in the face of a shift to the right which advocates growth-oriented authoritarianism, as well as the continued presence of fossil fuel–driven and green capitalism. It is also important to convince those who represent the

---

14 Pollin, 'De-growth vs a Green New Deal'; Giorgos Kallis, 'A Green New Deal Must Not Be Tied to Economic Growth', truthout.org, 10 March 2020; Aaron Vansintjan, 'Degrowth vs. the Green New Deal', Briarpatchmagazine.com, 29 April 2020; James Wilt and Max Ajl, 'Either You Are Fighting to Eliminate Exploitation or Not: A Leftist Critique of the Green New Deal', Canadiandimension. com, 14 June 2020.

15 Christos Zografos and Paul Robbins, 'Green Sacrifice Zones, or Why a Green New Deal Cannot Ignore the Cost Shifts of Just Transitions', One Earth 3, no. 5 (2020): 543–6; Stan Cox, The Green New Deal and Beyond: Ending the Climate Emergency While We Still Can (San Francisco: City Lights Books, 2020).

16 Jasper Bernes, 'Between the Devil and the Green New Deal', Commune, 25 April 2019: 151–60; Francis Tseng, 'Inside Out', Phenomenalworld.org, 17 April 2020; Kate Aronoff et al., A Planet to Win.

'Spirit of Porto Alegre' – but are also oriented towards productivism – of the merits of a degrowth society. In this way, degrowth advocates must navigate the multiple political realities that arise through repeated crises of the capitalist system and people's responses to these.

This book is one attempt at navigating these challenges: by showing how degrowth can respond to the crises we face, we seek not only to introduce the various critiques of growth and the vision, policies, and strategies of degrowth, but also make a case for a degrowth that specifically addresses capitalism and societal hierarchies, and to argue why the left should support it.

Where did degrowth come from?

Criticism of economic growth is almost as old as the phenomenon of economic growth itself. But the term 'degrowth', as it is used today, can be traced to relatively recent beginnings. Let us take a short look at its history. Some traditions of growth criticism date back to the late eighteenth century and ranged from Luddite riots against the machines of industrialization to romantic unease with modernity or anti-colonial dissections of European civilization. Yet, in the second half of the twentieth century, changed public perceptions of the finiteness of resources on this planet also led to a popular surge in critiques of economic growth. The first report to the Club of Rome in 1972 initiated a global debate on 'The Limits to Growth' which has not yet subsided. The birth of the word *décroissance*, translated into English as 'degrowth', can also be dated back to the year 1972. The political theorist André Gorz already asked at that time: 'Is the earth's balance, for which no-growth – or even degrowth – of material production is a necessary condition, compatible with the survival of the capitalist system?'[17] Other intellectuals of this

---

17 Quoted in Giacomo D'Alisa, Federico Demaria, and Giorgos Kallis, *Degrowth: A Vocabulary for a New Era* (London: Routledge, 2014), 17; See also Barbara Muraca and Matthias Schmelzer, 'Sustainable Degrowth: Historical Roots of the Search for Alternatives to Growth in Three Regions', in *History of the Future of Economic Growth: Historical Roots of Current Debates on Sustainable Degrowth*, ed. Iris Borowy and Matthias Schmelzer (London: Routledge, 2017), 174–97.

period influenced the early degrowth discussion – particularly important was the Romanian-American mathematician and economist
Nicholas Georgescu-Roegen, who integrated an understanding of physics and thermodynamics into economic theory. The debate on growth at
the time extended far beyond environmental movements and included
governments of industrialized countries, trade unions, and anti-colonial
debates about development. One aspect of current degrowth ideas has
been, for example, articulated by US revolutionary intellectuals and civil
rights activists James and Grace Lee Boggs, who argued in 1974 that 'the
revolution to be made in the United States will be the first revolution in
history to require the masses to make material sacrifices rather than to
acquire more material things,' because, they continue, these were
'acquired at the expense of damning over one-third of the world into a
state of underdevelopment, ignorance, disease and early death.'[18] Still,
during this time, the term 'degrowth' was rarely used, and did not
become a frame for a wider set of ideas until much later – and with the
end of the oil crisis and the rise of neoliberalism since the 1980s, broader
criticism of economic growth receded into the background.[19]

This only changed in the early 2000s. At the height of the neoliberal
penseé unique (Margaret Thatcher's 'There is no alternative') and the
hegemony of 'sustainable development' in environmental debates (the
claim that economic growth can be reconciled with sustainability),
degrowth was formed as a political project to open up cracks for
systemic alternatives. In 2002, a special issue of the French magazine
S!lence was published with the title 'Decroissance soutenable et convivi-
ale' (sustainable and convivial degrowth). In the introduction of the
issue, Bruno Clémentin and Vincent Cheynet coined the term *décroissance soutenable* explicitly as a counter-term to 'sustainable

---

18 James Boggs and Grace Lee Boggs, *Revolution and Evolution in the
Twentieth Century* (New York: Monthly Review Press, 1974), 163, cited in Jamie
Tyberg and Erica Jung, *Degrowth and Revolutionary Organizing* (New York: Rosa
Luxemburg Foundation, 2021).

19 Matthias Schmelzer, *The Hegemony of Growth: The OECD and the Making
of the Economic Growth Paradigm* (Cambridge: Cambridge University Press,
2016). During the 1990s, (eco-)feminist and post-development critics developed
key arguments that were later taken up in the degrowth debate (see chapter 3).

development', the buzzword at the time. In pairing the words 'degrowth' and 'sustainability', the authors highlighted the fact that ending the pursuit of growth should not point to collapse or recession – as the word 'degrowth' may suggest to many – but to a democratic process of transformation to a more just, sustainable, and less material and energy-intensive society. And the reference to degrowth as 'convivial' (a French term, based on Latin *con vivere*, to live together) emphasized that it referred to a positive vision of the good life defined by cooperative social interrelations with each other and with nature, a vision insisting that another world is indeed possible.[20]

In this new use of the term, 'degrowth' was both a provocation and a political proposal meant to challenge mainstream economic assumptions of development and to lay out a path for the future. Initially, it combined two intellectual strands: first, a socio-metabolic and thermo-dynamic analysis of capitalist growth, which highlighted the need for the countries of the Global North to exit the irrational and unsustainable growth race and subvert the related hegemony of the 'growth paradigm' that claimed GDP growth was good, imperative, and limitless; second, the radical critiques of the 'post-development' school of thought, which criticized capitalist 'development' and the idea that progress requires growth as a misguided, destructive, and universalizing Western ideology.[21] The term gained currency in France in the following years, especially through the work of French economist, philosopher, and critic of development Serge Latouche.[22] By 2008, the

20 Timothée Parrique, *The Political Economy of Degrowth: Economics and Finance* (Clermont: Université Clermont Auvergne, 2019); Serge Latouche, *Renverser nos manières de penser: Métanoïa pour le temps present* (Paris: Mille et Une Nuits, 2014); Vincent Liegey and Anitra Nelson, *Exploring Degrowth: A Critical Guide* (London: Pluto Press, 2020).

21 Valérie Fournier, 'Escaping from the Economy: The Politics of Degrowth', *International Journal of Sociology and Social Policy* 28, no. 11 (2008): 528–45, Muraca and Schmelzer, 'Sustainable Degrowth'; Barbara Muraca, 'Decroissance: A Project for a Radical Transformation of Society', *Environmental Values* 22, no. 2 (2013): 147–69; Jason Hickel, *Less Is More: How Degrowth Will Save the World* (London: William Heinemann, 2020).

22 Serge Latouche, *Farewell to Growth*, trans. David Macey (Cambridge: Polity Press, 2009).

English term 'degrowth' had received international attention, with the first 'International Degrowth Conference on Ecological Sustainability and Social Justice' in Paris. From this point onwards, the degrowth concept spread from France to Spain, Italy, the rest of Europe, and beyond.[23]

In its origins, the movement was rooted in anarchist environmental groups, campaigns for car-free cities and against large-scale industrial infrastructure, as well as in local collective projects such as collective housing groups and eco-villages. Yet it was the biannual International Degrowth Conferences which served as meeting points, places for discussion, and the slow formation of an international degrowth framework. In 2014, the Fourth International Conference in Leipzig attracted 3,000 participants. By 2020, the Seventh International Conference, held online due to the COVID-19 pandemic, attracted over 4,000 participants. Research on the subject has multiplied, with hundreds of peer-reviewed academic journal articles being published on the topic. Each year, degrowth summer schools organized by different institutes and collectives across Europe attract dozens and sometimes hundreds of participants, and the Global Degrowth Day in June is an opportunity for local organizations and initiatives to organize festivals and conferences around the world.

While degrowth continues to be a largely academic and activist concept, the critique of growth as an overarching priority is gaining popularity in the public realm as well. While polls have to be taken with a grain of salt, a 2018 poll taken in France showed that 54 per cent of respondents supported degrowth, compared to 46 per cent who supported green growth; in another poll, also in France, 55 per cent of respondents were for a degrowth future, compared to 29 per cent who preferred a more secure, stable continuation of the present and 16 per cent who were for a neoliberal, digitalized future.[24] In another poll, a majority of Europeans agreed that the environment

23 Muraca and Schmelzer, 'Sustainable Degrowth'; Parrique, *The Political Economy of Degrowth*.

24 'Les Français, plus "écolos" que jamais', Odoxa.fr, 3 October 2019; Philippe Moati, 'L'utopie écologique séduit les Français', Lemonde.fr, 22 November 2019.

should be a priority, even if that hampered economic growth.[25] Surveys such as these do not necessarily translate to, for example, voting patterns – it is still hard to imagine a degrowth party taking double-digit percentages of the vote in French or let alone European elections. But they are an indication of the fact that there is some concern and receptiveness by the public, and that there could be room for degrowth to prosper and develop further as a new eco-social common sense competing against eco-modernist and green growth ideas.

Research on degrowth is by now quite diverse and empirically robust. It spans disciplines such as economics and the humanities, political science, climate sciences, technology studies, and some natural and engineering sciences, and it includes hundreds of scientific articles on issues ranging from economic modelling to analyses of international socio-metabolic datasets, to case studies of squats in Barcelona. More and more books for a general audience are being published in English on the subject since 2014, as well as dozens of edited books and special issues that focus on diverse topics such as housing, technology, political economy, tourism, food, democracy, social movements, feminism, anthropology, and history.[26]

However, while degrowth goes beyond the ecological and economic perspectives that are dominant in the literature, there is

25 Mark Rice-Oxley and Jennifer Rankin, 'Europe's South and East Worry More about Emigration Than Immigration – Poll', Theguardian.com, 1 April 2019.

26 For a review of the existing literature, see: Giorgos Kallis et al., 'Research on Degrowth', *Annual Review of Environment and Resources* 43 (2018): 291–316; Martin Weiss and Claudio Cattaneo, 'Degrowth: Taking Stock and Reviewing an Emerging Academic Paradigm', *Ecological Economics* 137 (July 2017): 220–30; Matthias Schmelzer and Andrea Vetter, *Degrowth/Postwachstum zur Einführung* (Hamburg: Junius, 2019). *Degrowth: A Vocabulary for a New Era,* published in 2014, has since been translated into over a dozen languages and has proved to be particularly influential; designed as a handbook, it presents a large number of core terms that are central to the discussion of degrowth and gives room for some very disparate perspectives. D'Alisa, Demaria, and Kallis, *Degrowth.* Other influential books include Hickel, *Less Is More*; Giorgos Kallis et al., *The Case for Degrowth* (Cambridge: Polity Press, 2020); and Liegey and Nelson, *Exploring Degrowth.*

not much writing that explores degrowth in its full breadth, including analyses from the social sciences and humanities centre stage. And while the degrowth movement is clearly progressive or even largely anti-capitalist, there are few books exploring degrowth from a perspective explicitly critical of capitalism that engages with wider debates on the left – that is, one that sees systems of domination such as patriarchy, colonialism, imperialism, racism, and capitalism as the central, structural problems facing us today. This is what we seek to do in this book. In doing so, we argue that degrowth represents a crucially important, and internally coherent, framework for just futures – one that must supplement and possibly transform progressive proposals like the Green New Deal. While 'degrowth' as a term need not be taken up by emancipatory social movements and the broader left, we argue that its perspectives, its critiques, and its core proposals should form an integral part of the larger 'movement of movements' that is necessary for a globally just future for all.[27]

What is degrowth?

These days, with growing interest in degrowth, it seems that almost every other week another humourless columnist for a major newspaper writes a criticism of degrowth. This is to be expected and even, to a certain extent, welcomed: the more those in positions of power rail against degrowth, the more people who might be sympathetic to it, who would otherwise not have heard about it, are exposed to it. And, indeed, it also fulfils degrowth's initial goal as a provocation, a conversation starter, a shit-disturber. Yet, usually, these columnists show little understanding of what degrowth means – and so their objections tend to badly miss the mark.

What better way to find out the meaning of degrowth than to ask those most interested in it? The largest empirical survey of degrowth proponents, a survey at the 2014 Leipzig conference in which one of us was involved, found that respondents held several positions in common:

---

27 On this, see also Burkhart, Schmelzer, and Treu, *Degrowth in Movement(s)*.

they largely agreed that economic growth without destruction of nature is an illusion and that therefore industrialized countries need to equitably downscale production and consumption; they also mostly agreed that consequently the rich will have to do without some amenities to which they have become accustomed, and that the transformation to a degrowth society must come from below, will be peaceful, and will require overcoming capitalism and patriarchy.[28] This basic consensus across many different perspectives among conference attendees highlights that degrowth proponents are fundamentally critical of growth, capitalism, and industrialism, want to overcome other forms of domination, and advocate a radical restructuring of the economy in industrialized countries, requiring the selective downscaling of certain industries and production. This clearly distinguishes degrowth from many other political positions – not only from conservative currents (e.g., preserving the status quo, green fascism, or green growth) but also from leftist productivist positions such as most Green New Deals or visions of post-capitalism, which are less precise on the need to transform capitalism, dynamics of growth, global justice, and excess consumption.

Yet, these basic agreements aside, degrowth is not a unified concept – it can better be understood as a multivalent term. One of its characteristics is that it is not only a scientific research paradigm but also a political project. This becomes very clear at the International Degrowth Conferences and the degrowth summer schools, which stress exchanges among academics, activists, practitioners of alternative economic projects, and political actors. This exchange often goes both ways: scientific work and collective action can be mutually beneficial. Much of the scientific research done by degrowth scholars can be called 'activist research' or 'post-normal science', which highlight the political implications of academic work in times of necessary social change and

---

28 Matthias Schmelzer and Dennis Eversberg, 'Beyond Growth, Capitalism, and Industrialism? Consensus, Divisions and Currents within the Emerging Movement for Sustainable Degrowth', *Interface: A Journal for and about Social Movements* 9, no. 1 (2017): 327–56; Dennis Eversberg and Matthias Schmelzer, 'The Degrowth Spectrum: Convergence and Divergence within a Diverse and Conflictual Alliance', *Environmental Values* 27, no. 3 (2018): 245–67.

calls for the involvement of laypersons in the production and critical evaluation of knowledge.[29]

Another aspect of this multivalence is that degrowth is simultaneously a critique of the present and a visionary goal. As we lay out in this book, degrowth has its roots in diverse, wide-ranging analyses of the present – including ecological, feminist, anti-capitalist, and decolonial approaches. Degrowth, we argue, can be understood as the combination of a specific set of critiques of growth. But, straddling both academia and social movements, and building on these multiple critiques, degrowth also poses the question of what characteristics, institutions, infrastructures, and relationships a utopian growth-independent society should have. In this way, degrowth is explicitly a utopian project: it embraces the need to think, and act, beyond the present and to propose alternative futures. Degrowth thus involves a set of common principles for what that future could look like, policies for how to get there, and strategies for transformation. We begin the book with specific critiques of growth, then lay out proposals for a degrowth future, and finally discuss how we can get from here to there.

A central target of the degrowth critique, it must be noted, is the discipline of economics. Degrowth's relationship to economics is in many ways quite ambivalent. On the one hand, degrowth often analyses questions that are traditionally dealt with by economists – such as trends in global economic patterns, secular stagnation, or the relationship between productivity, resource use, and GDP growth – and degrowth-inspired research has offered important contributions to the field. Degrowth can thus be understood as an attempt to *reconfigure economics*.[30] On the other hand, degrowth is also a radical critique of economics itself, a critique of economic thinking as a form of

---

29 Silvio O. Funtowicz and Jerome R. Ravetz, 'Science for the Post-normal Age', *Futures* 25, no. 7 (September 1993): 739–55.

30 This perspective is particularly prominent within the ecological economics writings on degrowth. See, for example, Giorgos Kallis, *Degrowth* (Newcastle upon Tyne: Agenda Publishing, 2018); Herman E. Daly, *Beyond Growth: The Economics of Sustainable Development* (Boston: Beacon Press, 1996); Tim Jackson, *Prosperity without Growth: Economics for a Finite Planet* (London: Earthscan, 2016).

knowledge that became dominant with the growth economy, is closely interconnected with it, and stands in the way of thinking and talking about other economic and social orders freed from the logics of growth and 'the economy'.[31] Degrowth thus aims at 'escaping from the economy',[32] which importantly also includes a *critique of economics* – of the perspectives, methods, and basic assumptions of the discipline claiming to explain economic activities. Even as we incorporate theories and insights from heterodox economics, in this book we focus especially on the latter perspective, because we think degrowth offers a critique of economic thinking and of the dominance of economics that is especially useful for the left.

Beyond being both a critique and a proposal, degrowth also functions as an enabler of certain conversations. On the one hand, degrowth is a provocation: a way to rile people up and a way to begin asking transformative questions – the French historian Paul Ariès calls it a 'missile word'.[33] On the other hand, degrowth is also a meeting space for various concepts, arguments, and communities. Thus, the Italian economic historian Stefania Barca prefers the less militaristic metaphor of degrowth as an 'umbrella term': not just because it encapsulates many different critiques, proposals, and strategies, but also because, like an umbrella, it protects. As Barca explains,

> In a world constantly hit both by the heavy rains of ecological degradation, impoverishment, [and] austerity measures, and by the implacable heat of overconsumption, overproduction and the financialisation of everything, opening an umbrella and creating a space for different movements to converge and talk about (or practice) the alternatives that they want is exactly what the degrowth term has been doing in the past decade, especially in Europe.[34]

---

31 Schmelzer, *The Hegemony of Growth*.

32 Fournier, 'Escaping from the Economy'.

33 Paul Ariès, *Décroissance ou barbarie* (Lyon: Golias, 2005); Giorgos Kallis, 'The Left Should Embrace Degrowth', Newint.org, 5 November 2015.

34 Stefania Barca, 'In Defense of Degrowth: Opinions and Minifestos/ Doughnut Economics: Seven Ways to Think Like a 21st-Century Economist', *Local Environment* 23, no. 3 (2018): 379.

Building on this image of degrowth as an umbrella, we aim to hold space for the many interconnected, overlapping, yet not always harmonious concepts and ideas, lines of research, and political projects that are brought together under degrowth. In so doing, we argue that degrowth must be understood as a holistic term that both draws from a wider tradition of critical thought and offers a new framework that is indispensable for overcoming the crises we face.

What degrowth is not

That said, being such a provocative term, 'degrowth' is often misinterpreted or deliberately misrepresented, even by many who generally share the objectives of degrowth. We thus want to discuss some of the most widespread misunderstandings upfront. One common misconception is that degrowth is either a proposal for recession, imposed austerity, or that it will necessarily result in economic collapse and social catastrophe. Since economic growth is seen as the only possible way to improve living standards, whenever an economic crisis happens, critics of degrowth will say, often disingenuously, 'see, this is what happens when you degrow'.[35] And, since our economy depends on economic growth, and economic crisis is catastrophic for many people's livelihoods, people assume that degrowth would similarly be a catastrophe and lead to full-scale collapse. Both assumptions are, of course, false. Degrowth is the opposite of recession: recessions are unintentional, while degrowth is planned and intentional; recessions make inequality worse, degrowth seeks to reduce it; recessions typically lead to cuts in public services while degrowth is about de-commodifying essential goods and services; recessions often cause bold policies for sustainability to be abandoned for the sake of restarting growth, while degrowth is explicitly for a rapid and decisive transformation.[36] Hence the

---

35 See, for example, McAleenan, 'Coronavirus Reveals the Misery of Degrowth'; or the debate between Branko Milanovic and Jason Hickel, in Jason Hickel, 'Why Branko Milanovic Is Wrong about Degrowth', jasonhickel.org, 19 November 2017. For a collection of some controversies around degrowth, see 'Controversies', timotheeparrique.com.

36 Jason Hickel, 'What Does Degrowth Mean? A Few Points of Clarification', *Globalizations* 18, no. 7 (2021): 1105–11.

slogan of the French *décroissance* movement: 'Their recession is not our degrowth'. Such a transformed, just, and growth-independent economy is the core of the degrowth project. Further, degrowth is explicitly framed to build a system not structurally bent towards crisis. Crises like the 2008 financial crisis, the coronavirus pandemic, the fires engulfing the Amazon, and the past and ongoing genocide of Indigenous peoples indicate that growth-driven capitalism already is a catastrophe. More than ever, the choice is between degrowth – a multidimensional set of transformations based on sufficiency, care, and justice – or barbarism. In other words, we talk about degrowth in order to avoid the catastrophe that awaits us and which is already a daily reality in many parts of the world. Degrowth is not the crisis; capitalism is.

Another critique of degrowth is that it is reactionary, that it is against modernity and against progress.[37] For example, the Greek economist and politician Yanis Varoufakis recently characterized degrowth as some kind of regressive nostalgia aiming for a return to pre-industrial times that mainly argues that 'now we need to go back to the bush'. Similarly, the Serbian American economist of inequality Branko Milanovic vilified degrowth as 'an asceticism reminiscent of the early Christendom' and a proposal for the 'immiseration of the West'.[38] That little 'de-' in the word often rubs people the wrong way. And many – even on the left – fall for the ideology of growth and conflate modernity, development, emancipation, and improvement with economic growth, with more stuff, and with a continuous development of productive forces. It makes sense when conservatives, centrists, and liberals advance this criticism: for these people, any criticism of the present is all-too-often accused of being dismissive of the advances that we have made. 'If you don't like it, go live in a cave and see how you like that.' This all-or-nothing argument is the last resort of those who aim to preserve the status quo. But when it is put forward by leftists, it seems rather insincere. Rather than being

---

37 Leigh Philips, *Austerity Ecology and the Collapse-Porn Addicts: A Defence of Growth, Progress, Industry and Stuff* (Winchester: Zer0, 2014).

38 Timothée Parrique, 'A Response to Yanis Varoufakis: *Star Trek* and Degrowth', timotheeparrique.com, 3 January 2021; Branko Milanovic, 'Degrowth: Solving the Impasse by Magical Thinking', glineq.blogspot.com, 20 February 2021.

against modernity and progress, degrowth claims that a system built on economic growth obstructs meaningful progress towards global justice, well-being, and sustainability. And, as we will argue, degrowth posits that defending and strengthening the social, political, and cultural rights that modern movements have won requires moving beyond economic growth. Furthermore, far from being reactionary or against all modern technologies or conveniences, degrowth aims at democratizing the development of productive forces and social metabolism in order to achieve public abundance. And, far from being about 'belt-tightening sacrifice', degrowth is about strengthening more meaningful and less destructive forms of happiness, new forms of the joy of life (the oldest degrowth periodical is called *Le journal de la joie vivre*), or what has been called 'alternative hedonism'.[39] Degrowth is not against progress; rather, holding on to continuous economic growth undermines real progress.

In a similar vein, 'degrowth' is also often understood as simply another word for 'austerity': it is claimed that degrowth advocates use ecological arguments to say that we should have less, to deprive us of good stuff and make us tighten our belts – in particular, poor people's belts.[40] Even proponents of a Green New Deal, who are critical of growth, have asked, 'Who will march for green austerity?'[41] This is a curious criticism because austerity (or as the International Monetary Fund and World Bank call it euphemistically, 'structural adjustment') has always been imposed on populations *for the sake of growth*. We have been convinced, for half a century now, that cutting public services is good for us *because* it will increase competitiveness, balance the budget, and eventually lead to growth.[42] By contrast, degrowth targets the assumption that it is economic growth that we need and focuses instead

39 See chapters 4 and 5. Timothee Parrique, 'A Response to Branko Milanović: The Magic of Degrowth', 25 February 2021, timotheeparrique.com; Kate Soper, *Post-growth Living: For an Alternative Hedonism* (London: Verso, 2020).

40 'Ep 011 Destroying Degrowth with Facts and Logic (feat. Matt Huber)', 11 April 2021, Spacecommune.com, podcast; or Philips, *Austerity Ecology*.

41 Kate Aronoff et al., *A Planet to Win*, 12.

42 Mark Blyth, *Austerity: The History of a Dangerous Idea* (Oxford: Oxford University Press, 2013).

on a radical redistribution of income and wealth, on global justice, and on what actually ensures well-being. While austerity increases inequality by thrashing public services and benefitting the rich, degrowth policies focus on democratizing production, curbing the wealth and over-consumption of the rich, expanding public services, and increasing equality within and between societies. As we'll explain in this book, under degrowth, public services would flourish, rather than see cuts – degrowth is about private sufficiency and public abundance. Certainly, life would look a lot different, many people would likely possess fewer material objects – but others would have access to more and society would be more sustaining, just, convivial, and fulfilling. In essence, degrowth aims at a society in which well-being is mediated less by capitalist market transactions, exchange values, or material consumption – and more by collective forms of provisioning, use values, and fulfilling, meaningful, and convivial relationships.[43] As one degrowth slogans states: *'moins de biens, plus de liens'* (fewer transactions, more relations).

One of the most common misconceptions assumes that degrowth would imply an across-the-board, undifferentiated reduction of all types of production or consumption – a patently absurd idea. On the one hand, it is argued, degrowth's critique of 'growth as such' does not differentiate between essential and superfluous production and consumption and proposes to reduce all. As recently claimed by Kenta Tsuda,

> Degrowthers tend to elide the colloquial meaning of consumption, as something like discretionary 'retail therapy', with the term's economic definition: the final use of a resource as a good or service. The latter sense encompasses not only the ostensibly superfluous resource uses that degrowthers would reduce or ban, but also unambiguously essential ones: nutritious food, commodious shelter, healthcare and childcare.[44]

43 See chapter 4. Hartmut Rosa, *Resonance: A Sociology of Our Relationship to the World* (Medford, MA: Polity, 2019).

44 Kenta Tsuda, 'Naive Questions on Degrowth', *New Left Review* 128 (2021): 111–30, 128.

However, degrowth is not against consumption as such, but rather criticizes the dominance of a consumer culture, in which consumption governs social and political life (wherein proposals to the current crises are framed as individual choices), and the absurdity of 'positional consumption' based on status competition. Degrowth also takes aim at policies promoting GDP growth precisely *because* growth does not differentiate between useful and destructive, essential and superfluous. In contrast, degrowth differentiates between certain economic activities and forms of production and consumption, proposing policies for the downscaling of some and the flourishing of others – depending on how they address social needs, justice, care, and sustainability (see chapters 4 and 5).

On the other hand, proponents of ecological modernization or a Green New Deal have repeatedly argued that degrowth does not make sense because, as recently argued by Noam Chomsky, a 'shift to sustainable energy requires growth: construction and installation of solar panels and wind turbines, weatherization of homes, major infrastructure projects to create efficient mass transportation, and much else'.[45] Literally all degrowth proposals do include policies for the selective expansion of all these things. Yet degrowth also asks whether this would necessarily result in an increase of the size of the economy as measured in GDP when combined with the required contraction of other sectors and activities. Put differently, degrowth aims to disassociate socially and ecologically necessary improvements from the idea of economic growth – which often leads people to mix up well-being with economic growth as measured through GDP, while obscuring the material and energetic throughput that economic growth depends on.

Another common misunderstanding is that degrowth for poorer countries does not make sense, since it is in particular the poor that need material development – and that therefore degrowth is a neo-colonial plot, or just magical thinking, that will keep global inequality

---

45 Chomsky and Pollin, *Climate Crisis*, 118. See also Pollin, 'De-Growth vs a Green New Deal'.

as it is.[46] Again, however, the opposite is the case – degrowth starts explicitly from a global justice perspective that aims to decolonize the Global North so as to make space for the Global South.[47] Indeed, a degrowth perspective aims at the convergence of living standards at an equitable and globally sustainable level. While degrowth has allies in the Global South within the broader framework of 'alternatives to development', it mainly focuses on the Global North or, more specifically, on the affluent who maintain what has been called the 'imperial mode of living'.[48] Furthermore, as we argue in this book, degrowth embraces proposals for a decolonization of North–South relations, reparative justice and transfers of resources, technology, and money, and a self-determined increase of material and energy use by the dispossessed in the Global South (and those that have too little in the Global North).[49] This should suffice to make clear that degrowth is also *not* a critique of population growth (arguments that centre overpopulation are squarely refuted by degrowthers), a depoliticizing call for 'humanity' to live more sufficiently, or an initiative to conserve 'Half-Earth' (which tends to misdiagnose the causes of ecological disruption and disregard Indigenous land rights).[50] Some authors have also warned that degrowth's rise in popularity could reproduce neo-colonial asymmetries by setting a global agenda that dominates and renders invisible diverse perspectives from the Global South. Degrowth would thus 're-enact the presumed superiority of Modern developments over

46 Branko Milanovic, 'Degrowth: Solving the Impasse by Magical Thinking', *Global Inequality* (blog), 20 February 2021, glineq.blogspot.com; Max Roser, 'The Economies That Are Home to the Poorest Billions of People Need to Grow If We Want Global Poverty to Decline Substantially', Ourworldindata.org, 22 February 2021; Noah Smith, 'Against Hickelism: Poverty Is Falling, and It Isn't Because of Free-Market Capitalism', noahpinion. substack.com, 2 April 2021.

47 Hickel, 'What Does Degrowth Mean?'

48 Ashish Kothari et al., *Pluriverse: A Post-development Dictionary* (Delhi: Authors Up Front, 2019); Ulrich Brand and Markus Wissen, *The Imperial Mode of Living: Everyday Life and the Ecological Crisis of Capitalism* (London: Verso, 2021).

49 See chapter 5. Ajl, *A People's Green New Deal.*

50 See chapters 3 and 5 for more details.

alternative topologies of the pluriverse'.[51] While this might be a danger that needs careful attention, degrowth explicitly rejects imperial and Western hegemony and advocates for 'liberation from the one-sided Western development paradigm, as a precondition for enabling a self-determined shaping of society and a good life in the Global South', and enters into active alliances within the broader pluriversal framework of 'alternatives to development'.[52]

Some understand degrowth – or more often 'post-growth' – merely as a descriptive concept that characterizes societies that are not or are no longer growing. For example, in their recent book on a Global Green New Deal, Robert Pollin and Noam Chomsky analyse degrowth as a proposal for stagnating or shrinking economies, arguing that the 'fundamental problems with degrowth are well illustrated by the case of Japan' – which has for decades been a capitalist and growth-dependent, though slow-growing, economy.[53] If degrowth or post-growth are understood as merely analytical terms, they can indeed be used to characterize some advanced capitalist countries with long-term growth rates close to or below zero. Degrowth would thus also describe the trend of falling growth rates characterized by economists as 'secular stagnation' – contracting economies in crisis, showing the structural problems capitalist economies face without expansion.[54] However, degrowth is not a description of, for example, the tendencies of

51 Saurabh Arora and Andy Stirling, 'Degrowth and the Pluriverse: Continued Coloniality or Intercultural Revolution?', steps-centre.org/blog, 5 May 2021; Padini Nirmal and Dianne Rocheleau, 'Decolonizing Degrowth in the Post-development Convergence: Questions, Experiences, and Proposals from Two Indigenous Territories', *Environment and Planning E: Nature and Space* 2, no. 3 (2019): 465–92.

52 Corinna Burkhart, Matthias Schmelzer, and Nina Treu, 'Degrowth: Overcoming Growth, Competition and Profit', in *Degrowth in Movement(s): Exploring Pathways for Transformation*, 143–58, 147; Kothari et al., *Pluriverse*.

53 Chomsky and Pollin, *Climate Crisis*, 118; see also David Roberts, 'Noam Chomsky's Green New Deal', Vox.com, 21 September 2020.

54 Klaus Dörre, *Die Utopie des Sozialismus: Kompass für eine Nachhaltigkeitsrevolution* (Berlin: Matthes & Seitz Verlag, 2021); Aaron Benanav, *Automation and the Future of Work* (London: Verso, 2020); Schmelzer, *The Hegemony of Growth*.

crisis-ridden late capitalist industrial societies that, without growth, tend towards neo-feudal hierarchies and exploitation, also called societies of 'social decline' by sociologists.[55] On the contrary, degrowth is an explicitly normative concept. It delineates the contours of a desirable, democratic transformation process, which focuses explicitly on analysing, criticizing, and then overcoming growth dependencies. Degrowth does in fact argue that because growth rates are declining in some advanced economies, it is high time to restructure these economies along the lines proposed by degrowth in order to avoid structural problems such as rising unemployment, inequality, and debt, which are partly caused by growth dependencies. In other words, it is only *because* our economies are dependent on continuous growth that stagnation is seen as problematic by economists. Degrowth proposes to break out of this bind by decoupling well-being from the imperative to grow. It is the contours of such a concrete utopia that we work out in this book.

Finally, next to these misunderstandings – and there are many others that will be covered throughout the book – there is also an intense debate on the usefulness or pitfalls of the term 'degrowth'.[56] In fact, many who may agree with the general thrust of degrowth's radical ecological transformation still complain that the term is too focused on undoing growth and that it activates the problematic semantic frame of 'growth' (conflating it with more of the good things) that should rather be avoided. Some have thus argued that we should remain agnostic about the question of growth – in other words, about the increase or reduction of GDP – and simply focus on the policies and transformations needed.[57] Instead of 'degrowth', 'agrowth' has

---

55 Hartmut Rosa, Stephan Lessenich, and Klaus Dörre, *Sociology, Capitalism, Critique* (London: Verso, 2015); Robert Gordon, *Rise and Fall of American Growth: The U.S. Standard of Living since the Civil War* (Princeton, NJ: Princeton University Press, 2016); Oliver Nachtwey, *Germany's Hidden Crisis: Social Decline in the Heart of Europe* (London: Verso, 2018).

56 On common critiques of degrowth, see Kallis et al., *The Case for Degrowth*; and a collection of degrowth controversies at timotheeparrique.com/ degrowthcontroversies.

57 Kate Raworth, *Doughnut Economics: Seven Ways to Think Like a 21st-Century Economist* (White River Junction, VT: Chelsea Green Publishing, 2017), chapter 7.

been proposed as a better term (as cognate with 'atheism'), since it makes little sense to orient oneself to GDP statistics, which are largely meaningless for well-being.[58] Others still prefer 'post-growth', emphasizing that the goal is not to contract but to become growth-independent in an era 'after growth'.[59] 'Post-growth', when used as a normative rather than a descriptive term, is often seen as a safer, less negative, and more aspirational concept. As a result, post-growth often is agnostic about the role of GDP and its relationship to environmental and social impacts.

While there is certainly some truth to these arguments, and eventually there may come a time to drop the term 'degrowth', they miss one of the key goals of degrowth: to tear down the cracked edifice of the hegemony of growth. As we explain in chapter 2, growth is the cornerstone of an ideological construct justifying uneven global relations, growth dependencies, and policies that uphold private profits. Thus, it cannot simply be ignored; it must be dealt with head-on. Also, as discussed in more detail throughout the book, if a decoupling of GDP growth from ecological destruction is not possible, and if modern societies are structurally dependent on expansion, then it would be highly irresponsible to *not* address these structural growth dependencies, because they will always block effective environmental policies that would hamper growth.[60] As James Baldwin said, 'Not everything that is faced can be changed, but nothing can be changed until it is faced.'[61] Without facing the ideology of growth head-on, we will not be able to manifest the radical transformation of society that we need. Despite

---

58 Latouche, *Farewell to Growth*; Jeroen van den Bergh and Giorgos Kallis, 'Growth, A-growth or Degrowth to Stay within Planetary Boundaries?', *Journal of Economic Issues* 46, no. 4 (2012): 909–20; Jeroen van den Bergh, 'Environment versus Growth: A Criticism of "Degrowth" and a Plea for "A-growth" ', *Ecological Economics* 70, no. 5 (2011): 881–90.

59 Irmi Seidl and Angelika Zahrnt, *Postwachstumsgesellschaft: Neue Konzepte für die Zukunft* (Marburg: Metropolis, 2010).

60 Or, for the sake of argument, if environmental policies were effective, structural growth dependencies would push societies into recession, eco-austerity, and crisis. See the arguments and literature in chapter 4.

61 James Baldwin, 'As Much Truth as One Can Bear', *New York Times Book Review*, 14 January 1962.

some of the confusions that often emerge from using the negative term '*de*-growth', we believe it remains useful as a term that is more difficult to co-opt (see the fate of the term 'sustainable development'), that names the enemy, and, through its provocative framing, is extremely productive in starting conversations about systemic alternatives. As we argue in this book, degrowth is differentiated, first, through its principled criticism of capitalism and economic logics, and second, because the degrowth policies that aim at global ecological justice and the necessary reductions in material and energy throughput necessary to achieve it will in all likelihood also lead to a reduction in the size of 'the economy' as measured in GDP – and it is good to be prepared and do this in a planned manner.[62]

It is true that the aspirational character of 'post-growth' also has its benefits in certain contexts – for example, European Green parties have used the term 'post-growth' as a less confrontational way to advance degrowth ideas. 'Post-growth' is somewhat more open than 'degrowth' because it does not activate the growth frame as much, and all the complex debates this stirs up, but focuses on a future *beyond* economic growth. Yet, a debate on growth is still very necessary. As Giorgos Kallis puts it in a discussion with Kate Raworth on whether 'degrowth' is a good word: 'the missile has landed, but it hasn't worked, so it is not yet "the time to move on".'[63] The issue is also partly a linguistic problem. While in France, where the term *décroissance* was born and gained widespread prominence, in German, using *De-* or *Ent-* alongside *Wachstum* is awkward, and so *Postwachstum* is usually preferred. In Japan, *datsu seichou* (roughly, 'degrowth') is used; in Dutch, *ontgroei* (roughly, 'ungrowth'); and in Scandinavian countries, people usually use the English term, 'degrowth'. In this book we use the term 'degrowth', though neither are we against people using 'post-growth' instead.

---

62 Van den Bergh and Kallis, 'Growth, A-growth or Degrowth'; see also chapter 4.
63 Giorgos Kallis, 'You're Wrong Kate, Degrowth Is a Compelling Word', oxfamblogs.org, 2 December 2015.

What we argue

This book offers offer a systematic introduction to the dynamic, trans-disciplinary debate on economic growth, critiques of growth, the many currents of degrowth, degrowth policies, and a political strategy for degrowth from a decolonial, feminist, and anti-capitalist perspective. Throughout the book, we respond to the 'naïve questions on degrowth' that are often raised by its critics (e.g., Is green growth not more realistic? How could a planned contraction be implemented? What should grow and what should degrow?[64]). Many questions may remain, but we aim to provide context for readers to think more deeply about the challenges posed by the critiques of growth.

What distinguishes degrowth, we claim, is that it holds together social, cultural, and ecological questions and in this way advances new ideas that could provide answers to the pressing questions of the twenty-first century. The peculiarity and the potential of the degrowth discussion is that these various forms of criticism are taken up, recognized, brought into mutual productive exchange, and understood as parts of a common space of discourse. This book is therefore not only an introduction to the vision of degrowth but necessarily also an introduction to the dynamics of growth and the critiques of growth in modern societies. We argue that degrowth contributes what other leftist proposals do not: a holistic critique and proposal capable of deconstructing the dominant ideology driving capitalism today – the ideology of growth – and showing ways forward for unmaking growth and capitalism in our everyday lives, in our societal institutions, and in our economic structures.

We thus devote chapter 2 to the concept of 'growth'. Here, we highlight some foundational claims for the degrowth debate. Economic growth, we argue, appears as the ideological, social, and biophysical materialization of capitalist accumulation. To understand and dismantle the politics of growth today, we need to analyse economic growth as three interlinked processes that have evolved dynamically over time. First, economic growth as a policy goal, as well as the broader societal

---

64 Tsuda, 'Naïve Questions on Degrowth'.

obsession with growth as we know it today, are relatively new developments that can be traced to attempts in the middle of the twentieth century to stabilize and plan capitalist economies through state intervention, to measure capitalist economies against state socialist ones, and to appease the increasingly militant working class. It was only through the new idea that 'the economy' could be measured through GDP that it became possible to justify the belief that growth is natural, necessary, good, and unlimited. However, focusing on the new hegemony of growth alone would obscure the social and material roots of growth. Thus, second, we argue that growth is also a social process that preceded the hegemony of growth and which results in cultural norms, specific modes of production and living, and a set of class interests oriented towards increase, acceleration, and escalation – subsequently leading modern societies to become dependent on growth and its dynamics of accumulation. And third, growth is a material process – the ever-expanding use of land, materials, and energy – that is rooted in patriarchy, colonialism, and capitalism, resulting in an accelerated material and energetic throughput and exploitation for the sake of profit. 'Economic growth' can thus be understood as both an increase in economic production and as an interlocking, self-reinforcing cultural, social, and material process which has transformed life and the planet over the past centuries.

Having defined growth, in chapter 3 we explore the critique of growth. People often think that degrowth is only about limiting resources; however, it is much more complex. Degrowth, we argue, can be understood as the attempt to integrate a number of different strands of growth critique – we focus on seven. Economic growth, according to these critiques, (1) destroys the ecological foundations of human life and cannot be transformed to become sustainable; (2) mismeasures our lives and thus stands in the way of well-being and equality of all; (3) imposes alienated ways of working, living, and relating to each other and nature; (4) depends on and is driven by capitalist exploitation, competition, and accumulation; (5) is based on gendered over-exploitation and devalues reproduction; (6) gives rise to oppressive and undemocratic productive forces and techniques; and (7) necessarily relies on and reproduces unjust relations of domination, extraction, and exploitation between capitalist centre and periphery.

A historical analysis of growth, and a discussion of the critiques thereof, comprises the first half of the book. In the second half, we start from the position that degrowth is not only a critique but also a visionary proposal, an attempt to create 'concrete utopias' and to combine them with resistant practices and alternative ways of life in the here and now. In the last decade, there has been much debate on what degrowth stands for, with emphasis being put on different aspects of the theory. Chapter 4 provides an overview of the different visionary currents of degrowth and draws them together in a common definition. Degrowth, we argue, describes the democratic transition to a society that – in order to enable global ecological justice – has a much smaller throughput of energy and resources, and thus also a smaller economy; ensures justice, self-determination, and a good life for all under this changed metabolism; and does not depend on growth and continuous expansion. In essence, the degrowth vision is about pushing back against the dominant economic logic and economic calculation – namely, the question of whether everything pays off financially – as the dominant basis for decision-making in society. The aim is thus to repoliticize and democratize social institutions as well as power and property relationships, in order to abandon the social dominance and logic of 'the economy'.

Following this, we ask: how do we get there? In chapter 5 we consider the policies that could make degrowth a reality. Degrowth offers many concrete proposals for 'non-reformist reforms' (André Gorz) or a 'revolutionary Realpolitik' (Rosa Luxemburg).[65] This refers to reforms that take advantage of existing institutions and bureaucratic regulations and yet also lead to immediate gains for social movements and even point beyond the capitalist, growth-oriented mode of production and centralized technocratic states. They ultimately strengthen the struggles that

---

65 On the concept of 'non-reformist reforms', see Mark Engler and Paul Engler, 'André Gorz's Non-Reformist Reforms Show How We Can Transform the World Today', Jacobinmag.com, 22 July 2021; Rosa Luxemburg, 'Karl Marx', in *Gesammelte Werke*, vol. 1.2 (Berlin: Dietz, 2000): 369–77, 373.

help us overcome these same institutions, eventually helping to bring about revolutionary change.[66]

We focus on transformational changes in six areas: (1) *democratizing the economy*, which includes, for example, strengthening the commons and solidarity economy, transferring utilities like water or electricity into democratic ownership, providing institutional support for cooperative workplaces, or proposals for macroeconomic coordination and participatory planning; (2) *redistribution and social security*, which includes policies guaranteeing access to basic services such as health care, public transport, food, and education for all, or as the French *décroissance* movement has called it, *dotation inconditionelle d'autonomie* – universal basic services; (3) *democratizing technology*, supported by policies such as assessing the impact of technologies on society and the environment over their entire life cycle, or opening repair centres in every community; (4) *revaluation of labour*, including policies such as radical reduction in working time, and eliminating useless or socially harmful jobs (like advertising or the fracking industry) while recentring the economy around needs and care work; (5) *democratization of social metabolism*, meaning that large areas of production and consumption will need to be dismantled, while other systems will need to be developed in their place – this could include, for example, reforming taxation systems to disincentivize harmful industrial activity, or moratoria on planned fossil fuel infrastructure such as airports or mega-highways; (6) *international solidarity*, which could include, for example, restructuring the international monetary system to dismantle uneven hierarchies between nations, or cancelling the debts of Global South countries and transferring resources, technology, and money as reparations for climate debt. This wide selection of policies shows how degrowth is not just about proposing a single policy that could potentially change everything (as many basic income

---

66 A strategy of non-reformist reforms, Gorz argues, 'aims by means of partial victories to shake the system's equilibrium profoundly, to sharpen its contradictions, to intensify its crisis, and, by a succession of attacks and counterattacks, to raise the class struggle to a greater intensity, at a higher and higher level'. André Gorz, *Strategy for Labor: A Radical Proposal* (Boston: Beacon Press, 1967), 181.

advocates argue, for example) but, instead, offers a holistic package where each policy complements the others.

However, policies alone cannot bring about a society-wide transformation: we need a strategy for societal change. While the discussion about how to combine policies, electoral campaigns, social movements, and local initiatives is still only developing, chapter 6 aims to advance this debate by offering a transformative approach to linking movement-building, a strengthening of existing cooperative alternatives, and non-reformist policy change. Drawing on the analysis of sociologist Erik Olin Wright,[67] we distinguish three different, complementary transformation strategies: *interstitial strategies* that create more cooperative economic practices and spaces that do not follow the logics of capitalism, growth, and competition within existing structures; *non-reformist reforms* that transform policies and institutions and fundamentally democratize the economy, thus strengthening the scope for alternatives and struggles; and strategies for *building counter-hegemony and parallel institutions of power* that, through confrontational tactics such as strikes, blockades, citizen assemblies, autonomously organized municipalities, and alternative forms of government, make it possible to break with the logic of growth in individual sectors and regions of society.[68] We argue that the transformation towards a degrowth society requires an interplay of these three types of transformation strategies. We stress, however, that building counter-hegemony and parallel structures of power – in other words, pursuing a strategy of dual power – is paramount, despite being under-explored within the degrowth debate. It is only through collective power and the development of new kinds of common sense that it becomes possible to productively relate the other transformation approaches to envision degrowth becoming reality.

Degrowth, we believe, is a critique, a proposal, and a politics whose time has come. After the term was taken up in France, Spain, Italy, and

---

67 Erik Olin Wright, *Envisioning Real Utopias* (London: Verso, 2010).

68 The word 'citizen' has strong connotations with formal citizenship tied to membership of nation-states. In this context, however, we use the word 'citizen' as a broader category referring to any individual who has the capacity to engage in politics, which does not exclude undocumented migrants, refugees, or the stateless.

Germany, it spread beyond Europe. There are now groups, events, festivals, and publications in North America, India, and Mexico, among others, and degrowth is increasingly taken up in various social struggles. Though degrowth discussions initially developed surprisingly independently of one another, the degrowth community is increasingly interconnected globally and becoming more prominent in the mainstream. This, however, does not mean that it should not be further developed. In the concluding chapter, we highlight four areas which could be better integrated within the degrowth debate: class and race, geopolitics and imperialism, information technology, and democratic planning.

In this book, we propose that degrowth is well positioned to help us navigate the crises that face us. Degrowth is unique in offering both an analysis of how we got here and a way to get to the root of the crises we face. Over the last five centuries, a material, cultural, and political system has developed that depends on growth and further drives it. This is a system geared towards collapse. Neither green growth nor left productivism are desirable options: growth cannot solve the problems it creates, and, to face the impending crises, we need an economy that values rather than exploits, disposes of, and invisibilizes, women and people of the global majority. As far as the Green New Deal goes, this is an admirable and encouraging development on the left – and its growing popularity is a promising indicator of the possibility of mass appeal for transformative, radical projects. Here, a degrowth perspective can be a compass for determining what kind of policies a truly transformative – that is, a caring, internationalist, post-growth, and socially just – political project would entail. Our intention is that this book provide both a compass and a navigational guide for how to get there.

2
Economic growth

What words come to mind when you read the word 'growth'? Perhaps: economy, progress, prosperity, Gross Domestic Product (GDP), improvement, well-being, wealth, jobs. In the news, we might read about the predicted effects of a crisis on the annual rate of GDP, right next to an article about the importance of meditation for personal growth. All in one word, 'growth' is identified with many things: social and political goals, the dynamics of the economy, individual or social achievement. It forms what the cognitive linguist George Lakoff calls a 'cognitive frame': in which a cluster of ideas is triggered by the mention of a single word.[1] As one example, 'regulation' might denote something positive for those on the left of the political spectrum, signifying the curbing of corporate greed and greater protections for the poor, while, on the right, it has negative connotations: more control by the state over people's personal lives, authoritarianism, socialism. 'Growth', however, as a cognitive frame, is as yet less contested. In many corners of the political spectrum, it still signals improvement, development, more opportunities, more money, and so on. This cluster of interconnected ideas, where growth basically

---

1 George Lakoff, 'Why It Matters How We Frame the Environment', *Environmental Communication* 4, no. 1 (2010): 70–81.

means 'more of the good stuff' or 'progress', is today almost ubiquitous and largely unchallenged.

Because it is both so ubiquitous *and* ambiguous, we need to be very clear and define what we mean by growth before we can even begin talking about degrowth. But this gets complicated when we consider that growth is often – almost purposefully, it seems – poorly defined by the people who advocate for it, even as it is obsessed over. And, given that it seems often simply to mean 'more good things', it is often hard to argue against.

In this book, we analyse growth as a core feature of capitalism. As we discuss in more detail in chapter 3, capitalism can be understood as society driven by accumulation. From this perspective, growth can be understood as the *materialization* of this dynamic of accumulation. To put it differently, capitalism appears as growth – and this materialization is not only *social*, but also *biophysical* or material. In this chapter, we argue that, to understand and dismantle the politics of growth today, we need to analyse economic growth as three interlinked processes that have evolved dynamically over time. First, growth is a relatively recent idea, the hegemony of which is the core ideology of capitalism, justifying the belief that growth is natural, necessary, and good, and that growth, as the increase of output and the development of productive forces, is linked to progress and emancipation. Second, growth is a *social process* that has long preceded the current hegemony of growth in contemporary society: a specific set of social relations resulting from and driving capitalist accumulation that stabilizes modern societies dynamically and at the same time makes them dependent on expansive dynamics of growth, intensification, and acceleration. Third, growth is a material process – the ever-expanding use of land, resources, and energy and the related build-up of physical stocks – which fundamentally transforms the planet and increasingly threatens to undermine the foundations of growth itself.[2]

---

2 See Iris Borowy and Matthias Schmelzer, 'Introduction: The End of Economic Growth in Long-Term Perspective', in *History of the Future of Economic Growth: Historical Roots of Current Debates on Sustainable Degrowth*, ed. Iris Borowy and Matthias Schmelzer (London: Routledge, 2017), 1–26; Eric Pineault, 'The Growth Imperative of Capitalist Society', in *Degrowth in Movement(s):*

Our central argument is that these three each have their own self-reinforcing dynamics, which are nevertheless interlinked, fundamentally shaping how we live. 'Economic growth' thus not only describes the increase and acceleration of the monetary production economy – that which is measured as GDP – but also a comprehensive material, social, and cultural process of mutually constitutive dynamics of expansion. This process of expansion has transformed life and the entire planet over the last five centuries. For a part of humanity, especially in the Global North, this has drastically improved material living conditions and enabled successful social struggles for participation. For others, this process was accompanied by exploitation and the destruction of livelihoods. Today, at the beginning of the twenty-first century, these intertwined dynamics of expansion are increasingly reaching their limits because they undermine the ecological, social, and political foundations on which they are based. We have been told that the rising tide of growth will lift all ships if we do not rock the boat (meaning if we do not disturb the progressive unfolding of the forces of growth and accumulation). However, in the face of the ecological crises of 'existential' proportions, the opposite seems more accurate: If we do not rock the boat of growth and pull the emergency lever, all lower decks will soon drown. If we do not switch tracks now, we will continue to be rocked by crisis after crisis until growth itself throws society from its own rails – violently. This leads us to the next chapter, where we outline the various critiques of growth upon which the degrowth literature has drawn.

2.1. Growth as an idea

One of the more basic, and important, ways to understand growth is as an ideological construction – a collective myth that shapes modern societies and how we are told to see the world and ourselves in it. While growth is also much more than this – as we explore further below

Exploring Pathways for Transformation, ed. Corinna Burkhart, Matthias Schmelzer, and Nina Treu (Winchester: Zer0, 2020), 29–43.

– many people do not realize that the concept of growth itself, applied to the economy, is a surprisingly recent invention. Even though there are various precursors – such as 'development', 'progress', or the much quoted 'wealth of nations' by Adam Smith – the term 'economic growth' has only been used since the middle of the twentieth century. It was not until the invention of GDP in the 1930s that growth in the modern sense could be measured, and it was not until the 1950s that it became the key ideology of capitalist and actually existing socialist societies. Since then, the idea that growth was desirable, necessary, and essentially infinite has become common sense: self-evident and far-reaching, fundamentally shaping the political, social, and economic developments on planet Earth.[3] This increasingly global ideology, which plays a central role in the hegemonic stabilization of modern societies, is what we call the 'growth paradigm'.[4] Yet, as we explore in the following sections, this is only one, and a relatively more recent, dimension of growth. In order to go beyond a simplistic critique of GDP, we must analyse how the modern growth paradigm builds on and is interlinked with growth as a social and material process, going back at least to colonization and early capitalism.

The invention of 'the economy'

An important prerequisite for economic growth becoming so central to state governance was the invention of 'the economy', as an independent sphere of social life based on specific laws which can be statistically recorded and measured. As early as the eighteenth and nineteenth centuries, political economists in England and France postulated economic development as a relatively autonomous sphere that balances itself through the famous 'invisible hand'. This process was considered

---

3 Here we won't get into debates on the differences between hegemony and ideology; see Terry Eagleton, *Ideology: An Introduction* (London: Verso, 1991); and Matthias Schmelzer, *The Hegemony of Growth: The OECD and the Making of the Economic Growth Paradigm* (Cambridge: Cambridge University Press, 2016).
4 Borowy and Schmelzer, *History of the Future of Economic Growth*; Schmelzer, *The Hegemony of Growth*; Gareth Dale, 'The Growth Paradigm: A Critique', *International Socialism* 134 (2012), isj.org.uk.

to be clearly separated from nature and politics and to be determined by its own laws. The separation between economic, political, and natural laws is at the basis of liberalism, a doctrine advancing minimal state intervention into the autonomous sphere of economic activities.[5] But it was not until the 1930s and 1940s that economic experts, politicians, and, increasingly, the public began to understand 'the economy' as a self-contained totality where flows of money regulate the relationships between the production, distribution, and consumption of goods and services within nationally organized borders.[6] This idea, which today is widely taken for granted, replaced the older view in which economic processes were conceptualized as physical material and energy flows, which naturally gave rise to limits to growth. In contrast, the new measures, which aimed at 'the speed and frequency with which paper money changed hands', seemed to be able to expand without limit, without being limited by physical or territorial boundaries.[7]

The development of accounting techniques and statistical tools, in particular national accounts and GDP, was central to this understanding of 'the economy'. The latter was developed in the 1930s and 1940s in conjunction with Keynesian efforts to combat the Great Depression and as a tool for planning war economies and arms production in the United States and England during the Second World War. In GDP, the formerly fuzzy sphere of 'the economy' was crystallized into a technical object with clearly defined contents and boundaries. Put simply, GDP measures the sum of the monetary value of goods and services, produced by paid labour, sold in a given period of time (e.g., one year) in a given economic area (e.g., Greece, or the world). Often, GDP is divided by the number of inhabitants of a country or region and then expressed as per capita GDP. Over time, this became a much-used

5 Philip Mirowski, *More Heat Than Light: Economics as Social Physics, Physics as Nature's Economics* (Cambridge: Cambridge University Press, 1989); Wendy Brown, *Undoing the Demos: Neoliberalism's Stealth Revolution* (Boston: MIT Press, 2015).

6 Timothy Mitchell, 'Economentality: How the Future Entered Government', *Critical Inquiry* 40, no. 4 (2014): 479–507.

7 Ibid.; Timothy Mitchell, *Carbon Democracy: Political Power in the Age of Oil* (London: Verso, 2011); Schmelzer, *The Hegemony of Growth.*

measure of prosperity – and used especially as a metric to compare different countries or different time periods.[8]

As we discuss in more detail in the third chapter, GDP has been criticized from different perspectives. In essence, the criticism is that GDP only measures the *monetary value* of goods and services produced through *gainful employment*: it does not distinguish between the *positive and negative effects* of these products and services on the well-being of a society and makes everything that is not paid for invisible. In addition, GDP measurements fail to take into account *who gets paid for which work*, and how this is *distributed* within a society. This means that unpaid activities such as housework and care, self-sufficiency and subsistence, or voluntary work, as well as stewardship of the land, are not included. An increase in car accidents, for example, can therefore increase GDP through medical treatment, car repairs, and so on – and so can environmental destruction, if it leads to more paid work. The growing production of wasteful packaging, discarded electronics, and damaged and non-repairable equipment, or the monetarization of entire areas of society that were previously not regulated by money, such as ride-sharing, all contribute to economic growth.[9]

Far less well known is the fact that all these controversies about the correct measurement of wealth and the economy can be traced back to the period of development and international standardization of GDP in the late 1940s and early 1950s. Almost all leading economists in the middle of the twentieth century, including the ones who invented GDP, spoke out against using it as a yard-stick for the prosperity of nations

8 Diane Coyle, *GDP: A Brief but Affectionate History* (Princeton, NJ: Princeton University Press, 2014); Lorenzo Fioramonti, *Gross Domestic Problem: The Politics behind the World's Most Powerful Number* (London: Zed Books, 2013); Philipp Lepenies, *The Power of a Single Number: A Political History of GDP* (New York: Columbia University Press, 2016); Dirk Philipsen, *The Little Big Number: How GDP Came to Rule the World and What to Do about It* (Princeton, NJ: Princeton University Press, 2015); Schmelzer, *The Hegemony of Growth*.

9 Stephen J. Macekura, *Mismeasure of Progress: Economic Growth and Its Critics* (Chicago: University of Chicago Pr., 2020); David Pilling, *The Growth Delusion: Wealth, Poverty, and the Well-Being of Nations* (New York: Crown, 2018); Marilyn Waring, *Counting for Nothing: What Men Value and What Women Are Worth* (Toronto: University of Toronto Press, 1999).

and for international or historical comparisons.[10] There were a number of conceptual differences between national traditions for measuring GDP and fundamental disagreements about the measurement method. Debates revolved around concepts such as externalities, unpaid housework, and subsistence. Accordingly, different countries defined income in different ways. Some, for example, did count unpaid housework or, in addition to monetary values, accounted for material flows such as processed steel in kilograms. But governments and international organizations (especially the OECD and the UN) streamlined these intense academic debates, as they urgently needed comparative statistics to manage membership dues and international aid payments, and unified existing approaches by standardizing a particular version of GDP measurement in the early 1950s.[11] Since then, this statistical measuring method established itself in the capitalist West and then globally, making GDP the 'world's most powerful number'.[12] Although the statistical measurement method has been constantly updated and adapted within the framework of the UN – primarily to deal with changes in the importance of trade and technological innovations – the core logic of '(mis-) measuring our lives' through GDP has remained the same to this day.[13]

This modern, *dematerialized* understanding of 'the economy' made invisible how present-day economies fundamentally depend on an ever-increasing flow of energy and matter. Its implementation is closely linked to technical and geopolitical shifts in the twentieth century, which led to the explosion of the global energy supply and the total materials and land used in subsequent decades.[14]

---

10 Schmelzer, *The Hegemony of Growth*; Fioramonti, *Gross Domestic Problem*; Coyle, *GDP*.

11 Schmelzer, *The Hegemony of Growth*.

12 Fioramonti, *Gross Domestic Problem*.

13 Joseph Stiglitz, Amartya Sen, and Jean-Paul Fitoussi, *Mismeasuring Our Lives: Why GDP Doesn't Add Up* (New York: New Press, 2010). See also Philipsen, *The Little Big Number*, and Fioramonti, *Gross Domestic Problem*.

14 Will Steffen et al., 'Trajectories of the Earth System in the Anthropocene', *Proceedings of the National Academy of Sciences* 115, no. 33 (2018): 8252–9; Mitchell, *Carbon Democracy*; Fridolin Krausmann et al., 'Growth in Global Materials Use, GDP and Population during the 20th Century', *Ecological Economics* 68, no. 10 (August 2009): 2696–705.

Bear in mind that GDP is far more than a technical tool for measuring economic activity. It generates a whole grammar that not only shapes economics but also structures shared ideas of the world – above all, through its close connection to the growth paradigm. So, while economic growth is a highly ambivalent and elusive concept, its semantic core is statistically fixed: it is defined as the annual increase in GDP or per capita GDP and is usually expressed in percentages.

The growth paradigm

The international standardization of statistical measurements of the economy was central to making growth a policy objective. Only through this universalized concept of 'the economy', commensurable over time and space, did it become conceivable to measure what was to grow: the sum of market transactions within national borders. Only then did the idea that long-term, stable, and unlimited growth was at all possible and desirable become established.

In fact, in the political discussions of the early post-war period, the idea of economic growth was conspicuously absent. Rather, the central themes were full employment, stability, and reconstruction. Before 1950, there was almost no interest at all in economic growth as a policy goal in political statements or economic literature.[15] In the following years, however, growth was catapulted to the top of the hierarchy of political goals. At the time, movements for decolonization were arising in former colonies around the world, the Cold War was in full swing, and it became imperative to pacify class struggles in both the Global North and South. Something needed to be done to stabilize Western economic dominance and capitalist class relations. There needed to be a way to show conclusively the progress of capitalist economies. First declared the goal of national economic policy by the chairman of the US Council of Economic Advisers in 1949, it became the globally accepted measure of progress from the mid-1950s onwards. The sociological modernization theories developed by North American and

---

15 Dale, 'The Growth Paradigm'; Mitchell, 'Economentality'; Schmelzer, *The Hegemony of Growth.*

European white men were framed as an irreversible and unilinear process of economic growth.[16] Cold War competition further fuelled the race for growth, through which governments could show their economic dominance. Growth became the yard-stick for comparing the productivity of capitalist and socialist economies. Emblematic of this crucial phase of the development of the growth paradigm is a 1958 statement by Nikita Khrushchev, chairman of the Council of Ministers of the Soviet Union: 'Growth of industrial and agricultural production is the battering ram with which we will smash the capitalist system.'[17] Nation-states thus entered into competition not for equality, emancipation, or jobs, but for the rising quantity of goods and services they could produce. By the late 1950s, growth had become a central goal of economic policy and the most important indicator, tying growth and welfare together and equating them with the continuous expansion of market transactions. In this constellation, GDP became the first and general indicator of the modernity, prosperity, standard of living, development, and prestige of countries.

The hegemony of growth fundamentally transformed the state's tasks, purpose, and legitimacy, all of which became linked to growth and thus to the economy. This process occurred much earlier than is usually believed. Wendy Brown, for example, situates the threefold economization of the state in the 1980s and links it to the rise of neoliberalism:

> The state secures, advances, and props the economy; the state's purpose is to facilitate the economy, and the state's legitimacy is linked to the growth of the economy – as an overt actor on behalf of the economy. State action, state purpose, and state legitimacy: each is economized by neoliberalism.

---

16 Arturo Escobar, *Encountering Development: The Making and Unmaking of the Third World* (Princeton, NJ: Princeton University Press, 1995); Ariel Salleh, *Ecofeminism as Politics: Nature, Marx and the Postmodern* (London: Zed Books, 2017).

17 Cited in Schmelzer, *The Hegemony of Growth*, 163; see also Dale, 'The Growth Paradigm'.

A focus on the rise of the growth paradigm, however, shows that already from the 1950s onwards the expansion of the economy became what could be described as the *raison d'état*.[18] Government interventions all over the world became largely focused on maintaining a stable growth path and on creating and maintaining favourable investment conditions. The growth state stood at the centre of the democratic-capitalist constellation of the 'golden age', the long phase of stability and rising prosperity in the second half of the twentieth century.

The growth paradigm has played a key role in transforming the social discourse on how to distribute wealth: from a zero-sum game in which a fixed amount is distributed (so what some win, others lose), to a seemingly positive-sum game in which everyone benefits from the growing economic product and therefore has a common interest in economic growth.[19] Growth promised to turn difficult political conflicts over distribution into technical, non-political management questions of how to collectively increase GDP – an ideology that only partially reflected reality within the capitalist core during the 'golden age', and much less so from a global socio-metabolic perspective.[20]

By thus transforming class and other social antagonisms into so-called win–win situations, it provided what could be called an 'imaginary resolution of real contradictions' and played a key role in producing the stable post-war consensus around embedded liberalism.[21] In the West, growth made it possible to redirect the demands of the workers' movement towards more participation and equality. In the East, it justified the lack of democracy and the failure of revolutionary ambitions. In the 'developing countries' – a category itself developed through the logic of the growth paradigm – it served in combination

18 Brown, *Undoing the Demos*, 64; Schmelzer, *The Hegemony of Growth*.

19 Dale, 'The Growth Paradigm'.

20 Eric Pinault has proposed analysing the 'material trajectory of advanced capitalism as a zero-sum game' during this period. See Eric Pineault, 'The Ghosts of Progress: Contradictory Materialities of the Capitalist Golden Age', *Anthropological Theory* 21, no. 3 (2021): 260–86, 260.

21 Eagleton, *Ideology*; Schmelzer, *The Hegemony of Growth*; Charles S. Maier, 'The Politics of Productivity: Foundations of American International Economic Policy after World War II', *International Organization* 31, no. 4 (1977): 607–33.

with the idea of 'development' as justification for the smashing of subsistence and traditional economies and the implementation of large-scale technical infrastructures after the formal end of colonialism, and further as a way to justify structural adjustment and the stripping of public goods.[22] Growth thus helped to overcome the political focus on equality and redistribution, depoliticizing the economy. As noted by an American economist and advisor to President Eisenhower: 'Growth is a substitute for equality of income. As long as there is growth there is hope, and that makes large income differentials tolerable.'[23]

In fact, growth became presented as the common good, thus justifying the particular interests of those who benefitted most from the expansion of market transactions and capital accumulation as beneficial for all. The historian Charles S. Maier puts it in a nutshell: 'The true dialectic was not one of class against class, but waste versus abundance.'[24] Drawing on the definition of hegemony, as developed by the Italian Marxist Antonio Gramsci, growth appears as an unquestionable, positive value at the centre of a network of ideas and everyday common sense which justifies, and silently coerces people into, contemporary relations of power and hierarchy – including social relations of production such as wage work.[25] As discussed in more detail below, by tightly linking ideas of emancipation and progress to economic growth, the growth paradigm became the normative ideal of modernity – not just in liberal circles, but also in socialist thought. Indeed, the power of this

---

22 Schmelzer, *The Hegemony of Growth*; Escobar, *Encountering Development*; Wolfgang Sachs, *The Development Reader: A Guide to Knowledge and Power* (London: Zed Books, 1992); Giorgos Kallis, *Degrowth* (Newcastle upon Tyne: Agenda Publishing, 2018).

23 Henry C. Wallich, 'Zero Growth', *Newsweek*, 24 January 1972, 62.

24 Cited in Schmelzer, *The Hegemony of Growth*, 117.

25 The hegemony of growth is thus a comprehensive social practice that not only accepts growth as a necessary prerequisite for improving the living conditions of wage earners, but also sanctions dominant forms of ownership and rule. As we will explore in the third chapter, these power relations include class, race, gender, and South–North uneven development. Antonio Gramsci, *Prison Notebooks*, ed. by Joseph A. Buttigieg, vols. 1–3 (New York: Columbia University Press, 2011). See also Giacomo D'Alisa and Giorgos Kallis, 'Degrowth and the State', *Ecological Economics* 169 (2020): 106486; Schmelzer, *The Hegemony of Growth*.

myth became so strong that it captured most intellectual currents and social movements on the progressive left that wanted to overcome capitalism – which, as put by Eric Pineault, 'have remained imprisoned in the imaginary of growth'.[26]

2.2. Growth as a social process

We can now understand growth as a hegemonic idea that emerged quite recently, discursively tied to GDP. But growth is far more than an increase in GDP, as it is normally defined. In fact, GDP is only the tip of the iceberg, the surface phenomenon of a whole set of social processes related to capitalist accumulation that drive growth, and of ever-increasing biophysical flows that are mobilized by this global economy. To see the whole picture of this world system, we must go much further back than the twentieth century, because this newer ideology of growth is itself rooted in both *social* and *biophysical* processes that go back to the beginnings of capitalism and colonialist expansion. This deeper understanding of the nature of growth distinguishes degrowth from more vague critiques of economic growth, which focus on the pitfalls of GDP alone and are limited to proposing alternative ways of measuring economic output, rather than addressing the roots of growth itself. In the following sections we analyse growth as a social process: a specific set of social relations resulting from capitalist accumulation, which not only drive the reproduction of capitalism but also act as a central stabilizing mechanism in modern society. To understand this aspect of growth, we need to engage with the humanities, social sciences, and political economy. In this section, we begin by discussing how capitalism emerged and analyse how growth led to specific class structures which, in turn, brought about a dynamic relationship between class formations and material growth. We argue that 'dynamic stabilization' is a core feature of modern

---

26 Pineault, 'The Growth Imperative of Capitalist Society', 32. See also Schmelzer, *The Hegemony of Growth*; Giorgos Kallis, 'Socialism without Growth', *Capitalism Nature Socialism* 30, 2 (2019): 189–206.

societies – where, in order to remain stable and reproduce their social structures, growth societies require continuous economic expansion, technological innovation and escalation, and social-cultural acceleration. Dynamic stabilization explains how and why growth societies are fundamentally dependent on growth.

Unleashing capital: the dynamics of accumulation

The social materialization of capitalist accumulation can be analysed as an economy driven by the production of profit – in which societal wealth 'presents itself as an immense accumulation of commodities'.[27] The annual production of these commodities is, more or less, what GDP measures. Within capitalism, money moves through society and mobilizes machines, resources, and labour power to produce commodities. As will be discussed in more detail in chapter 3, the expansion of the output of this commodified societal wealth rests on capital being invested (the 'input') to increase the capacity to produce and circulate commodities (the 'output').

Many analyses and critiques of capitalism deal with the structural relations, tensions, and contradictions resulting from the dynamics between these factors, mainly capital and labour, and focus on the period when the monetary production economy became dominant with industrialization. However, the analysis of capitalism that has shaped the degrowth debate not only starts much earlier, with the rise of capitalist enterprises in the context of colonialism. It also centres other processes shaping capitalist growth, mainly related to the commodification and appropriation of nature and care, processes of devaluation, cheapening and externalization, and to the dynamic stabilization of capitalist society through growth. While this analysis will further unfold throughout the rest of the book, the following sections

27 Karl Marx, *Capital: A Critique of Political Economy, Volume 1*, trans. Ben Fowkes (New York: Vintage, 1976), 27; Ulrich Brand et al., 'From Planetary to Societal Boundaries: An Argument for Collectively Defined Self-limitation', *Sustainability: Science, Practice and Policy* 17, no. 1 (2021): 265–92; Augusto Graziani, *The Monetary Theory of Production* (Cambridge: Cambridge University Press, 2003).

sketch some historical background that might help illustrate this perspective.[28]

Homo sapiens have lived on this planet for about 200,000 years. For most of human history, all humans have lived nomadically as hunters and gatherers. Agriculture existed for about 10,000 years as a regionally dominant production method, and since then phases of social development have alternated with phases of decay in various regions of the world. However, there was no, or close to no, economic growth in its modern sense. This only started to change with the beginning of colonialism, the rise of capitalist enterprise, and then industrialization.[29] For most of human history, communities' relationships and self-reproduction were based on systems of mutual obligations, power, or wealth, but not on the logic of capitalism, the ceaseless accumulation of capital. Over thousands of years, humans have experimented with a vast array of social formations, some of which included large and complex civilizations organized on surprisingly egalitarian lines, others involving merchants investing in the expansion of trade – yet on the whole, those dealing with capital remained marginal to those societies. This started to change beginning with the emergence of the 'world system' in the sixteenth century.[30]

---

28 Jason Hickel, *Less Is More: How Degrowth Will Save the World* (London: William Heinemann, 2020); Pineault, 'The Growth Imperative of Capitalist Society'; Utsa Patnaik and Prabhat Patnaik, *Capital and Imperialism: Theory, History, and the Present* (New York: NYU Press, 2021).

29 Of course, all the problems of GDP accounting discussed in this book multiply when economists try to reconstruct long-term growth trends going back hundreds of years to economies where most work was done outside of markets and wage relations. But – as far as this can be measured retrospectively at all – preindustrial growth of GDP was very slow, with annual per capita rates measured in fractions of a per cent. See Vaclav Smil, *Growth: From Microorganisms to Megacities* (Boston: MIT Press, 2019), chapter 5; Jürgen Osterhammel, *The Transformation of the World: A Global History of the Nineteenth Century* (Princeton, NJ: Princeton University Press, 2014); Desmond C. M. Platt, *Mickey Mouse Numbers in World History: The Short View* (Basingstoke: Macmillan, 1989).

30 David Graeber and David Wengrow, *The Dawn of Everything: A New History of Humanity* (New York: Farrar, Straus and Giroux, 2021); Sven Beckert, *Empire of Cotton: A Global History* (New York: Alfred A. Knopf, 2014); Immanuel

At that time, early venture capital companies, driven by the arms race of the early modern European states and their enormous capital requirements, financed expansionary voyages to the Americas, importing raw materials such as cotton and silver. From these early colonial enterprises, trading companies emerged, which later developed into joint-stock companies whose central purpose was, and remains, the endless accumulation of capital. Increasingly, capitalists started to invest in agriculture and industry, thus permeating the world of human labour with the logic of continuous accumulation and – where they could, as with the plantation regime around cotton – remaking the entire mode of production to their benefit. By appropriating raw materials, based on both slave and wage labour, and by integrating these through trade flows that spanned from Europe to the Africas, Asia, and the Americas, they created a dynamic world system that has since reshaped the entire planet.[31]

This accumulation took place at the expense of people in different parts of the world in different ways. In the Americas, genocides were perpetrated against Indigenous peoples, and millions of people from African regions were sold into slavery. The entire colonial enterprise, so intricately linked to the emergence of capitalism, was justified by racism – the systematic dehumanization of certain groups of people for the benefit of others – which came to form an integral part of the social dynamics of capitalism to this day. Through the privatization of the commons, the rural population in Europe lost the basis for their subsistence production. These enclosures also created the everyday scarcity that is still the basis of capitalist growth today – limiting people's ability to use their surroundings for subsistence and generation of communal wealth. Stripped of the land and their means of subsistence production, people were forced into wage labour – a process of violent 'primitive

Wallerstein, *World-Systems Analysis: An Introduction* (Durham, NC: Duke University Press, 2004).

31 Ibid.; Amitav Ghosh, *The Nutmeg's Curse: Parables for a Planet in Crisis* (Chicago: University of Chicago Press, 2021); Jason W. Moore, *Capitalism in the Web of Life: Ecology and the Accumulation of Capital* (London: Verso, 2015); Fabian Scheidler, *The End of the Megamachine: A Brief History of a Failing Civilization* (Winchester: Zer0, 2020).

accumulation' (Karl Marx) or incorporation of non-capitalist social worlds (Rosa Luxemburg) that continues in ever-changing forms to this day. States played a key role in all of this – not only in the 'war capitalism' of the earlier period, but also by driving land seizure around the world and by using their powers in the 'cheapening' of key resources, in imperial wars underlying capitalist development, or in guaranteeing the property rights that made capitalist production possible in the first place.[32] As we discuss at length in the next section, the entire dynamism within the world system changed when, beginning in the eighteenth century, the plantation revolution in the Americas was linked with emerging industrial capitalism in Europe, which in turn started to be increasingly powered by a truly revolutionary technology: coal-fired steam engines.[33]

These social and economic changes went hand in hand with the emergence of a set of perspectives and ideas that legitimized, enabled, and even drove the expansion of the world system – and which also laid the foundation for the later development of the modern growth paradigm. To begin with, the idea of the 'development' or 'progress' of human societies in a linear course of time had to be actively produced. Most known cultures of the past – as well as some contemporary communities – had a cyclical understanding of time as 'eternal recurrence', interpreted their present as an abandonment from a mythical ideal past to be restored, or had some other non-linear conception of time. Yet beginning with the Renaissance and building on Christian apocalypticism, which assumed an absolute end point of human societies with the Last

32 Marx, *Capital, Volume 1*, 873; Rosa Luxemburg, *The Accumulation of Capital* (London, New York: Routledge, 2003 [1913]); Silvia Federici, *Caliban and the Witch: Women, the Body and Primitive Accumulation* (New York: Autonomedia, 2004); Patnaik and Patnaik, *Capital and Imperialism*; Karl Polanyi, *The Great Transformation* (Boston: Beacon Press, 1944); Moore, *Capitalism in the Web of Life*; Cedric J. Robinson, *Black Marxism: The Making of the Black Radical Tradition* (Chapel Hill: University of North Carolina Press, 2005); Hartmut Rosa, Stephan Lessenich, and Klaus Dörre, *Sociology, Capitalism, Critique* (London: Verso, 2015).

33 Andreas Malm, *Fossil Capital: The Rise of Steam Power and the Roots of Global Warming* (London: Verso, 2016); Beckert, *Empire of Cotton*; Kenneth Pomeranz, *The Great Divergence: China, Europe, and the Making of the Modern World Economy* (Princeton, NJ: Princeton University Press, 2000).

Judgment, concepts of abstract time and space emerged in Europe, in particular since the seventeenth century. The spread of the mechanical clock promoted changes in the understanding of time as objective, linear, and countable. Geometry and cartography also enabled a new conceptualization of land and territory as abstract, borderless, uniform, and measurable space that can be emptied or filled as needed, clearly demarcated, and traded as a commodity through property rights.[34] Early modern natural sciences not only promoted the idea of abstract nature but also argued that humans could dominate nature. In a mechanistic view of the world, nature and human labour were conceived of as mechanisms governed by laws and flows of energy that could correspondingly be manipulated and controlled (see section 3.6).[35]

Concepts and practices of linear time, abstract space, and mechanical nature became key ideological building blocks of the capitalist colonization of the planet. The practical treatment of all things and living beings as comparable, interchangeable, and tradable, as well as the mechanistic understanding of nature based on linear thinking, were consolidated in colonialism. The plundering of the planet was thus justified by the idea that land, natural resources, the work of women and the colonized, and all life are to serve mankind (and this was usually meant only the white men who claimed ownership of it[36]) and can therefore be possessed, exploited, and changed at will (see sections 3.1 and 3.5).[37] Beginning with the seventeenth century, these ideas

34 Scheidler, *The End of the Megamachine*; Dale, 'The Growth Paradigm'; Malm, *Fossil Capital*; Carolyn Merchant, *The Death of Nature: Women, Ecology, and Scientific Revolution* (San Francisco: Harper and Row, 1980).

35 Merchant, *The Death of Nature*; Joachim Radkau, *Nature and Power: A Global History of the Environment* (Cambridge: Cambridge University Press, 2008); George Caffentzis, *In Letters of Blood and Fire: Work, Machines, and the Crisis of Capitalism* (Oakland: PM Press, 2012).

36 *White* is not a biological property, but rather the privileged position within the dominant structures of racism. Alan H. Goodman, Yolanda T. Moses, and Joseph L. Jones, *Race: Are We So Different?* (Hoboken, NJ: John Wiley & Sons, 2019); Cedric J. Robinson, *On Racial Capitalism, Black Internationalism, and Cultures of Resistance* (London: Pluto Press, 2019).

37 Ghosh, *The Nutmeg's Curse*; Richard H. Grove, *Green Imperialism: Colonial Expansion, Tropical Island Edens and the Origins of Environmentalism, 1600–1860*

underwent a secularized reformulation: a linear narrative of progress divided people into 'civilized' and 'primitive' based on racist metrics, thus legitimizing colonial expansions. At the height of imperialism and in early 'development' discourse, poor countries were seen to be in need of outside intervention by European or American experts, to speed up their 'development' on a linear path of social and economic improvement. In the twentieth century, the linear narrative was economized, as general social progress was increasingly conflated with the expansion of production.[38] Under capitalism, growth became the secular promise of redemption.

The mechanistic understanding of nature also laid the foundation for eighteenth-century European economists' understanding of 'the economy' as a separate area of social life that is measurable and predictable like clockwork – and which corresponded to changes in the world of work.[39] This sector of the formal economy was characterized throughout the nineteenth century by the spread of gainful employment as a male-dominated sector separate from the rest of life. At the same time, unpaid reproductive work became 'housewifely' – devalued, but necessary for the reproduction of labour power. Thus the invisibility and appropriation of unpaid reproductive work associated with wage labour still characterizes gender relations and the world of work today (see section 3.6).[40] Different disciplinary technologies, manifested in institutions such as factories, the military, prisons, and

---

(Cambridge: Cambridge University Press, 2010); Naomi Klein, *This Changes Everything: Capitalism vs. the Climate* (London: Penguin UK, 2014).

38 Escobar, *Encountering Development*; Walter Mignolo and Catherine E. Walsh, *On Decoloniality: Concepts, Analytics, Praxis* (Durham, NC: Duke University Press, 2018); Gilbert Rist, *The History of Development: From Western Origins to Global Faith* (London: Zed Books, 1996); Schmelzer, *The Hegemony of Growth*.

39 Dale, 'The Growth Paradigm'. For more historical literature, see Giorgos Kallis et al., 'Research on Degrowth', *Annual Review of Environment and Resources* 43 (2018): 291–316.

40 Veronika Bennholdt-Thomsen and Maria Mies, *The Subsistence Perspective: Beyond the Globalized Economy* (London: Zed Books, 1999); Maria Mies and Vandana Shiva, *Ecofeminism* (London: Zed Books, 1993); Moore, *Capitalism in the Web of Life*; Salleh, *Ecofeminism as Politics*.

schools, promoted the proletarianization of labour. This change in work led to the monetarization of more and more spheres of life and was accompanied by the suppression of relationships of reciprocity.[41] This proletarianization of previously subsistence-based communities, rooted in the system of wage labour, created a lock-in effect, where workers, too, depend on growth to satisfy their most basic needs as they are no longer able to survive outside of the capitalist system.[42]

The social implementation of abstract concepts of time and space, a process that took centuries to reach the entire globe, symptomatically stands for the abstract logic of capitalist modernity: the practice of the – scientific, and above all economic – production of equivalences between completely different concrete realities. The fact that labour, land, and many other things were made measurable and comparable, largely by means of an abstract standard of comparison expressed in money, created the conditions for exchanging everything for everything else.[43] Growth, in this sense, is also a process of the relentless and often violent commodification and repeated colonization of natures, life worlds, and reproductive activities, all of which became increasingly shaped by market-mediated social relations – a process that is still ongoing.[44]

Growth as dynamic stabilization

Modern societies dynamically stabilize through a continuous process of expansion and intensification in terms of space, time, and

41 David Graeber, *Bullshit Jobs: A Theory* (New York: Simon & Schuster, 2018); Osterhammel, *The Transformation of the World*.

42 Pineault, 'The Growth Imperative of Capitalist Society'; Adelheid Biesecker and Sabine Hofmeister, 'Focus: (Re)productivity: Sustainable Relations Both between Society and Nature and between the Genders', *Ecological Economics* 69 (2010): 1703–11.

43 Max Horkheimer and Theodor W. Adorno, *Dialectic of Enlightenment* (London: Verso, 1996).

44 Raj Patel and Jason W. Moore, *A History of the World in Seven Cheap Things: A Guide to Capitalism, Nature, and the Future of the Planet* (Berkeley: University of California Press, 2017); Hickel, *Less Is More*.

energy.[45] This means that modern societies inherently rely on growth to stabilize their institutions. These dynamics, while being based on processes of appropriation and exploitation as analysed above, did provide material prosperity to more and more people. While initially largely reserved to *white* men in the middle and upper classes in Europe, these sustained dynamics of growth also enabled successful social and political struggles that made this material standard of living accessible to an increasingly larger part of humanity, especially in the Global North, but also in the middle and upper classes of the Global South. This increasing democratization of material prosperity – from consumer goods such as sugar and tea for European workers in the nineteenth century to larger private homes, household appliances, cars, and travel in the twentieth century – again laid the foundation for the continued acceleration of economic growth. And – as a stabilizing mechanism for capitalism – the promise of rising levels of material prosperity through economic growth served to pacify social conflicts and to create consent for the technocratic, productivist politics of growth societies.[46] This does not only apply to the capitalist core countries. Even the real existing socialist societies of the twentieth century were – albeit under different circumstances – fundamentally productivist growth societies. Under the pressure of competition between the Western and Eastern blocs, they also relied on increasing economic output and growing material prosperity in order to guarantee their social stability.[47] And, as we will explore throughout the book, the promise of a better life through growth also

45 Rosa, Lessenich, and Dörre, *Sociology, Capitalism, Critique*; Radkau, *Nature and Power*; Moore, *Capitalism in the Web of Life*; Hartmut Rosa, *Resonance: A Sociology of Our Relationship to the World* (Cambridge: Polity Press, 2019).

46 Frank Trentmann, *Empire of Things: How We Became a World of Consumers, from the Fifteenth Century to the Twenty-First* (New York: Harper Perennial, 2017); Schmelzer, *Hegemony of Growth*; Kallis, *Degrowth*; Tim Jackson, *Prosperity without Growth: Economics for a Finite Planet* (London: Earthscan, 2016).

47 Radkau, *Nature and Power*; Wallerstein, *World-Systems Analysis*; Ekaterina Chertkovskaya and Alexander Paulsson, 'The Growthocene: Thinking Through What Degrowth Is Criticising', *Entitle Blog*, 19 February 2016, entitleblogdotorg3 .wordpress.com.

legitimized and thus stabilized uneven development globally – the promise of future growth made inequalities seem acceptable.

Furthermore, dynamic stabilization goes beyond material prosperity. In fact, many of the social and political achievements people in modern welfare states have access to today, such as the right to vote, a minimum wage, health care, and a five-day workweek, were fought for by strong social movements and trade unions in the context of expansive and fossil fuel–driven modernity. The power of the strike in the twentieth century, for example, was closely linked to the need for the labour force to operate the facilities necessary for the mining, transport, and processing of coal and, consequently, their ability to effectively paralyse them. To highlight the intimate entanglements between the material properties of coal, which enabled coal workers to become the spearhead of a strong workers movement that successfully fought for welfare and participation, and the resulting mass democracy, the historian Timothy Mitchell has termed modern representative systems 'carbon democracies'.[48] The historian Dipesh Chakrabarty makes a similar argument: emancipation movements went hand in hand with the dynamics of fossil fuel–powered growth and were based on it: 'The mansion of modern freedoms stands on an ever-expanding base of fossil fuel use. Most of our freedoms so far have been energy-intensive.'[49] And similar arguments can be made regarding other modern achievements. Indeed, the public institutions of modern societies – including the welfare state itself, which sought to pacify and constrain capitalism and which emerged from the great emancipatory struggles of the nineteenth and twentieth centuries – stabilize themselves through economic growth: they emerged within, contributed to, and are structurally dependent on expanding economies.[50] This includes institutions such as pension systems, health insurance, unemployment benefits, long-term care insurance, public education systems, universities, and public infrastructures (roads and railways, water and sewage pipelines,

---

48 Mitchell, *Carbon Democracy*.

49 Dipesh Chakrabarty, 'The Climate of History: Four Theses', *Critical Inquiry* 35, no. 2 (2009): 208.

50 Rosa, Lessenich, and Dörre, *Sociology, Capitalism, Critique*.

electricity and telecommunications networks). Increasing production created surpluses and thus facilitated struggles for the distribution of wealth, the shortening of working hours, and social security systems.[51] As also argued by Thomas Piketty, the structural tendency within capitalism to increase inequality could historically be counteracted in phases of high growth.[52] It must be noted, however, that these achievements, rights, and freedoms were not the direct outcome of capitalist growth, but rather resulted from struggles from below. As the economic historian Stefania Barca points out, '*health, wealth, longevity and security* are not the result of global trade and capital, but of those forces which have opposed them.'[53] Nonetheless, these struggles did occur within the context of economic growth and were fundamentally shaped by it – and this has important implications for a future beyond growth.

In the nineteenth and twentieth centuries, the economic and social model of an expansive modernity, characterized by growth, was thus not only very successful in material terms but also enabled rising and hitherto-unknown levels of social, political, and cultural achievements and rights, mostly within the early industrialized capitalist centres, but in parts also in emerging countries and globally. The fact that key democratic, social, and cultural rights were thus fought for in the context of expansive modernity, and that within the growth paradigm societal progress became conflated with GDP growth, has laid the foundation for a powerful common sense, based on lived experience, that social improvements do indeed require economic growth and the development of the productive forces. This applies in particular to the Fordist regime, which prevailed mainly in industrialized countries from the 1920s to the 1970s. Fordism was a social constellation of production methods and

51 See, for example, Bernd Sommer and Harald Welzer, *Transformationsdesign: Wege in eine zukunftsfähige Moderne* (München: Oekom, 2014); Rosa, Lessenich, and Dörre, *Sociology, Capitalism, Critique*; Imre Szeman and Dominic Boyer, eds., *Energy Humanities: An Anthology* (Baltimore: Johns Hopkins University Press, 2017).

52 Thomas Piketty, *Capital in the Twenty-First Century* (Cambridge, MA: Harvard University Press, 2014).

53 Stefania Barca, *Forces of Reproduction: Notes for a Counter-hegemonic Anthropocene* (Cambridge: Cambridge University Press, 2020), 17.

power relations based on standardized factory labour (largely male bread-winners), rising productivity (based on fossil fuels and standardization), and rising wages (enabling increasing mass-consumer markets to absorb the rising output), which temporarily pacified the conflict between capital and labour mainly in industrialized countries. The very high growth rates of this period helped to create consumer societies built around a work-and-spend ethics and ample markets to increase production, which was key for capital to expand – as put by Henry Ford himself: 'Cars don't buy cars'. At the same time, high growth rates did translate to a certain democratization of prosperity – it was the period in which Western lifestyles of building houses in suburbs, driving cars, and owning washing machines became dominant.[54] Today, even after decades of neoliberal welfare cuts and austerity, social memory of this era still powerfully links hopes of social improvement to growth.

This experience of the democratization of prosperity, which was powerfully associated with growth, became the formative experience of entire generations in industrialized countries. Recently, the term 'imperial mode of living' was introduced to describe how this way of life, which has great capacity to stabilize capitalist centres, requires an uneven, imperial global structure that ensures global access to cheap resources, energy, and labour, while at the same time externalizing its ecological costs to Global South regions and the future. Driven by the global spread of its media representation, the imperial mode of living, with all its fossil fuel–based comforts and capitalist consumer goods, also became a global dream for many, even in the peripheral regions, who had thus far laboured to provide the foundations of this prosperity but were excluded from its benefits (see section 3.7).[55] It is this experience of Fordist democratization of prosperity and its attachment to consumer lifestyles which the critique of growth today has to work its way through, at least in the early-industrializing countries. In fact, the legitimating narrative of the progressive nature of growth and the

---

54 Eric Pineault, 'From Provocation to Challenge: Degrowth, Capitalism and the Prospect of "Socialism without Growth"; A Commentary on Giorgios Kallis', *Capitalism Nature Socialism* 30, no. 2 (2018): 1–16.

55 Ulrich Brand and Markus Wissen, *The Imperial Mode of Living: Everyday Life and the Ecological Crisis of Capitalism* (London: Verso, 2021).

development of productive forces is so powerful that it also shapes the outlook of parts of the left. And the function of growth as a stabilizing mechanism remains one of its key justifications.

However, this common sense is increasingly eroding: contemporary growth since the 1970s is showing diminishing social returns. In the capitalist core, ever higher economic output has failed to translate into a proportionate increase in well-being; this growth has not led to more equality (except in parts of Asia), because the fruits of growth have largely been captured by a small global elite; and, most importantly, continuous growth and the spread of consumer-oriented lifestyles throughout the world are producing ever more visibly devastating ecological and social effects globally.[56] These make clear that while continuous growth stabilizes social conditions in the core – where the benefits accrue – and has the capacity to mediate contradictions between capital and labour through the redistribution of production and surplus, this constellation becomes increasingly precarious with economic conditions deteriorating for many, even in the centres. And it comes at a price. Such contradictions are actually displaced towards other spheres of life and to the Global South. In effect, the globalization of the 'imperial mode of living' threatens to destroy the very achievements on which its ideological power rests. Growth is a powerful stabilizing mechanism of capitalist modernity – yet it also destabilizes the ecological foundations of human life on this planet.

2.3. Growth as a material process

Growth, we have argued, is a culturally hegemonic idea in modern society. And growth is also a social process driven by accumulation, characterized not only by the relations internal to capitalism, such as capital and labour, exploitation, or alienation, but also by relations that define the struggles on its frontiers, such as appropriation, externalization, and

---

56 Lucas Chancel et al., *World Inequality Report 2022* (Harvard University Press, 2022); Richard Wilkinson and Kate Pickett, *The Spirit Level: Why Greater Equality Makes Societies Stronger* (New York: Bloomsbury Press, 2011).

unequal exchange. Growth, as a social process, dynamically stabilized modern societies. In this section, we discuss growth as a material, biophysical process: the accelerating movement and use of more and more resources, energy, land, consumable goods like food or smartphones, and the resulting waste products and emissions – all of which are considered part of the 'social metabolism' of society. Going beyond critically analysing the ideology of growth and the monetary production economy, a critical theory of growth also includes analysing how growth appears in the material world, as a biophysical process, and how its expansive nature produces socio-ecological contradictions.[57]

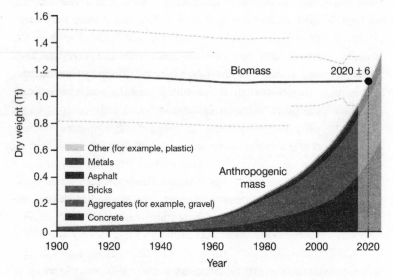

Figure 2.1. Biomass and anthropogenic mass estimates since the beginning of the twentieth century on a dry-mass basis. Source: Emily Elhacham, Liad Ben-Uri, Jonathan Grozovski, Yinon M. Bar-On, and Ron Milo, 'Global Human-Made Mass Exceeds All Living Biomass', *Nature* 588, no. 7838 (2020): 442–4.

57 John Bellamy Foster, *Marx's Ecology: Materialism and Nature* (New York: Monthly Review Press, 2000).

One way to get an impression of this material dimension of growth is through scientific analyses that measure the weight of all the mass of the objects produced by humans – from buildings and infrastructure to plastic bottles and smartphones. This research in industrial and political ecology has generated some striking results: since around 1900, this 'anthropogenic mass', which consists mainly of concrete, aggregates, bricks, asphalt, and metals, has increased rapidly, doubling roughly every twenty years (see Figure 2.1). Today, human-made stuff equal to each person's body weight is produced every single week for everyone alive globally. This 'anthropogenic mass', which at the beginning of the twentieth century accounted for only about 3 per cent of all biomass (all the trees, shrubs, other plants, animal bodies, and so on) on Earth, surpassed the overall biomass around the year 2020. The mass of produced plastics alone is double the mass of all the terrestrial and marine animals, including the bodies of humans.[58] How can we conceptualize this material dimension of economic growth – and what ecological and social repercussions does it have?

Accumulation as biophysical growth

Economic growth not only appears as the 'immense accumulation of commodities' – the ever-expanding stream of commodified things and beings and the social relations making these possible. Growth is also experienced as biophysical and material change and as the accumulation of stuff. This includes transformations in our environments, as – driven by rising demand for energy – coal mines swallow villages and forests in Germany, the oil industry destroys livelihoods in the Niger delta, or rare earth mining in northern China – critical for electric cars – produces radioactive earth dumps, poisoned groundwater, and replaces Indigenous

58 Emily Elhacham et al., 'Global Human-Made Mass Exceeds All Living Biomass', *Nature* 588, no. 7838 (2020): 442–4; see also Fridolin Krausmann et al., 'Global Socioeconomic Material Stocks Rise 23-Fold over the 20th Century and Require Half of Annual Resource Use', *Proceedings of the National Academy of Sciences* 114, no. 8 (2017): 1880–5; Heinz Schandl et al., 'Global Material Flows and Resource Productivity: Forty Years of Evidence', *Journal of Industrial Ecology* 22, no. 4 (2018): 827–38.

populations. Material growth is also experienced through ever larger cities, rising buildings, urban sprawl, or the construction of more highways. Or it appears as diverse agro-economic or pastural systems being continuously replaced by industrial agriculture, factory farming, or monocultural crop production for global agrobusiness.

To understand this biophysical dimension of growth, degrowth offers an analytical apparatus that builds on biophysical and ecological economics (see also section 3.1). Centrally, growth can be analysed as the flows of energy and matter that are passing through societies – extracted in some useful form, put to work or consumed, and eventually emitted as waste. In this metabolic process, these flows are not only sustaining human and non-human bodies, but also the infrastructures and material artefacts that humans have built, which require energy and materials to be sustained and are analysed as 'stocks'. From this ecological and materialist perspective, economic growth necessarily requires increasing throughput of energy and matter – a fact that tends to be disguised by the focus on GDP or 'the economy' in terms of monetary flows.[59] As will be discussed in more detail throughout the book, while efforts to dematerialize the economy through increased efficiency and the use of renewable energy and resources might change the equation somewhat, they cannot escape the necessary materiality of economic growth.[60]

The social metabolism of capitalism relies mainly on non-circular flows of energy and materials that constantly run through 'the economy' and build up as rising stocks or are released as waste. This means that for production to happen, energy and matter must be extracted at

---

59 Marina Fischer-Kowalski and Karl-Heinz Erb, 'Core Concepts and Heuristics', in *Social Ecology: Society-Nature Relations across Time and Space*, ed. Helmut Haberl et al., *Human-Environment Interactions* (Cham: Springer International Publishing, 2016), 29–61; Herman E. Daly and Joshua C. Farley, *Ecological Economics: Principles and Applications* (Washington: Island Press, 2011); Pineault, 'The Growth Imperative of Capitalist Society', Anke Schaffartzik et al., 'The Transformation of Provisioning Systems from an Integrated Perspective of Social Metabolism and Political Economy: A Conceptual Framework', *Sustainability Science*, 18 (2021).

60 Schandl et al., 'Global Material Flows'.

a 'source', which creates ecological effects such as the depletion of ecosystems. And after the throughput has been transformed and consumed, it is excreted as waste into a 'sink' and must be reintegrated into ecosystems and biological cycles. Again, this causes ecological and biogeochemical effects such as plastic waste polluting oceans or, most critically, carbon emissions driving the climate catastrophe. At sources and sinks, where capitalism encounters nature, the ecological contradictions resulting from accumulation and growth as a material process manifest most clearly – presenting both resistance to capital as well as opportunities for further innovation and renewal. Yet, as will be discussed in depth later, flows are subject not only to economic dynamics, but also to the laws of physics and thermodynamics – which has far-reaching repercussions for the prospects of infinite growth of throughputs, and thus also for the prospects of endless accumulation (see section 3.1).

Within capitalism, the flow of energy and matter through the economy must constantly be kept going or accelerated to increase the output of commodities and thus avert the ever-present spectre of overproduction. As argued by Eric Pineault, to absorb surplus capacity in the form of unused machines (fixed capital) or uninvested profits, output in mass consumer societies is managed in specific ways that allow for more growth:

> Commodities, even the most basic, are designed to maximize output consumption: they don't last long, they are overwrapped, they are disposable or they depend on energy and matter thirsty artefacts that households must collect to enjoy them ... It is not only that the output must be absorbed and consumed, but it must be consumed in such a way as to make room for the absorption of a continuously expanding output. This is growth.[61]

Of course, this material growth, which is driven by competitive efforts to impede the structural crisis of overaccumulation, has disastrous

---

61 Pineault, 'The Growth Imperative of Capitalist Society', 40. See also Foster, *Marx's Ecology*; Trentman, *Empire of Things*.

effects at both source and sink. New research has calculated the total amount of resources and energy that is wasted due to throughput being directed by accumulation; it concludes that every year the global economy 'mismanage[s] around ... 49% of the food produced, 31% of the energy produced, 85% of ores and 26% of non-metallic minerals extracted, respectively'. Consequently, natural resources are being depleted, ecosystems are polluted, and livelihoods depending on these are destroyed.[62]

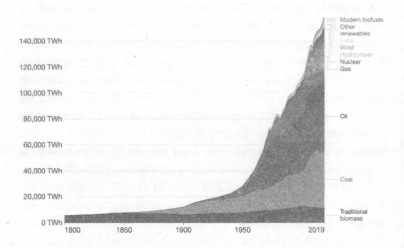

Figure 2.2. Global direct primary energy consumption.
Even as renewables increase exponentially, they
are dwarfed by increased use of fossil fuels. Source:
Vaclav Smil, *Energy Transitions: Global and National
Perspectives* (Santa Barbara: Praeger, 2017), and BP
Statistical Review of World Energy; Our World
in Data, https://ourworldindata.org/
grapher/global-primary-energy.

62 Marín-Beltrán et al., 'Scientists' Warning against the Society of Waste', *Science of the Total Environment* (2021), 151359. See also section 3.1.

Fossil fuels play a particularly central role in the social metabolism of capitalism.[63] Previous societies were dependent on renewable forms of energy. These are ultimately derived from solar energy concurrently in circulation – mostly biomass and land, but also wind and water, and are limited in their ability to scale up production and cannot easily be transported. Thus, people were primarily dependent on available land, biological processes, the specific temporality of plant and animal life, and unchangeable phenomena such as the weather. Fossil fuels fundamentally transformed all that – by giving access to the stored energy of millennia of past photosynthesis, these underground reserves provided an extremely concentrated, powerful, and cheap form of energy. Thus, the entire dynamic of capitalism changed when, in the early nineteenth century, British industrialists started to systematically use coal to fire steam engines. By creating a powerful 'prime mover' that over time came to power anything from the spinning jenny in the cotton factory to Elon Musk's spacecraft, a particularly dynamic and expansive social formation was unleashed: 'fossil capitalism'.[64]

Fossil fuels made it possible to produce increasingly independently of time and space by enabling a constantly available flow of highly concentrated energy that could be increased almost at will, regardless of the specificities of a location. It thus dramatically increased the power of capitalists over the workforce and the production process, which could move wherever labour was cheap and obedient. It also provided the material and energetic basis not only for the expansion of industrial wage labour, but also a previously unknown increase in productivity, an entire range of new mass-produced materials such as steel, cement, and plastic and new forms of increasingly rapid mobility.[65] During the nineteenth and twentieth centuries, the continuously increasing use of fossil fuels has fundamentally transformed almost all areas of modern societies – from the way we live, fight wars, or grow food to the specific forms of nation-states and

63 Elmar Altvater, 'The Growth Obsession', *Socialist Register* 38 (2009): 73–92.

64 Malm, *Fossil Capital*.

65 Cara Daggett, *The Birth of Energy: Fossil Fuels, Thermodynamics, and the Politics of Work* (Durham: Duke University Press, 2019); Ghosh, *The Nutmeg's Curse*; Osterhammel, *The Transformation of the World*; Radkau, *Nature and Power*.

geopolitics, gender roles, or the prevalent 'carbon culture'.[66] Fossil fuels
have powered not only economic expansion during this period, but also
the increase in societal throughput and the acceleration of other core variables of the Earth system and related social trends. The capitalism of
continuous economic growth that we know is fundamentally a fossil capitalism. And while renewable energy has grown exponentially in recent
years, this is still comparatively minor and partly offset by the simultaneous growth of fossil fuel energy – instead of a global energy transition, we
are largely seeing energy additions (see Figure 2.2).[67]

The great acceleration and ecological crises

The material and social dynamics ushered in by this economic expansion
are often illustrated with the now iconic 'great acceleration' graphs. Scientists
have calculated and visualized a series of socio-economic and Earth system
trends between the years 1750 and 2010.[68] They show that sustained growth
in its various dimensions is a relatively new phenomenon. Only since the
nineteenth century have key measurable variables – such as population,
water consumption, fertilizer consumption, urbanization, the construction
of dams, transport, and so on – begun growing significantly. This process
accelerated even more in the middle of the twentieth century, and its trajectory remains largely unbroken to the present day (see Figure 2.3). To understand the trends of the great acceleration, we need to interpret them not only
in relation to the physical growth of societies, but as resulting from the
dynamics of accumulation as discussed in the previous sections.[69]

---

66 Cara Daggett, 'Petro-Masculinity: Fossil Fuels and Authoritarian Desire',
Millennium 47, no. 1 (2018): 25–44; Bob Johnson, *Carbon Nation: Fossil Fuels in
the Making of American Culture* (Lawrence, KS: University Press of Kansas, 2014);
Mitchell, *Carbon Democracy*.
67 On this aspect, see in particular the works by Vaclav Smil. For example,
Vaclav Smil, *Energy Transitions: Global and National Perspectives* (Santa Barbara:
ABC-CLIO, 2017); Vaclav Smil, *Growth: From Microorganisms to Megacities*
(Cambridge: MIT Press, 2020).
68 Steffen et al., 'Trajectories of the Earth System'. See also Smil, *Growth*.
69 Christoph Görg et al., 'Scrutinizing the Great Acceleration: The
Anthropocene and Its Analytic Challenges for Social-Ecological Transformations',
Anthropocene Review 7, no. 1 (2020): 42–61.

This great acceleration has irreversibly changed human life and planet Earth. The concept of the 'Anthropocene', coined by Paul Crutzen and embraced by natural scientists, ecologists, geologists, and historians, describes the age in which humanity itself has become the dominant geological force on Earth. But it is not the abstract 'anthropos' (human being) who is responsible for ecological changes or who has produced them, but a specific mode of (re-)production based on growth and expansion. Some therefore speak of a 'capitalocene' or 'growthocene'.[70] And despite efforts to delink the growth of GDP from material growth (emissions, material throughput, and energy use), these trends have continued to go up in the aggregate, quickly pushing the global Earth system beyond the limits recommended by scientists.

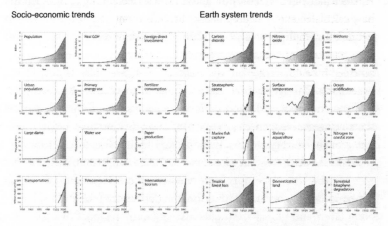

Figure 2.3. The great acceleration. Source: Will Steffen, Wendy Broadgate, Lisa Deutsch, Owen Gaffney, and Cornelia Ludwig, 'The Trajectory of the Anthropocene: The Great Acceleration', *Anthropocene Review* 2, no. 1 (2015): 81–98.

70 Jason W. Moore, 'The Capitalocene, Part I: On the Nature and Origins of Our Ecological Crisis', *Journal of Peasant Studies* 44, no. 3 (2017): 594–630; Andreas Malm and Alf Hornborg, 'The Geology of Mankind? A Critique of the Anthropocene Narrative', *Anthropocene Review*, no. 1 (2014): 62–9; Chertkovskaya and Paulsson, 'The Growthocene'.

Indeed, a multiplicity of studies show clearly that most of these trajectories of material growth cannot continue. Already in 1972, the 'Limits to Growth' report to the Club of Rome used an at-the-time ground-breaking computer model to show that continuous rates of growth of economic and material variables would most likely lead to the depletion of key resources by the 2030s. The material limits to growth, this much-discussed report stated, would also imply limits to economic growth in general. In the decades since, different groups of scientists have repeated the modelling from the report with contemporary data and showed that with the exception of some aberrations, current data map quite accurately to the models from 1972.[71] Since then, more and more scientific evidence has cast doubt on the prospects of continuous biophysical growth over the next decades – the growth of stocks and flows of human-made matter, or of the use of energy. This research strengthened the claim that physical limits will eventually also imply an end to economic growth itself.[72]

In 2009, Johan Rockström's team at the Stockholm Resilience Centre identified nine different 'planetary boundaries' – thresholds which, when crossed, would trigger unpredictable ecological breakdown. Research has since shown that the global economy has already crossed five: *irreversible* climate change, *mass* species extinction, *excessive* land use, the *overburdening* of the nitrogen cycle, and *pollution* by novel entities including plastics and chemicals. The global transformation of nature has already exceeded the 'safe operating space for humanity'. Regarding the other four boundaries – ocean acidification, the depletion of the stratospheric ozone layer, and global freshwater usage – only regional overuse has

---

71 Tim Jackson and Robin Webster, *Limits Revisited: A Review of the Limits to Growth Debate* (London: All-Party Parliamentary Group on Limits to Growth, 2016); Graham Turner, *A Comparison of The Limits to Growth with Thirty Years of Reality*, Socio-economics and the Environment in Discussion Working Paper Series (Canberra: CSIRO Sustainable Ecosystems, 2008); Gaya Herrington, 'Update to Limits to Growth: Comparing the World3 Model with Empirical Data', *Journal of Industrial Ecology* 25, no. 3 (2021): 614–26.

72 Helmut Haberl et al., 'Contributions of Sociometabolic Research to Sustainability Science', *Nature Sustainability* 2, no. 3 (2019): 173–84; Görg et al, 'Scrutinizing the Great Acceleration'; Schandl et al., 'Global Material Flows'; Jackson, *Prosperity without Growth*; Hickel, *Less Is More*.

occurred thus far, but the situation is deteriorating.[73] Exceeding only two of these planetary boundaries – namely, climate change and the loss of biodiversity – has the potential to fundamentally destabilize the Earth system. However, it must be noted that these planetary 'boundaries' are not absolute barriers whose transgression immediately leads to general ecological catastrophes or the end of growth. In particular, the significance of these boundaries is fiercely contested because they affect people very differently, above all depending on their geographical location and their positions in relations of power and domination. However, they do provide a good indication of which systems we are pushing to their limits, beyond which we end up in a future of uncharted, non-linear tipping points. These scientific, empirically rigorous findings justify the conclusion that it is well past time for wide-scale, assertive, and comprehensive action. And, if they were to be reconceptualized as 'societal boundaries' resulting from capitalist social relations, they demonstrate how societies can react differently to these boundaries, including through self-limitation.[74]

Even just to limit climate change driven by human activity – which alone could endanger the survival of large parts of the future human race and other living beings – greenhouse gas emissions must be reduced to zero in less than three decades. A formidable challenge, given the centrality of fossil fuels to the social metabolism of capitalism discussed above. Yet, even if this were to happen, it is uncertain whether self-reinforcing feedback cycles would not continue to drive the Earth system beyond planetary tipping points, preventing climate stabilization and leading to continuous warming and a 'hothouse Earth'.[75]

But it is not just climate change that we are up against. The great

73 Kate Raworth, *Doughnut Economics: Seven Ways to Think Like a 21st-Century Economist* (White River Junction, VT: Chelsea Green Publishing, 2017); Johan Rockström et al., 'A Safe Operating Space for Humanity', *Nature* 461, no. 7263 (2009): 472–5 ; Linn Persson et al., 'Outside the Safe Operating Space of the Planetary Boundary for Novel Entities', *Environmental Science and Technology* 56, no. 3 (2022): 1510–21.

74 Brand et al., 'From Planetary to Societal Boundaries'.

75 Will Steffen et al., 'Trajectories of the Earth System in the Anthropocene', *Proceedings of the National Academy of Sciences* 115, no. 33 (2018): 8252–9.

acceleration is affecting all aspects of human–nature interactions – from our water systems to the air we breathe, biodiversity, soil health, the sixth mass extinction, and increased risk of zoonosis, where encroachment into animal habitats leads to novel viral strains causing global pandemics. The writer Charles Eisenstein calls this process a 'death of a thousand cuts',[76] where climate change itself is just one aspect of the multi-faceted degradation of global ecosystems.

Of course, these are only some of the most prominent frameworks that analyse how growth as a biophysical process is disrupting biogeo-chemical natural systems, approaching, or even surpassing dangerous and partly irreversible tipping points. Yet there is clear and mounting evidence that this process of material expansion – which began with the beginning of industrial, fossil fuel–driven capitalism and accelerated in the 1950s, coinciding with the development of the growth paradigm – is today running up against multiple limits. One of the most distinct signs of the approaching limits is the rising social resistance against the ideol-ogy of growth, against social dynamics of accumulation, and against their material form – biophysical growth. People all around the world are resisting, as part of a diverse and growing network of movements against environmental injustice: land defenders, peasants, workers, and Indigenous peoples fighting against successive incursions on their land, against extraction of resources, against demeaning and alienating jobs, and for collectively defined self-limitations and a just transition to a dignified and ecologically sustainable economy.[77]

2.4. The end of growth?

What is the future of growth? Of course, no one knows. But the idea that the global economy will continue to grow at 3 per cent each year,

---

76 Charles Eisenstein, *Climate: A New Story* (Berkeley: North Atlantic Books, 2018).

77 See the Environmental Justice Atlas, at ejatlas.org; John Robert McNeill and Peter Engelke, *The Great Acceleration: An Environmental History of the Anthropocene since 1945* (Cambridge, MA: Harvard University Press, 2016); Brand et al., 'From Planetary to Societal Boundaries'.

thus matching some projections and the expectations of what is considered 'normal' in economics and public discourse, might turn out not only to be a nightmare (ecologically, but also for many other reasons, as discussed in the next chapter) but also a fantasy. Compounding a 3 per cent annual growth doubles the size of the economy every twenty-four years and, by the end of this century, would lead to a global economy eight times larger. How this can be squared with ecological and social limits is difficult to conceive.

However, since the 1970s, economic growth itself has started slowing, beginning in the early industrialized countries. In the US, Europe, and Japan, growth rates have been declining significantly since the 1970s, a process discussed as 'secular stagnation' by economists. The reasons for this are manifold and intertwined. They range from the political structural break from social welfare states towards the neoliberal model, to the tendencies for markets for goods to be saturated, intensified international competition, declining productivity growth, and the financialization of the global economy. Another important factor has been rising resource prices – it is no coincidence that secular stagnation was triggered by the oil crisis of the 1970s. And since the global economy has now become a behemoth, relative growth can only be achieved with ever greater expenditure on materials and energy, which is becoming ever more expensive to provide, in particular with declining rates of productivity.[78] In the long run, the economy does not seem to be developing in the way of the 'hockey stick' we have become accustomed to – stagnating for much of human history and then accelerating into a continuous and almost vertical ascent, like the curve of a 'J'. Instead, the regions in which capitalist industrialization began earliest now show a transition to a trajectory that can be more adequately described as an 'S'-curve, in which acceleration slows down and finally comes to a standstill. It could be that, in the long term, the rapid growth of parts of the world economy between the nineteenth and twentieth centuries turns out to be a historical exception.[79]

---

78 Robert J. Gordon, *Rise and Fall of American Growth: The U.S. Standard of Living since the Civil War* (Princeton, NJ: Princeton University Press, 2016).

79 Borowy and Schmelzer, *History of the Future of Economic Growth*; Barry

But also in the short term, the future of growth is uncertain – not only given the crisis-tendencies inherent to the social process of accumulation, but also due to the various ecological, social, and material limits of growth. As we look towards the next decades, we will be facing multiple, simultaneous crises, each a result of a global economy based on growth – and increasingly one based on growth in crisis. On the one hand, we are already facing economic stagnation, which is sending tremors through the system of 'dynamic stabilization' and upending the expectations of those enjoying an 'imperial mode of living', leading to new forms of popular reaction in industrialized and middle-income countries, as well as increasing social divisions. On the other hand, our current energy system, based on fossil fuels, is fast causing a breakdown in the stability of the climate – itself a foundational precondition for welfare, prosperity, and even the very existence of complex human societies. Beyond climate change largely caused by carbon emissions, many parts of the world are facing ecological breakdown and public health crises due to ecosystem degradation, pollution, and high levels of toxicity in food and the environment. All these ecological crises hit the poorest – as well as those oppressed by intersectional hierarchies such as race, class, and gender – first and hardest. These multiple crises are the result of a system dependent on, and driven by, growth.

The main objection to the analyses presented here, which highlights how intricately interwoven the material dimension of growth is with the social process of accumulation, posits that while growth might have been very material and destructive in the past, it is already and can further be dematerialized in the future. The hope is that by shifting to renewable energies, increasing energy and resource efficiency, and through recycling, GDP can be decoupled fast enough from both the use of resources (the 'source' problems) and the creation of waste and emissions (the 'sink' problems). And all of this is already happening in some industrialized countries, the narrative of green, dematerialized, and cyclical growth

---

Eichengreen, 'Secular Stagnation: A Review of the Issues', in *Secular Stagnation: Facts, Causes and Cures*, ed. Richard Baldwin and Coen Teulings (London: CEPR Press, 2014), 41–6; Jackson, *Prosperity without Growth*; Schmelzer, *The Hegemony of Growth*.

claims. However, this hope is based on false assumptions and lacks evidence. While research shows how carbon emissions, GDP, and material footprint have become slightly less coupled, they are still all increasing at a critically dangerous rate (see Figure 2.4). As will be discussed in detail throughout the book (in particular, section 3.1), all the signs of dematerialization or decoupling, as welcome as they are, are simply not enough – growth is still sending us over a cliff.

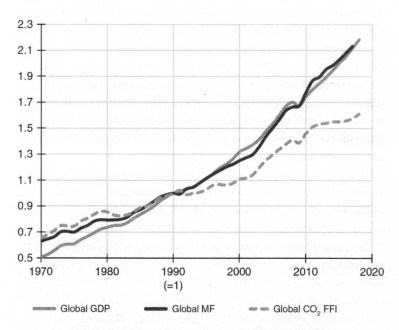

Figure 2.4. Relative change in key global economic and environmental indicators from 1970 to 2017. The graph shows how the global material footprint (MF, equal to global raw material extraction) and global CO_2 emissions from fossil fuel combustion and industrial processes (CO_2 FFI) changed compared with global GDP (constant 2010 USD). Indexed to 1 in 1990. Source: Thomas Wiedmann, Manfred Lenzen, Lorenz T. Keyßer, and Julia K. Steinberger, 'Scientists' Warning on Affluence', *Nature Communications* 11, no. 1 (2020): 1–10.

In this chapter, we have discussed growth as expanding social metabolism of society with nature, which in ever faster rhythms allows more and more resources to flow through 'the economy' and remain as waste and emissions. We have also discussed growth as a social process of mutually reinforcing and dynamically stabilizing forces of acceleration, escalation, and intensification. And we analysed growth as an ideology, focusing on the making and power of the growth paradigm. With regard to each of these, growth ultimately undermines the foundations on which it is based. Yet the hegemony of the growth idea still persists. This is where the critiques of growth come in, which we will discuss in detail in the third chapter and which continue the arguments only outlined here. For a transition to a degrowth society – as we will discuss in chapters 4, 5, and 6 – all three dimensions of growth must be addressed. First, degrowth takes seriously the material dimension of growth in all its complexity, drawing attention to what this means for a future of global justice. Second, degrowth must seriously examine the question of how the self-reinforcing growth dynamics of expansive modernity can be overcome without jeopardizing the social, cultural, and democratic achievements that have been accomplished, largely through social struggles, but also within the context of growth societies. And third, degrowth must critically engage with and dismantle but also transform the promises, myths, and hopes associated with the growth paradigm.

3

Critiques of growth

When first confronted with the word 'degrowth', many people react by calling its proponents anti-modern (You want us to go back to living in caves!), privileged (You want people to have less but many people are already poor!), or apolitical (You don't talk about the root of the problem, which is capitalism!). In part, people often react this way because growth continues to be seen as the provider of all the good things that society offers, so to go against this common sense raises many people's ire, both on the right and on the left.

Another reason is that, while it is easy to react negatively to the word 'degrowth', truly understanding the degrowth framework takes a much more dedicated engagement with the arguments it advances – which are based on both scientific evidence and political theory. In the previous chapter, we took you through some of the history of growth – from its more recent rise as a paradigm of governance to its deeper roots, both material and social, within capitalism. Uniquely among leftist critiques of capitalism, degrowth offers a rigorous understanding of these growth dynamics. In this chapter, we describe the various critiques of growth upon which degrowth literature has drawn, assembling in one place the different frameworks that together make up a degrowth perspective.

Degrowth, we argue, can be understood as a synthesis of different strands of growth critiques, which analyse the dynamics of growth in modern societies from various perspectives. This is not to say that degrowth does not offer any positive proposals beyond critique. In the next chapter, we present the vision and proposal at the core of degrowth. In this chapter, however, we focus on critique. We claim that there are, central to degrowth, seven distinct and overlapping lines of argumentation each critical of growth: ecological, socio-economic, cultural, anti-capitalist, feminist, anti-industrialist, and South–North critique (see Table 3.1). A comprehensive degrowth perspective should incorporate all of them.[1]

That said, we do acknowledge that there is some truth to the criticism that growth critiques can be anti-modern or regressive. Certainly critiques of growth can lead to apolitical or misanthropic conclusions. For example, without a critique of capitalism or a positive vision of human societies, growth critiques can easily go down the road of focusing only on false causes like population growth or 'human nature', so prominent within Western environmentalism.[2] Alternatively, without a feminist perspective, growth critiques tend to reproduce gender inequalities, stereotypes, and binaries and strengthen rather than undermine the gendered division of labour. These reactions to the problems of growth can only advocate overcoming the problem in limited, even regressive, ways. Even if the main thrust of degrowth differs markedly from right-wing extremism, it is still necessary to continue to ward against such contaminants. As the sociologist Dennis Eversberg notes,

---

1 On various traditions of degrowth, see Giacomo D'Alisa, Federico Demaria, and Giorgos Kallis, *Degrowth: A Vocabulary for a New Era* (London: Routledge, 2014); Federico Demaria et al., 'What Is Degrowth? From an Activist Slogan to a Social Movement', *Environmental Values* 22, no. 2 (2013): 191–215; Barbara Muraca and Matthias Schmelzer, 'Sustainable Degrowth: Historical Roots of the Search for Alternatives to Growth in Three Regions', in *History of the Future of Economic Growth: Historical Roots of Current Debates on Sustainable Degrowth*, ed. Ingrid Borowy and Matthias Schmelzer (London: Routledge, 2017): 174–97.

2 Thomas Robertson, *The Malthusian Moment: Global Population Growth and the Birth of American Environmentalism* (New Brunswick, NJ: Rutgers University Press, 2012). For a degrowth analysis, see Giorgos Kallis, *Limits: Why Malthus Was Wrong and Why Environmentalists Should Care* (Stanford, CA: Stanford University Press, 2019).

growth-critical positions are particularly at risk of being appropriated from the right, who often focus on blaming the interest rate, the monetary system, or overpopulation for global problems and frame the solution as the return to an allegedly better, more sustainable state of 'natural' or 'original' communities.[3]

In contrast to these perspectives, the central thrust of degrowth should be understood as a global justice perspective. As we argue in the conclusion of this chapter, only a holistic approach, one which takes into account the several critiques we outline here, can safeguard degrowth against right-wing appropriation and respond effectively to the current crises.

Before we go further, we would like to offer some clarifications on these different strands of the degrowth framework. In this chapter we focus, on the one hand, on critiques of growth that are often seen as key 'sources' of degrowth.[4] On the other hand, however, we also discuss critical approaches that are less frequently heard but that are key to framing degrowth accurately – or likewise those that have been important historically in debates concerning growth. All these forms of critique come from different historical and social contexts, and their argumentation takes place on different levels and with different degrees of abstraction. There are overlaps and cross-fertilizations. Not all forms of criticism are completely critical of growth, and only some of the authors see themselves as part of the degrowth spectrum – and some formulated their arguments long before the emergence of a degrowth discourse. But they all make a specific contribution to a comprehensive critique of growth adequate for our current predicaments.

---

3 Dennis Eversberg, 'Gefährliches Werben: Über Anschlussfähigkeiten der Postwachstumsdebatte gegenüber dem autoritären Nationalismus – und was sich dagegen tun lässt', *Forschungsjournal Soziale Bewegungen* 4 (2018): 52–60, our translation.

4 See for example D'Alisa, Demaria, and Kallis, *Degrowth: A Vocabulary for a New Era*; Serge Latouche, *Farewell to Growth*, trans. David Macey (Cambridge: Polity Press, 2009); Fabrice Flipo, 'Les racines conceptuelles de la décroissance', in *La décroissance économique pour la soutenabilité écologique et l'équité sociale*, ed. B. Mylondo (Bellecombe-en-Bauges: Croquant, 2009), 19–32.

Critiques of growth	Economic growth . . .
Ecological critique	. . . destroys the ecological foundations of human life and cannot be transformed to become sustainable
Socio-economic critique	. . . mismeasures our lives and thus stands in the way of well-being and equality of all
Cultural critique	. . . produces alienating ways of working, living, and relating to each other and nature
Critique of capitalism	. . . depends on and is driven by capitalist exploitation and accumulation
Feminist critique	. . . is based on gendered over-exploitation and devalues reproduction
Critique of industrialism	. . . gives rise to undemocratic productive forces and techniques
South–North critique	. . . relies on and reproduces relations of domination, extraction, and exploitation between capitalist centre and periphery

Table 3.1: The seven forms of growth critique central to degrowth

The common basis of these different growth critiques is the deconstruc-tion of the hegemonic belief that economic growth per se is a good thing. To this end, the logic and central assumptions of orthodox neoclassical economics are attacked with various arguments. All critiques point to the fact that human and non-human living beings are part of complex, inter-dependent networks of relationships. A purely economic description cannot adequately capture them and conceals rather than explains the actual logics of social and socio-ecological relations. Degrowth thus criti-cizes the universalization of economic rationality as manifested in its ideological orientation towards growth and the replacement of complex networks of relationships by an all-determining number: GDP.

In the following, we present each of the seven forms of critique in a separate section. We begin each section with a summary of the core arguments, briefly describe the historical development of this critique, and then explain some key arguments in more detail. Finally, we discuss their significance for the broader degrowth discourse, once again exploring how degrowth critiques can inoculate themselves against reactionary, conservative approaches.

3.1. Ecological critique

Infinite growth is not possible on a finite planet. The core message of the ecological growth critique can be summarized in this oft-repeated commonplace argument. Even if this is only one of several forms of criticism that make degrowth necessary, for many it is the starting point of a critical engagement with economic growth – therefore we will start with it as well. Ecological growth criticism, however, goes beyond this popular statement. On the one hand, it shows that economic growth is not sustainable and cannot be made sustainable by any other modulations of growth (i.e., 'green', 'qualitative', or 'smart' growth), by technological progress (increases in efficiency, digitalization, and so on), or by merely shifting the resource and energy base (via renewable energies, say, or recycling). On the other hand, the ecological growth critique does analyse the reasons for this structural unsustainability of the growth-oriented, productivist, and capitalist economic system. Rebound effects, entropy, criticism of the green economy, and environmental justice are central keywords. Another important aspect is the analysis of the fundamental level at which human societies are shaped by their metabolic relationship with nature and how these society–nature relations are deeply inscribed in modern societies.

Ecological growth critiques take up arguments from environmental and environmental justice movements, sharpen them, and bring them in exchange with scientific discussions. Even though, in their modern forms, these date back at least to the nineteenth century, the discussion about the connection between economic growth and ecology has gained momentum only since the 1970s. In chapter 2 we already discussed a critical theory of growth, whose analysis of the material dimension of growth integrates some of the ecological growth critiques. Further strands of the ecological critique came, first, from the developing field of ecological economics, and especially from the thermodynamic arguments of Nicholas Georgescu-Roegen. They also came, second, from the environmental justice movement and from eco-Marxist analyses of social metabolism. Third, they relied on empirical material flow analyses, studies on resource scarcity, and studies on decoupling environmental impact from economic growth.

Ecological economics and the law of entropy

Ecological economics developed from critiques of neoclassical economics, which is oblivious to ecological processes and their importance to economic activities. Let us begin with how the laws of physics determine and shape growth. It may perhaps seem self-evident to say that the economy, like everything else, must obey the laws of physics. However, mainstream economics rarely acknowledges this fact. Neoclassical models conceptualize the economy as money-mediated and self-contained processes of circulation of labour and capital, money and goods between households and companies, all of which can reproduce themselves again and again. Growth, in this model, is due to savings and investments and the resulting increase in knowledge, technology, and capital. Such a circular-flow model of the economy, with which the textbooks of economics begin to this day, has been fundamentally challenged: to give one example, neither nature (in the form of energy, raw materials, and land) nor reproductive work (as indispensable prerequisites of the formal economy) appear in it. As an image central to ecological economics depicts, the economy is embedded in a society (in the form of laws, social institutions, or moral concepts) without which it could not function; and both the economy and society in turn are embedded in nature.[5]

The circular flow model is the 'original sin of modern economics', as the mathematician and economist Nicholas Georgescu-Roegen stated, because it creates the illusion that the economy does not depend on resources, energy, and sinks, and can thus continue to expand indefinitely.[6] In the 1960s and 1970s, he developed some of the central building blocks both for ecological economics and for later degrowth discourses through a rigorous analysis of the

5 Herman Daly and Joshua Farley, *Ecological Economics: Principles and Applications* (Washington, DC: Island Press, 2011); Tim Jackson, *Prosperity without Growth: Economics for a Finite Planet* (London: Earthscan, 2016). For a standard economics textbook, see N. Gregory Mankiw, *Principles of Economics* (Boston: Cengage Learning, 2016).

6 Nicholas Georgescu-Roegen, *The Entropy Law and the Economic Process* (Cambridge, MA: Harvard University Press, 1971).

biophysical side of economic activities. He argued that economic development is necessarily integrated into physical and biological processes and therefore cannot ignore the limits arising from physical laws, especially the law of entropy.[7] In *The Entropy Law and the Economic Process*, published in 1974, Georgescu-Roegen showed how what we call the economy, which is understood largely as a system of market exchange, is in fact a complex system of flows and stocks of energy and materials, each of which has different properties and potential for sustainable (re-)use. The expenditure of energy or the use of any material tends not to be fully renewable in the long term, since each time energy or material is transformed from one form to another, that substance becomes lower quality. Fossil fuel–driven economies are rapidly using the limited supply of highly concentrated energy stored during millennia of photosynthesis – the sun being the only source of energy entering the otherwise largely closed system of the earth. To switch to a fully renewable economy, we would need to transition to a largely solar-powered economy. However, Georgescu-Roegen argued that, unlike fossil fuels, solar energy 'comes to us with an extremely low intensity, like a fine rain, almost a microscopic mist'.[8] Imagine trying to catch fine rain: you cannot do it with a bucket. To do so, we would need to transform our current systems of energy capture and storage completely, creating a massive infrastructure (of solar panels, wind turbines, bioenergy plants, tidal turbines, and, most importantly, technologies to store that energy, such as batteries) that relies on material resources, which are, unlike sunlight, non-renewable. Such a solar-based economy

7 The second law of thermodynamics, also known as the law of entropy, states that in a closed system the potential benefits from a source of energy decreases continuously and irreversibly in the course of time. An example of this is the bathtub, which cools down until it is as cold as the room temperature (i.e., the heat is distributed throughout the room and thus loses its usefulness). Energy and material transformations thus are not arbitrarily reversible but are directed into space and time; they can only be reversed by an input of additional energy. See Georgescu-Roegen, *The Entropy Law*.

8 Nicholas Georgescu-Roegen, 'Energy and Economic Myths', *Southern Economic Journal* 41, no. 3 (January 1975), 371.

must manage with existing materials and will thus in the long term have to limit growth.

Technological progress and non-fossil energy sources (such as the sun, wind, water, or biomass) cannot beat the entropy law in the long term, especially since resources and land are inherently limited. From this analysis, Georgescu-Roegen deduced that if we begin from an analysis that is grounded in the laws of physics, we can only conceive of an economy that consumes less and less energy and material, since nothing can be 100 per cent recycled and since capturing renewable energy depends on material resources, which are themselves limited. Georgescu-Roegen also formulated initial thoughts on the form such an economy must take, anticipating some of the central degrowth proposals. Thus, it is no coincidence that the word *décroissance*, although Georgescu-Roegen did not use it himself, first became known through the title of a 1979 French translation of his writings titled *Demain la décroissance*.

These arguments highlight two basic facts. First, every economy is embedded within an environmental context and therefore is subject to natural laws such as those of physics and thermodynamics. Second, an economy that grows endlessly must make trade-offs with regard to material and energy use, since each form of energy has different characteristics in terms of storage, material intensity, renewability, transportation, and the time and space they require. While this does not prove in itself that endless growth is impossible, it shows how, the bigger an economy, the more difficult it becomes to maintain, and the more difficult it becomes to switch to more sustainable forms of energy that are not as dense, concentrated, and transportable as fossil fuels, without reducing overall energy use. This insight applies to all economic systems, not just our own.[9]

Vaclav Smil, in his recent book *Growth: From Microorganisms to Megacities*, brings the study of physics and economics of growth to a new level. In a wide-ranging analysis of growth in multiple systems – from the biological to cities to economic trends – Smil underlines that, in all systems, growth may look to be exponential but eventually tends to have decreasing growth rates until it reaches its material and

---

9 Georgescu-Roegen, *The Entropy Law*.

thermodynamic limits. Thus, societies currently experiencing growth may have the impression that things will continue as they are, but they usually are just within an exponential curve that will eventually flatten, or even result in whole-scale collapse. More broadly, Smil's work demonstrates in exhaustive detail how all economic activity, regardless of social organization, is subject to material, ecological, and physical limitations. In essence, his argument, which aligns closely with that of Georgescu-Roegen, is that all available evidence suggests that growth is finite. Any society that relies on compound rates of economic growth will eventually face ultimate limits, which manifest themselves in the breakdown of the complex ecosystems upon which growth relies. Smil stops short, however, of suggesting models for how to avoid collapse; and, what's more, his work does not take into account the role played by ideology and hegemonic, interlocking social dynamics in perpetuating growth. As we underline throughout this book, an important aspect of the degrowth framework involves combining a material analysis of the growth of the economy with an understanding of its structural roots.[10]

Another problem, related to the one highlighted above, is that increasing economic complexity also locks in future material and energetic throughput. For example, as more infrastructures organized around fossil fuels (such as highways and container shipping ports) are built, the more society becomes 'locked in' to non-renewable sources of energy, and the more work it takes to disassemble that system and create a system based on renewable energy. These mutually reinforcing dynamics of growth become increasingly coupled to each other, making it more and more difficult to change energy sources but also to address the increasing disorder (through pollution, environmental degradation, and social strife) created by a reliance on a single, highly concentrated source of energy – in our economy's case, fossil fuels.[11]

---

10 Vaclav Smil, *Growth: From Microorganisms to Megacities* (Boston: MIT Press, 2019).

11 Mauro Bonaiuti, *The Great Transition* (London: Routledge, 2014); Smil, *Growth*. For empirical evidence, see also Fridolin Krausmann et al., 'Global Socioeconomic Material Stocks Rise 23-Fold over the 20th Century and Require Half of Annual Resource Use', *Proceedings of the National Academy of Sciences* 114, no. 8 (2017): 1880–5.

Social metabolism and the metabolic rift

It was from this understanding – the scientific investigation into the physical basis of economies – that political economists started to develop an understanding of what is called 'social metabolism'. This is a key term in the degrowth literature and fundamental for an accurate understanding of the material conditions of growth. In physiology and biology, metabolism is understood as a system that exchanges and balances nutrients of an organism. A human organism, for example, takes in food, processes it to create energy, uses parts of it to continuously rebuild the body, and excretes the rest. The concept of metabolism began to be applied to wider ecological and social systems in the nineteenth century with the development of the science of ecology. Scientists began to use the term 'metabolism' (in German, *Stoffwechsel*) to apply to biochemical processes in natural systems, not just in organisms. Karl Marx, interested in the development of these new natural sciences, started to explore what he called *social* metabolism: the material and energetic exchange that allows a society to reproduce itself, produce, stabilize, and grow.[12] Marx, who coined the term 'social metabolism', described it as the dynamic relationship between humans and nature. This interchange was dependent on complex and ecologically specific dynamics, such as the nutrient capacity of the soil or the availability of various forms of energy. Since societies depend on biological and ecological functions, these limit the potential of economic activities. This suggests that capitalist development, which relies on infinite accumulation, has yet another tendency towards crisis.[13]

Marx, in his investigations of capitalism, also became concerned with the way in which a capitalist economy's social metabolic processes systematically disrupt natural metabolic processes – such as by

12 Karl Marx, *Capital: A Critique of Political Economy, Volume 3*, trans. David Fernbach (New York: Vintage, 1981), 949.

13 Kohei Saito, *Karl Marx's Eco-socialism: Capital, Nature, and the Unfinished Critique of Political Economy* (New York: NYU Press, 2017); John Bellamy Foster, 'Marx and the Rift in the Universal Metabolism of Nature', Monthlyreview.org, 1 December 2013.

producing waste (sewage, pollution, plastics) that can't be absorbed by
ecosystems but rather that degrades them. As Marx pointed out,

> [Capitalist production] disturbs the metabolic interaction between
> man and the earth, i.e., it prevents the return to the soil of its constit-
> uent elements consumed by man in the form of food and clothing;
> hence it hinders the operation of the eternal natural condition for the
> lasting fertility of the soil.[14]

John Bellamy Foster, in his study of Karl Marx's ecological politics,
has called this dynamic the 'metabolic rift'.[15] Thus, Marx's work and
a revival of eco-Marxism highlight the importance of understanding the material and ecological basis of any social system, and the
way by which social metabolism fosters or disrupts natural cycles
and metabolic exchanges, contributing to the dynamics of capitalist
crisis (see also section 3.4).

Following the development of ecological economics, scientists began
to trace the social metabolism of different economies by measuring
aggregate material and energetic 'throughput' – basically, the total 'stuff'
that economies consume. Different economic systems, historically, have
had vastly different rates and forms of metabolism.[16] The measurement of
social metabolism has become a key basis for the empirical evidence
underlying whether economic growth can be decoupled from material
and energy throughput. Indeed, with the advent of tools to empirically
measure metabolic impacts such as carbon and water footprints, scientists have also come closer to understanding how the aggregate throughput of a society is linked to environmental impact.[17]

---

14 Karl Marx, *Capital: A Critique of Political Economy, Volume 1*, trans. Ben
Fowkes (New York: Vintage, 1976), 637–8.

15 John Bellamy Foster, *Marx's Ecology: Materialism and Nature* (New York:
Monthly Review Press, 2000).

16 Alf Hornborg, John Robert McNeill, and Joan Martínez-Alier, *Rethinking
Environmental History: World-System History and Global Environmental Change*
(Lanham, MD: Altamira Press, 2007); Vaclav Smil, *Energy and Civilisation: A
History* (Boston: MIT Press, 2018).

17 Marina Fischer-Kowalski, 'Society's Metabolism: The Intellectual History

The study of social metabolism is important for our understanding of the material basis of the economy for several reasons. First, it highlights once again how nature and society are not separate objects but are connected through biological, chemical, and physical interchanges. It thus underlines how social dynamics can adversely affect ecological systems, and how this depends on complex interlocking systems, each of which has its own unique traits. For example, the social metabolism of speeding up the water cycle through erosion-prone agriculture has very different impacts on society than speeding up the carbon cycle through burning fossil fuels – since water and carbon each have different properties and effects (on the air, on the soil, in the ocean, and so on). Second, the theoretical perspective that focuses on 'social metabolism' and the empirical measurement of it bring to light a part of the economy that is veiled by most economic measurement tools like GDP. Third, measuring the aggregate social metabolism of a society becomes a political object in itself, as it has the potential to empirically assess the relationship between economic growth, material and energetic throughput, and ecological devastation – as well as to challenge unequal distributions of the negative effects of interlinked processes (see section 3.7). In summary, an understanding of social metabolism is necessary for comprehending the material form that any economy takes and determining whether it is sustainable or not.

Decoupling and rebound effects

A large number of empirical studies on the relationship between economic growth and environmental degradation or resource consumption are also at the foundation of the ecological growth critique. This leads us to perhaps the most important controversy in the ecological critique of growth: the question of decoupling. This field of research makes it increasingly difficult to deny that past economic growth has

of Materials Flow Analysis, Part I, 1860–1970', *Journal of Industrial Ecology* 2, no. 1 (1998): 61–78; Marina Fischer-Kowalski and Walter Hüttler, 'Society's Metabolism: The Intellectual History of Materials Flow Analysis, Part II, 1970–1998', *Journal of Industrial Ecology* 2, no. 4 (1998): 107–36.

been a central driver of economic destruction. What is controversial, however, is whether current and future economic growth can be decoupled from environmental impact. As we noted at the end of the previous chapter, a prominent thesis by advocates of green growth states that technological progress and an efficiency revolution can 'decouple' growth from environmental destruction. By switching to green sources of energy on a large scale, as well as by improving efficiency, countries could see green growth throughout the next decades and beyond, while environmental burdens decrease and emissions decline.[18]

Criticism of these claims is the central starting point for degrowth. The debate is complex and involves both theoretical and empirical arguments. To begin with, the widely held idea that productivity improvements due to technological innovations lead to savings in resources and energy is historically misleading and factually wrong. Productivity increases were, in effect, largely caused by the use and appropriation of cheap labour and nature, by the increasing use of fossil fuels, and by ecological plundering and the shifting of costs to the future and to the countries of the Global South. Furthermore, the 'rebound effect' has had an important role to play in the difficulty of reducing environmental impact while growth increases. The debate about the rebound effect goes back to the paradox discovered as early as 1865 by the British economist William Stanley Jevons: increasing the efficiency of energy and material use often leads to more, and not less, consumption of this energy or raw material. Even though this mechanism has long been neglected in neoclassical economics, a rising number of empirical studies have shown how rebound effects counteract decoupling. Rebound effects are defined as excess demand due to an increase in productivity. Studies show that, often, savings due to technological improvements are offset by an increase in demand. For example, more efficient combustion engines do not lead to lower energy use or CO_2 emissions when cars become heavier, people drive more, and the money saved on fuel is spent on other CO_2-intensive consumption. Rebound effects are extremely diverse, affect different levels

---

18 See Giorgos Kallis and Sam Bliss, 'Post-environmentalism: Origins and Evolution of a Strange Idea', *Journal of Political Ecology* 26, no. 1 (2019): 466–85.

(households, companies, economies), and sometimes reinforce one another. The sociologist Tilman Santarius distinguishes between financial, motivational, habitual, industrial, economic, and structural rebound effects. Empirical studies show that all these rebound effects together directly offset at least 50 per cent of the efficiency gains through new growth, and in some cases significantly more – even at times reaching what is called an 'overshoot', where efficiency improvements lead to additional net consumption.[19]

The debate on decoupling often lacks clarity on what kind of decoupling is actually necessary to achieve sustainability goals and have continuous growth. While there is wide evidence for some forms of decoupling, what we actually need is a decoupling in all key sustainability indicators (not only carbon emissions, but also biodiversity loss, land use, resource consumption, and so on) that is global (not just happening in some countries or regions), absolute (not just relative), permanent (and not just due to temporary circumstances, low-hanging fruits, and so on), fast enough (and not just possible in the long-term future), and strong enough to achieve agreed sustainability targets such as the 1.5°C limit for global warming, while taking global equity considerations into account.[20]

Fortunately, there are some signs of global relative decoupling and of some regional absolute decoupling. For example, the global energy intensity (amount of energy per unit of global GDP) today is almost 25 per cent below that of 1980, and the carbon intensity of the global economy (amount of CO_2 per unit of global GDP) has also declined by

19 Daly and Farley, *Ecological Economics;* Tilman Santarius, *Der Rebound-Effekt: Ökonomische, psychische und soziale Herausforderungen der Entkopplung von Energieverbrauch und Wirtschaftswachstum* (Marburg: Metropolis, 2015); Tilman Santarius, Hans Jakob Walnum, and Carlo Aall, *Rethinking Climate and Energy Policies: New Perspectives on the Rebound Phenomenon* (New York: Springer, 2016); Christopher L. Magee and Tessaleno C. Devezas, 'A Simple Extension of Dematerialization Theory: Incorporation of Technical Progress and the Rebound Effect', *Technological Forecasting and Social Change* 117 (2017): 196–205.

20 Timothée Parrique et al., *Decoupling Debunked: Evidence and Arguments against Green Growth as a Sole Strategy for Sustainability* (Brussels: EEB, 2019).

almost 1 per cent per year in recent decades.[21] However, while the carbon intensity of the global economy continues to decrease, CO_2 emissions have also continued to rise – by more than 60 per cent since 1990. What is needed is not *relative* decoupling, but *absolute* decoupling, in which resource consumption, environmental damages and emissions decrease in absolute terms and sufficiently fast, while the economy grows. And there is no evidence for *global* absolute decoupling of economic growth from environmental impacts, neither in terms of CO_2 emissions nor biodiversity loss, land-use change, plastic pollution, or the aggregate level of anthropogenic resource use (which is a key indicator for environmental damage generally).[22]

And while some temporary, localized absolute decoupling has taken place, in particular in some Global North countries with low growth rates, there is no evidence to show that it has, or can, occur at the scale needed to become permanent and global, nor to do so fast enough. For example, between 1980 and 2008, countries such as Canada, Germany, Italy, and Japan decoupled their domestic material use from economic growth, and the G8 as a whole halved their domestic material consumption. Yet, when measured in absolute terms and including embedded resources in trade, material footprint closely tracks GDP in all wealthy nations, and, despite dips in GDP rates, continues to grow at an unsustainable rate.[23] Furthermore, only fourteen countries have absolutely

21 Jackson, *Prosperity without Growth*, 141–3.

22 Helmut Haberl et al., 'A Systematic Review of the Evidence on Decoupling of GDP, Resource Use and GHG Emissions, Part II: Synthesizing the Insights', *Environmental Research Letters* 15, no. 6 (2020): 065003; IPBES, *Summary for Policymakers of the Global Assessment Report on Biodiversity and Ecosystem Services of the Intergovernmental Science-Policy Platform on Biodiversity and Ecosystem Services* (Bonn: IPBES, 2019); Parrique et al., *Decoupling Debunked*; Iago Otero et al., 'Biodiversity Policy beyond Economic Growth', *Conservation Letters* 13, no. 4 (2020): 12713; Brooke A. Williams et al., 'Change in Terrestrial Human Footprint Drives Continued Loss of Intact Ecosystems', *One Earth* 3, no. 3 (2020): 371–82.

23 Thomas Wiedmann et al., 'The Material Footprint of Nations', *Proceedings of the National Academy of Sciences* 112, no. 20 (2015): 6271–6; Julia K. Steinberger et al., 'Development and Dematerialization: An International Study', *PloS One* 8, no. 10 (2013): e70385; Heinz Schandl et al., 'Global Material Flows and Resource Productivity: Forty Years of Evidence', *Journal of Industrial Ecology* 22, no. 4 (2018): 827–38.

decoupled GDP growth from both production- and consumption-based CO_2 emissions – and this was aided by slow economic growth and, for several, was only temporary.[24] Yet even in these countries, achieved mitigation rates remain very far from what is necessary to achieve climate targets, in particular if equity considerations are taken into account. To put the case directly: the transformations of the Global North economies necessary to achieve annual emissions reductions of around 10 per cent, as is necessary to avert a climate emergency, can only be achieved without economic growth and will most likely result in a reduction of GDP.[25]

A recent systematic review of decoupling, synthesizing the evidence emerging from 835 peer-reviewed articles, concludes that while relative decoupling is common and while some small-scale and slow absolute decoupling can be seen in certain areas in recent years, the absolute decoupling we need is highly unlikely:

> Large rapid absolute reductions of resource use and GHG emissions cannot be achieved through observed decoupling rates, hence decoupling needs to be complemented by sufficiency-oriented strategies and strict enforcement of absolute reduction targets.[26]

24 Klaus Hubacek et al., 'Evidence of Decoupling Consumption-Based CO_2 Emissions from Economic Growth', *Advances in Applied Energy* 4 (2021): 100074; Corinne Le Quéré et al., 'Drivers of Declining CO_2 Emissions in 18 Developed Economies', *Nature Climate Change* 9, no. 3 (2019): 213–17.

25 Haberl et al., 'A Systematic Review, Part II'; Parrique et al., *Decoupling Debunked*; Hickel and Kallis, 'Is Green Growth Possible?'; Tere Vadén et al., 'Decoupling for Ecological Sustainability: A Categorisation and Review of Research Literature', *Environmental Science and Policy* 112 (2020): 236–44; William F. Lamb, 'Countries with Sustained Greenhouse Gas Emissions Reductions: An Analysis of Trends and Progress by Sector', *Climate Policy* (2021): 1–17; Le Quéré et al., 'Drivers of Declining CO_2 Emissions'; Ranran Wang et al., 'Energy System Decarbonization and Productivity Gains Reduced the Coupling of CO_2 Emissions and Economic Growth in 73 Countries between 1970 and 2016', *One Earth* 4, no. 11 (2021): 1614–24.

26 Haberl et al., 'A Systematic Review, Part II'.

Another analysis of historical trends and model-based projections concludes:

> (1) there is no empirical evidence that absolute decoupling from resource use can be achieved on a global scale against a background of continued economic growth, and (2) absolute decoupling from carbon emissions is highly unlikely to be achieved at a rate rapid enough to prevent global warming over 1.5°C or 2°C.[27]

Of course, this could theoretically change in the future – yet given what we know, this is highly unlikely, and the large-scale and high-speed energy transitions that would be necessary, including negative emission technologies, bear considerable risks regarding not only their feasibility, but also their sustainability and justice.[28] Furthermore, next to the rebound effects discussed above that will compensate some of the efficiency gains, there are other mechanisms that make sufficiently fast absolute decoupling very unlikely – among these are the possibility of rising energy and resource expenditures, problem shifting to other regions and timescales, the impacts of services, the limited potential for recycling, lack of technological innovations, and cost shifting by polluting industries to society and nature.[29]

This strong coupling of growth and emissions is also the reason why the only historical periods when total CO_2 emissions actually did go down were periods of economic decline: after the collapse of the Soviet economy in the early 1990s, during the global economic crisis from 2008 to 2010,[30] and during the coronavirus pandemic.[31] For some, the

---

27 Jason Hickel and Giorgos Kallis, 'Is Green Growth Possible?', *New Political Economy* 25, 4, 469–86, 469.

28 Ibid.; Lorenz T. Keyßer and Manfred Lenzen, '1.5 °C Degrowth Scenarios Suggest the Need for New Mitigation Pathways', *Nature Communications* 12, no. 1 (2021): 1–16; Jason Hickel et al., 'Urgent Need for Post-Growth Climate Mitigation Scenarios', *Nature Energy* 6 (2021), 1–3.

29 For an analysis of these seven mechanisms, see Parrique et al., *Decoupling Debunked*.

30 Jackson, *Prosperity without Growth*; Giorgos Kallis, *Degrowth* (Newcastle upon Tyne: Agenda Publishing, 2018).

31 Corinne Le Quéré et al., 'Temporary Reduction in Daily Global CO_2

social fallout from these crises are evidence that degrowth is never desirable. However, degrowth advocates point out that, within a growth-oriented economy, economic crises end up leading to more environmental impacts eventually, as environmental regulations are loosened and countries accelerate production after the crisis.[32] For degrowth advocates, economic crises are *not* degrowth; rather, they show that an economy dependent on growth is unable to satisfy both social and environmental needs. The point, instead, is to move towards an economy in which *well-being* can increase while environmental damage rapidly declines, thereby decoupling prosperity from ecological impact and thus also from economic growth.

Significance for degrowth: Avoiding apolitical ecology

While these ecological approaches shape today's degrowth discussion, classical conservation movements motivated by romantic unease about the destruction of 'untouched' nature, or Malthusian critiques that problematize population growth, are less important for degrowth. On the contrary, many degrowth authors criticize arguments that primarily focus on population growth as structurally racist. Demographic arguments are implicitly mostly directed towards the Global South, where the population is currently growing. But it is precisely the rich countries – where population is currently stagnating or declining – that are historically and today mainly responsible for the ecological crisis. Ecologically, lifestyle or per-capita consumption is much more important than the abstract number of living people.[33] Criticism of population growth under the given circumstances is therefore usually (sometimes only implicitly) a criticism of the high reproduction rates

---

Emissions during the COVID-19 Forced Confinement', *Nature Climate Change* (2020): 1–7; Manfred Lenzen et al., 'Global Socio-Economic Losses and Environmental Gains from the Coronavirus Pandemic', *PLOS ONE* 15, no. 7 (2020): e0235654.

32 Glen P. Peters et al., 'Rapid Growth in CO_2 Emissions after the 2008–2009 Global Financial Crisis', *Nature Climate Change* 2, no. 1 (2012): 2–4.

33 Ian Angus and Simon Butler, *Too Many People? Population, Immigration, and the Environmental Crisis* (Chicago: Haymarket Books, 2011).

of people in the Global South, although these live far more appropriately from a purely ecological point of view, and it thus diverts attention from what is much more important: affluence and the systemic drivers of growth.[34] Arguments based on population growth typically view humanity as having an aggregate, monolithic impact, which is a function of the number of people in the world. However, humans can develop societies that are carbon neutral or even carbon negative – storing carbon through building up soil, regenerating ecosystems, and building a world of abundance that does not transgress planetary boundaries and is based on ecological knowledge. Ecological arguments based solely on demographics and population growth deny this reality that we can, and should, create different social systems – they are thus limited to an apolitical ecology.

The ecological critique of growth impressively reveals a fundamental dilemma that is now increasingly becoming part of everyday consciousness and that also plays a role in almost all other growth critiques: if the ecological foundations of human life are not to be further destroyed, the material flows of the economy must be slowed down and reduced very quickly in the coming years – which is very unlikely and maybe not possible alongside simultaneous economic growth. In addition to efficiency and consistency, *sufficiency* – a reduction in the consumption of raw materials, energy, and land which nevertheless offers a basis for well-being – as a way to a sustainable society is therefore of primary importance.[35] To further stress this point: the ecological argument is not only one of limits and renunciation. Prioritizing socio-ecological interactions within our political systems offers the potential for building a world of sufficiency – enough for all – that satisfies both material needs of all humans globally and planetary boundaries – well-being within limits.[36]

---

34 Thomas Wiedmann et al., 'Scientists' Warning on Affluence', *Nature Communications* 11, no. 3107 (2020).

35 Ariel Salleh, *Eco-sufficiency and Global Justice: Women Write Political Ecology* (London: Pluto Press, 2009); Riccardo Mastini, 'A Sufficiency Vision for an Ecologically Constrained World', Greeneuropeanjournal.eu, 3 August 2018.

36 Daniel W. O'Neill et al., 'A Good Life for All within Planetary Boundaries', *Nature Sustainability* 1, no. 2 (2018): 88–95; Kallis, *Limits*.

3.2. Socio-economic critique

The OECD recently announced that 'for much of the twentieth century, the implicit assumption that economic growth was synonymous with progress prevailed: the assumption that a growing Gross Domestic Product (GDP) meant that life had to get better'.[37] The socio-economic growth critique calls this assumption into question: further economic growth in the Global North does not (any longer) improve the quality of life. Growth is therefore not desirable as such. Rather, quality of life depends on other factors, which do not need growth: equality, democratic participation, leisure time, revaluation of care work, or the overcoming of irrational, growth-oriented consumption habits such as positional consumption.[38] Based on a large number of empirical studies, this form of growth critique shows that the social and environmental costs of growth above a certain individual or societal income level are higher than its benefits. The socio-economic growth critique thus provides the basis for a degrowth perspective that sees the end of economic growth not as a threat, but as an opportunity for new forms of well-being and a good life for all.

Early economic critiques of growth and consumption

Socio-economic growth criticism became prominent in the middle of the twentieth century, with some earlier precursors. Since the 1970s, it has played a central role in heterodox (i.e., non-neoclassical) economics, especially in welfare economics and feminist economics but also in the interdisciplinary field of 'happiness research' and in social history. Being anchored mainly in academia with a more narrow argumentative thrust, it is less radical (in the sense of 'going to the roots') and critical of the existing systems than other lines of argumentation critical of growth, but it is also relatively accessible.

---

37 Cited in Matthias Schmelzer, *The Hegemony of Growth: The OECD and the Making of the Economic Growth Paradigm* (Cambridge: Cambridge University Press, 2016).

38 That is, consumption habits oriented towards reflecting one's status in society (e.g., driving a sports car or buying a yacht).

Some of the theses of the socio-economic growth critique go back to the British economist John Stuart Mill, who argued as early as 1884 that an end to economic growth, which he predicted would occur in the long term, did not mean the end of human progress. On the contrary, according to Mill: 'There would be as much scope as ever for all kinds of mental culture, and moral and social progress; as much room for improving the Art of Living, and much more likelihood of its being improved, when minds ceased to be engrossed by the art of getting on.'[39] This line of argument was also common among more radical thinkers like William Morris, who, influenced by Karl Marx, argued that an economy less oriented towards accumulation and material growth could nevertheless lead to fulfilling lives – as he sought to illustrate in his utopian novel *News from Nowhere*. Writing in 1896, he observed: 'But think, I beseech you, of the product of England, the workshop of the world, and will you not be bewildered, as I am, at the thought of the mass of things which no sane man could desire, but which our useless toil makes – and sells?'[40] In contrast to 'useless toil', Morris proposed a society that was based on useful, pleasurable work (rather than the total abolition of work), in great part because creative work is essential for human beings to thrive.[41]

Another early critic of growth and consumption was Thorstein Veblen, an eclectic and ground-breaking economist who is considered one of the forerunners of institutional economics, a field of heterodox economics that greatly influenced ecological economics. In his book *The Theory of the Leisure Class*, Veblen coined the term 'conspicuous consumption' to describe how the rich purchase goods or services mainly for the specific purpose of displaying their wealth and social status through luxury goods.[42] In Veblen's analysis, a dynamic emerges when poor people

---

39 John Stuart Mill, *Principles of Political Economy, with Some of Their Applications to Social Philosophy* (London: Longmans, Green and Co., 1920), 751.

40 William Morris, *Signs of Change* (London: Longmans, Green, 1896), 148–59.

41 John Bellamy Foster, 'The Meaning of Work in a Sustainable Society', Monthlyreview.org, 1 September 2017.

42 Thorstein Veblen, *The Theory of the Leisure Class* (London: Transaction Publishers, 1899).

mimic this behaviour, and the rich respond by consuming ever newer and more luxurious 'positional goods', leading to a society that is wasting time and resources in irrational ways. Institutional economists took Veblen's argument a step further to highlight how novel social norms – such as the institution of positional consumption – may eventually lead to cascading and self-reinforcing effects.[43] Several decades later, this field greatly informed the work of heterodox economists such as Elinor Ostrom, who drew on institutional economics to show how managing common resources requires looking beyond market transactions or private property (see section 4.1).[44]

Another, more famous forerunner of the socio-economic critique was John Maynard Keynes, one of the most influential economists of the twentieth century. In his famous essay 'Economic Possibilities for Our Grandchildren', Keynes formulated a series of long-term predictions about a good life beyond growth, drudgery, and endless accumulation. In discussing whether human needs are really insatiable, as is conventionally claimed, and thus require infinite growth, Keynes distinguished two classes of human needs:

> those needs which are absolute in the sense that we feel them whatever the situation of our fellow human beings may be, and those which are relative in the sense that we feel them only if their satisfaction lifts us above, makes us feel superior to, our fellows.[45]

43 Starting with the work of Thorstein Veblen and continuing until the 1950s, the field of institutional economics – which included economists such as John R. Commons, Walton Hamilton, Karl William Kapp, and Karl Polanyi, several of whom were instrumental in shaping the social welfare policies of the New Deal in the United States – sought to break from neoclassical economic orthodoxy and argued that social norms, culture, and forms of property rights also shape the social and environmental sustainability of the economy. Malcolm Rutherford, 'Institutional Economics: Then and Now', *Journal of Economic Perspectives* 15, no. 3 (2001): 173–94.

44 Elinor Ostrom, *Governing the Commons: The Evolution of Institutions for Collective Action* (Cambridge: Cambridge University Press, 1990).

45 John Maynard Keynes, *Essays in Persuasion* (New York: W. W. Norton & Co., 1963), 363.

Based on this distinction, he argues that although the need for what would later be dubbed 'positional consumption' may be insatiable, 'absolute' needs are finite: 'a point could be reached soon, much sooner perhaps than we are all aware, when these needs are satisfied in the sense that we prefer to devote our further energies to non-economic purposes.'[46] Based on this analysis, Keynes concludes that while economic production and living standards in industrialized countries would continue to rise well into the twenty-first century, by 2030 the grandchildren of his generation would have reached a state of abundance in which, instead of continuing to pursue profane activities such as saving, accumulating, or wage labour, they would devote themselves to higher goods such as leisure or the arts. Even in these very early analyses the idea emerged that continuous growth is not the end of history but, on the contrary, that at a certain point in the future, growth may even stand in the way of human progress. From then on, the increase in material prosperity will be replaced by the search for a good life, pleasure, meaning, and 'time prosperity' (drastically reduced working hours for all) or, as in the case of William Morris, more pleasurable and useful work.

Consumer criticism and positional goods

At the height of the 'golden age' of high growth rates in the post-war decades, a critique of prosperity and consumption developed which drew in great part from institutional economics and looked at the social, psychological, and ecological costs of prosperity. The increasing criticism of consumer society – expressed politically both by the left and by conservatives – came in the form of much-discussed popular science books such as Kenneth Galbraith's *The Affluent Society* (1958), David Riesman's *Abundance for What?* (1964), E. J. Mishan's *The Costs of Economic Growth* (1967), or Fred Hirsch's *Social Limits to Growth* (1977). These criticisms can be used politically in different ways. In their conservative, or classist, variant, their arguments are directed against the democratization of consumer practices previously reserved only for the social elite – mass tourism, for example, is a problem because no one may now enjoy the secluded beach as before. In a more critical variant, however, which can still be made productive today, the

---

46 Ibid., 365.

critique is directed against a series of social logics of increase, acceleration, and distinction that lead to greater consumption instead of a better quality of life. Building on earlier work, Fred Hirsch formalized the concept of 'positional goods' as goods that derive their value above all from their scarcity and, therefore, the more people consume them, the less their value. As an example of this 'abundance paradox' he cites tourism, or the desire for a home in the suburbs. In society as a whole, the competition mechanism leads to a wasteful competition for positions, in which everyone tries to gain a higher place in the social hierarchy even if this can only be accomplished at the expense of others. It is a zero-sum game: 'What winners win, losers lose.'[47] Based on these and similar concepts, modern happiness research analyses the functioning of the 'treadmills of happiness' caused by positional competition and social logics of increase and acceleration – and the possibilities of getting out of this hamster wheel.[48]

The paradox of happiness and income

While earlier contributions to a socio-economic growth critique argued mainly theoretically, a broad field of empirically oriented research has developed since the mid-1970s. In 1974, the US economist Richard Easterlin provocatively asked: 'Does economic growth improve the human lot?' His statistical analysis of the relationship between GDP and subjective feelings of happiness introduced the much-discussed 'Easterlin paradox', or 'happiness-income paradox', in economics debates. In essence, it states that, although to some extent quality of life is directly related to income (both within a country and between countries), quality of life does not increase in the longer term if a country's income exceeds a certain level. Four decades later, extensive studies have largely confirmed this thesis.[49]

47 Fred Hirsch, *Social Limits to Growth* (Cambridge, MA: Harvard University Press, 1976), 52.
48 Robert Skidelsky and Edward Skidelsky, *How Much Is Enough? Money and the Good Life* (London: Pengiun, 2012); Hartmut Rosa, *Alienation and Acceleration: Towards a Critical Theory of Late-Modern Temporality* (Malmö and Arhus: NSU Press, 2010).
49 Richard A. Easterlin et al., 'The Happiness-Income Paradox Revisited', *Proceedings of the National Academy of Sciences of the United States of America*

As a product of the socio-economic growth critique and the 'happiness-income paradox', a variety of alternative methods of measuring well-being have been developed since the 1970s. These were decisively inspired by feminist criticism of GDP (see section 3.5). These methods include those that complement the national accounts (roughly speaking, GDP) by including non-market factors such as unpaid labour, environmental degradation, and well-being (see, for example, the *Genuine Progress Indicator* or the *Index of Sustainable Economic Welfare*); those that measure 'social indicators' based on social values (such as housing conditions, education, environment, and health, for example the *Better Life Index* of the OECD); and those that directly survey subjective well-being through questionnaires.[50] Studies that compare different countries with each other and those that analyse changes in the quality of life within a country over time show that the relationship between GDP and quality of life is only stable up to a certain level of prosperity. In most industrialized countries, this was the case until the 1970s or 1980s, after which the relationship falls dramatically apart: even if the economy continued to grow, prosperity has stagnated or even started to decline over recent decades.[51]

How can these empirical results underlying the socio-economic critique be interpreted? Five explanations seem particularly central. On a material level, one reason is, first, that more is not always better. In economics, this is discussed as the 'diminishing marginal utility' of goods (or income), which means that any additional quantity of goods generates less additional satisfaction. An extra $100 in additional income will hardly make a person with an income of $5,000 any happier. However, for someone with an income of $600, or even $30, an additional $100 makes a huge difference. Second, the 'relative income effect' means that, even if more income does not make a country's population happier, it is still worth it for individuals to be richer than other people in their

107, no. 52 (2010): 22463–68; Jackson, *Prosperity without Growth*; Tim Jackson, *Post Growth: Life after Capitalism* (Cambridge: Polity, 2021), chapter 4.

50 Jackson, *Prosperity without Growth*; Schmelzer, *The Hegemony of Growth*; Marilyn Waring, *Counting for Nothing: What Men Value and What Women Are Worth* (Toronto: University of Toronto Press, 1999).

51 Kate Raworth, *Doughnut Economics: Seven Ways to Think Like a 21st-Century Economist* (White River Junction, VT: Chelsea Green Publishing, 2017).

vicinity. Inter-country comparisons show that absolute gains in life satisfaction through increased income are many times lower in richer economies than in poorer ones. To a large extent, they are offset or even
surpassed by senseless status competition throughout society and rising
social and ecological costs. Therefore, according to the British economist,
and author of the book *Prosperity without Growth*, Tim Jackson, a key
message of this research is that 'there is a strong case for the developed
nations to make room for growth in poorer countries' because, in the
latter, 'growth really does make a difference'.[52] Third, the disparity between
rising GDP and well-being is simply due to the fact that GDP is a poor
measure of well-being, since it neglects non-market labour, does not
measure the social and environmental costs of economic growth, neglects
inequality, and so on (see chapter 2). Fourth, in the 1970s and 1980s, the
'golden age' of Fordism or 'democratic capitalism' in most regions in the
Global North ended. It was replaced by neoliberal policies such as financialization, deregulation, privatization, and social cuts, which led to a
massive increase in social inequality and increasing precarity and the
flexibilization of working and living conditions. The prominent idea that
a rising tide lifts all boats has been disproved. There has been a marked
shift from what Ulrich Beck called 'elevator societies' – those with a lot of
upward social mobility – towards societies characterized by social
decline, exhaustion, and anxiety, in which a small elite is able to capture
an increasingly larger share of the output.[53] Fifth, and finally, the general
trend towards declining growth rates in the industrialized countries –
secular stagnation – without redistributive measures leads to an increase
in class inequality and a stagnation or decline in the quality of life of the
majority of the population (see Figure 3.1). In the long run, without
growth, capitalism changes into a neo-feudal market economy, capital
accumulation slackens, overcapacities increase, and inequalities
explode.[54] For these reasons – according to the socio-economic growth

52 Jackson, *Prosperity without Growth*, 41.

53 Oliver Nachtwey, *Germany's Hidden Crisis: Social Decline in the Heart of
Europe* (London: Verso, 2018); Lucas Chancel et al., *World Inequality Report 2022*
(Cambridge: Harvard University Press, 2022).

54 Thomas Piketty, *Capital in the Twenty-First Century* (Cambridge, MA:
Harvard University Press, 2014); Jackson, *Prosperity without Growth*, 107;

critique – politics cannot realistically rely on further economic growth in the rich countries in order to achieve gains in the quality of life. Thus, other sources of well-being, which do not depend on economic growth, must move to the centre of the discussion. This line of argumentation was also recently highlighted by the European Environment Agency – who in a 2021 report argued: 'The broader "post-growth" concept seems highly relevant for Europe and other developed regions as they face increasing uncertainties about future GDP growth' (see Figure 3.1). [55]

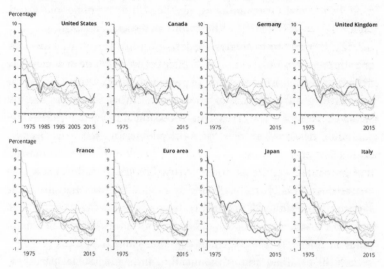

Figure 3.1. Annual growth of GDP (2010 USD), rolling average for previous ten years. Source: European Environment Agency, *Reflecting on Green Growth: Creating a Resilient Economy within Environmental Limits* (Copenhagen: European Environment Agency, 2021), 24; created using World Bank data.

Skidelsky and Skidelsky, *How Much Is Enough?*; Robert Brenner, *The Economics of Global Turbulence: The Advanced Capitalist Economies from Long Boom to Long Downturn, 1945–2005* (London: Verso, 2006); Aaron Benanav, *Automation and the Future of Work* (London: Verso, 2020).

55 European Environment Agency, *Reflecting on Green Growth: Creating a Resilient Economy within Environmental Limits* (Copenhagen: European Environment Agency, 2021), 24.

Significance for degrowth: In an economy
based on growth, any recession is a crisis

In the more contemporary degrowth debate, this research is interpreted as evidence that prosperity is possible without growth.
However – and this already indicates one of the central requirements
of a degrowth vision – the fact that growth does not (any longer)
bring additional prosperity does not necessarily mean that within
capitalism growth is meaningless for the well-being of people. For in
capitalist growth societies, the economic, social, institutional, and
mental infrastructures are designed based on, and are geared towards,
growth and accumulation – these institutions of modern society are
dynamically stabilized through expansion and only function in the
context of growth. A lack of growth is, if these structures are not
changed, first of all a crisis. The recession during the COVID-19
pandemic has been a crisis for most people, in great part because
declines in growth were not (or not adequately) paired with policies
that guarantee well-being and security. Empirical studies show that
life satisfaction falls drastically during economic crises, because while
expectations tend to go up quickly during boom cycles – we all want
to keep up with the Joneses – they are not adjusted downwards in
times of crisis. This shows that well-being and happiness are both
socially determined and economically contingent. Social participation in consumer societies also depends to a large extent – also for the
lower classes – on expressing identity, affiliation, lifestyle, and status
through consumer goods and the symbolic language embedded in
them. And modern welfare states basically function as growth states
– across the entire political spectrum, the promise of welfare is based
on growth raising the standard of living of poorer sections of the
population and at the same time providing the financial means for
welfare programmes via taxes.[56]

Thus it is necessary, beyond individual appeals for renunciation and
subjective discussions about happiness, to overcome the social foundations of growth societies based on status competition and a narrow

---

56 For the relevant literature, see chapter 4.

focus on gainful employment – and to replace them with a different social organization. That this is possible is shown by studies that have demonstrated that quality of life does not depend on growth but instead on factors such as equality, prosperity, trust, social security, political participation, and the appreciation of care work – none of which require GDP growth.[57] These studies have shown that, above a certain income level which industrialized countries have long since reached, gains in equality are much more important for a multitude of factors central to the quality of life (such as life expectancy, health, social mobility, trust, education, and so on) than rising incomes, for all in society, even the better-off.[58] This is one of the reasons for the importance of equality in the discussion on degrowth. These ideas have recently been developed further by philosopher Kate Soper, who calls for an 'alternative hedonism', which shares many of the core intuitions of the degrowth perspective. Alternative hedonism, Soper argues, is premised

> on the idea that even if the consumerist lifestyle were indefinitely sustainable it would not enhance human happiness and well-being beyond a certain point already reached by many. Its advocates believe that new forms of desire – rather than fears of ecological disaster – are more likely to encourage sustainable modes of consuming.[59]

---

57 Tim Jackson, 'Paradise Lost? The Iron Cage of Consumerism', Centre for the Understanding of Sustainable Prosperity blog, 23 December 2018, cusp.ac.uk; Milena Büchs and Max Koch, *Postgrowth and Wellbeing: Challenges to Sustainable Welfare* (London: Palgrave Macmillan, 2017); Frank Trentmann, *Empire of Things: How We Became a World of Consumers, from the Fifteenth Century to the Twenty-First* (New York: Harper Perennial, 2017).

58 See in particular Richard Wilkinson and Kate Pickett, *The Spirit Level: Why Greater Equality Makes Societies Stronger* (New York: Bloomsbury Press, 2011); see also Jackson, *Prosperity without Growth*; Jason Hickel, *Less Is More: How Degrowth Will Save the World* (London: William Heinemann, 2020); Giorgos Kallis et al., *The Case for Degrowth* (Cambridge: Polity Press, 2020).

59 Kate Soper, *Post-Growth Living: For an Alternative Hedonism* (London: Verso, 2020), 59.

So, beyond all the ecological justifications for degrowth, there are many other reasons, key among them declining actual growth rates and the need to adjust to these, as well as the human desire to improve well-being further, beyond the confines of consumerist lifestyles and economic growth.

3.3. Cultural critique

Suburbia, shopping, malls, sweatshops, branding, mass consumption: critique of consumer culture is by now a cliché and easily recognizable. While it is often shallow, there is quite a lot more to this line of critique than may appear at first. When done right, cultural critique can get at some of the deepest social issues and can be an accessible in-road for many people to develop a broader critique of the economy. Indeed, aside from ecological criticism, cultural criticism was the most influential strand of criticism of the first wave of growth-critical debates in the 1970s and 1980s. Here, we summarize various forms of this critique, which deal with how people are formed as subjects by growth societies. The question is to what extent an internalized growth logic is a major driver of growth, and in what way economic growth comes up against 'subjective limits' that lie within people themselves. Cultural critique is concerned with making visible the mechanisms and consequences of these internalized logics, which are often unconsciously acted out, and showing them to be contingent, or in other words, socio-culturally determined and subject to change. A central concept of cultural criticism is 'alienation'. Cultural critique also often deals with anthropological questions – that is, questions about what it means to be a human being and what kind of image of humanity we create when we talk about the economy.

Ecological humanism and the critique of modern society

A key source of thought for the degrowth movement is a field of progressive authors that can be put under the broad category of 'ecological humanism' (see also sections 3.6 and 4.1). More well-known culprits in this strain of thought include thinkers such as Henry David

Thoreau, Leo Tolstoy, Mahatma Gandhi, and, more contemporarily, Rachel Carson, E. F. Schumacher, and Jane Jacobs. What unites these thinkers is their ecological humanism – that is, combining an embrace of the diversity, uniqueness, and connectedness of the human experience, with a critique of modernity, and an advocacy of ecological awareness. This includes thinkers who are often, but not always, critical of capitalism.[60]

Importantly, much of this thought pushes back against the idea of the individual as an isolated being. Rather, rooted in an – often highly poetic – assessment of the human experience, these thinkers tend to stress the interdependence of human beings and ecosystems. Yet, this is often balanced, as in the work of Tolstoy, Erich Fromm, Mikhail Bakunin, and Murray Bookchin, with a recognition of the importance of freedom and autonomy and a rejection of authority and social hierarchies.

A second facet is the critique of modernity and modern life. Thinkers such as E. F. Schumacher, Jacobs, Ivan Illich, Lewis Mumford, and Kirkpatrick Sale, as well as Aldo Leopold, Wendell Berry, Thoreau, and Gandhi, stressed simplicity, political decentralization, and economic as well as technological organization at a human scale. For these thinkers, modern civilization also engendered a socio-economic system that was alienating and detrimental to human – both individual and collective – flourishing.

A third critique made by the ecological humanists is that an ecological understanding must be integrated within progressive analysis. Many of these thinkers, such as Rachel Carson and Murray Bookchin, were far ahead of their Western contemporaries in advancing an ecological critique of society itself. Running through their approaches was an understanding of the relationships between society and nature, as well as a deep understanding of ecological complexity and how modern society systematically degrades those relationships. Degrowth can be seen as taking up this diverse tradition, by stressing notions of interdependence and self-determination, as well as by advocating for an

---

60 Brian Morris, *Pioneers of Ecological Humanism* (Leicester: Book Guild, 2006).

ecological politics, which does not see progress as necessitating domination over or separation from nature.

The ecological humanist approach can run into trouble, however, when it is uncritically romantic and anti-modern, or when it lacks a critique of capital and colonial relations. For example, within the tradition of American ecological thinkers, there often was not a sufficient engagement with Indigenous epistemologies, whose own environments were relegated to the status of supposedly untouched wilderness. Indeed, much of cultural criticism emerged as a romantic discomfort with the 'cold' and 'rationalist' industrial world, informed by the eighteenth-century work of Jean-Jacques Rousseau, who upheld the ideal of the 'noble savage' and the flight to a pastoral life as a way of escaping modern society. There is also a risk of holding on to problematic justifications for gender inequality and paternalistic ideals of motherhood as a form of sacrifice. This is not to say that ecological humanism in general falls into romanticism – the work of thinkers such as Bakunin, Bookchin, Fromm, and Jacobs shows otherwise. Rather, it is to emphasize how an ecological critique of modern society must go deeper to appreciate the capitalist, patriarchal, and colonial roots of alienation and ecological degradation.

'Alienation' as a key term

In 1844, the young Karl Marx formulated theses on the 'alienation' of people through capitalist work and class society. In a capitalist society, people do not choose to go to work; they are forced to do so because – 'freed' from the means for subsistence – one needs to have an income to survive. And, thus, people become estranged from their humanity. As Marx described, work is alienating in great part because workers neither command the work process nor the fruits of their labour – their function is the same as a cog in a machine: to execute a particular part of the assembly line. For most, work is neither creative nor fulfilling; people are deprived of their ability to determine their own actions and destiny or their relations to other people and to the products of their own labour. Workers are thus turned into instruments; they function as a thing, not as a person.[61] Building on these arguments, thinkers such as Ivan Illich, the French anti-utilitarian group MAUSS (Mouvement anti-utilitariste dans les sciences sociales), the Situationist International, and authors such as Herbert Marcuse (in *One-Dimensional Man*) and Erich Fromm (in *To Have or to Be*) have argued that capitalist society produces not only unequal but also alienated relations – both to oneself and to the world. The critique of alienation is very present in degrowth debates and therefore distinguishes it from other leftist critiques. However, it also often provokes controversy over the legitimacy of this form of criticism, because it is often seen as an anti-modern or individualist approach, as we discuss in the conclusion of this section.

Today, we are further alienated in our workplace, as many of the jobs we have do not feel useful or productive at all. This was most recently argued by David Graeber, who introduced the concept of 'bullshit jobs' to describe how, in the regime of modern capitalism (which is supposedly efficient and competitive) much of our work is meaningless, unnecessary, or even harmful.[62] From a degrowth perspective, all these 'bullshit jobs' – from lobbyists to underemployed office workers to financial service providers or telemarketers – are not only profoundly alienating, but also superfluous. A society not structured around growth would not require people to work useless jobs that they hate.

Let us take a moment to expand briefly on the critique of alienation. More broadly, alienation is a 'silencing' of self and world relationships, which in extreme cases can be manifested in depression or burnout.[63] It can occur in and through work, consumption, or in relation to one's own body, such as through an eating disorder. The alienation of the worker from her own activity in industrial society is a central object of the criticism of industrialization (see section 3.6). However, critical theory has

61 Karl Marx, *Early Writings* (London: Penguin, 1974), 322–34.

62 David Graeber, *Bullshit Jobs: A Theory* (New York: Simon & Schuster, 2018).

63 Max Horkheimer and Theodor W. Adorno, *Dialectic of Enlightenment* (London: Verso, 1996); Rosa, *Alienation and Acceleration*; Hartmut Rosa, Stephan Lessenich, and Klaus Dörre, *Sociology, Capitalism, Critique* (London: Verso, 2015).

extended the concept of alienation to the field of consumption and to industrially prefabricated consumer and cultural experiences.[64] Typical for societies that are subject to a logic of growth is the contradiction between the exponentially increasing variety of options (for example, the possibility to purchase more and more consumer goods and services, to extend the range of one's own social interactions to the entire globe by smartphone) and the real – above all temporally but also physically limited – possibility of using them. As a result, some consumer goods are not bought primarily for use; instead, the event of 'shopping' and the promise that such goods carry with them come to the fore – a new or better pair of badminton rackets may promise afternoons of play, though we soon realize there is hardly any time for using them in everyday life.[65] This kind of absurd, compensatory consumer behaviour is at the centre of current growth-critical consumer critique – which thus differs from the paternalistic bourgeois post-war critique of consumerism that had complained in a classicist manner about the increase of the consumption of working people (see section 3.2).

Another critique of alienation important to mention here is that of the Situationist International, whose critique of the 'society of the spectacle' and of consumer society has also influenced degrowth theory. For Situationists like Guy Debord and Raoul Vaneigem writing in the 1950s and onwards, Marx's theory of alienation was basically correct but had to be extended to better fit the changing realities of contemporary society. For these thinkers, the alienation of the workplace had been extended to everyday life. Capitalist accumulation and exploitation was a feature of urban space – through ever-present advertising, vast shopping districts, and the redesign of cities to stimulate consumption – and of popular media, the radio, magazines, and so on. The Situationists noted how, increasingly, our relationships with one another are mediated through objects and media (and remember that their argument preceded, by a half-century, the arrival of social media, targeted advertising, and platform

---

64 Horkheimer and Adorno, *Dialectic of Enlightenment*.
65 Rosa, *Alienation and Acceleration*; Latouche, *Farewell to Growth*; Trentmann, *Empire of Things*.

capitalism). Individual expression takes the form of the consumption of commodities, rather than direct, authentic communication. Thus, the Situationists argued that, beyond the workplace, culture itself is a key site of control, pulling us into spectacular accumulation and competition with one another and ourselves.[66] As we explain in the next sub-section, the Situationists also proposed practical ways of cutting through the 'spectacle' of society, methods that would come to influence the degrowth movement as well.

Adbusting and culture jamming

'Be realistic, demand the impossible.' This was one of the many playful slogans spray-painted in the streets of Paris in 1968, leading up to and during the period of massive social unrest. The slogan was an early example of what later came to be part of a bigger movement in which people hacked and played with their surroundings and with the media in order to convey counter-cultural messages – practices collectively called 'adbusting' or 'culture jamming'. Indeed, these strategies were very influential in shaping the degrowth movement in the early 2000s. Adbusting describes the practice of intervening in, or playing with, advertisements in public space in order to change their meaning in an often critical or humorous way. The Situationists were early adopters of this approach, as one of the key methods they advocated for breaking through the consumption-oriented society of the spectacle was that of 'détournement' (meaning 'rerouting' or 'hijacking'), a strategy whereby one would take hegemonic ideas from mainstream culture and turn them against themselves. This would allow activists to sneak counter-cultural ideas into the mainstream through 'culture jamming', as it was practised by the punk movement, militant feminists such as the Guerrilla Girls, and, later and more famously, the magazine *Adbusters*, which played an important role in kickstarting the Occupy Wall Street protests.[67]

---

66 Raoul Vaneigem, *The Revolution of Everyday Life* (Oakland, CA: PM Press, 2012); Guy Debord, *Society of the Spectacle* (London: Bread and Circuses Publishing, 2012).

67 Vince Carducci, 'Culture Jamming: A Sociological Perspective', *Journal of Consumer Culture* 6, no. 1 (2006): 116–38.

To highlight the importance of this strategic perspective, the story of the degrowth movement's beginnings is worth briefly recounting here. As mentioned in the introduction, the term 'degrowth' was launched in 2002 by the editors of *Casseurs de pub* (the French version of *Adbusters*), who conceived of the phrase *décroissance durable* as a sly play on *développement durable* – which was the concept of the day as promoted by the World Trade Organization and the leaders of early industrialized nations – and as a reference to Georgescu-Roegen's early use of the term *décroissance* (see section 3.1). Pairing 'sustainability' and 'degrowth' in this way was not only meant to highlight the need for an equitable downscaling, but also a way to turn a mainstream hegemonic concept against itself – continuing the tradition of the Situationists and anti-establishment culture jammers. Thus, degrowth has its roots in counter-cultural movements and was, from its very inception, seen as a playful word, meant to destabilize mainstream cultural hegemony.[68] Degrowth has since continued to be a central concept behind the adbusting movement, and climate justice movements aligned with degrowth often use similar spectacular and playful methods to break through the spectacle of mass media.[69]

People as complex relationships

Beyond strategies for cultural intervention, degrowth has adopted an approach to culture that seeks to counter deep-seated Western assumptions. As analysed in chapter 2, to want more and more is not 'human nature'. On the contrary, unlimited consumer desires are functionally necessary for an ever-increasing demand and thus for the sustained

68 Serge Latouche, *Renverser nos manières de penser: Métanoïa pour le temps present* (Paris: Mille et Une Nuits, 2014); Vincent Liegey and Anitra Nelson, *Exploring Degrowth: A Critical Guide* (London: Pluto Press 2020); Timothée Parrique, *The Political Economy of Degrowth: Economics and Finance* (Clermont: Université Clermont Auvergne, 2019); Paul Ariès, *Décroissance ou barbarie* (Lyon: Golias, 2005).

69 Samuel Alexander, *Art against Empire: Toward an Aesthetics of Degrowth* (Melbourne: Simplicity Institute, 2017); Aaron Vansintjan, 'The New Ecological Situationists: On the Revolutionary Aesthetics of Climate Justice and Degrowth', Neverapart.com, 10 September 2018.

growth of markets, which allows capitalist crises of overaccumulation to be deferred. Today's consumer societies of the Global North did not come about because humans are insatiable but were in fact deliberately constructed at the end of the post-war period. Neoclassical economic theory rests on the assumption of a consumer who maximizes self-interest with every purchasing decision. In this, it is supported by popular and supposedly self-evident claims, like the idea that human beings are essentially selfish, greedy, and insatiable, that they, like other animals, are trying to prove themselves in a supposedly permanent competition of 'survival of the fittest'. This is crystallized in the concept of *Homo economicus* at the centre of neoclassical economic theory: that the human being rationally maximizes their own utility. Far from being scientific knowledge, this is an ideological construct.[70]

This ideology, nevertheless, creates realities, because people become subjects through social systems structured in large part by the directives of economics. People who are socialized in this way, in consumer society, can be characterized as 'growth subjects'. In analysing 'growth subjects', which are often conceptualized according to the model of the bourgeois white man, three characteristics are particularly noteworthy: (1) having the status of an apparently completely independent individual; (2) an orientation towards maximizing one's own 'world reach', or making ever larger parts of the world available to oneself, through for example, travel, consumption, media usage, and so on; and (3) striving for personal assertiveness in order to achieve these goals under competitive conditions.[71]

---

70 Marshall Sahlins, *The Western Illusion of Human Nature* (Chicago: Prickly Paradigm Press, 2008); Amitav Ghosh, *The Nutmeg's Curse: Parables for a Planet in Crisis* (Chicago: University of Chicago Press, 2021); John Gowdy, *Limited Wants, Unlimited Means: A Reader on Hunter-Gatherer Economics and the Environment* (Washington, DC: Island Press, 1998); Waring, *Counting for Nothing*.

71 Rosa, *Alienation and Acceleration;* Dennis Eversberg and Matthias Schmelzer, 'Mehr als Weniger: Erste Überlegungen zur Frage nach dem Postwachstumssubjekt', *psychosozial* 40, no. 2 (2017): 83–100; Matthias Schmelzer and Dennis Eversberg, 'Beyond Growth, Capitalism, and Industrialism? Consensus, Divisions and Currents within the Emerging Movement for Sustainable Degrowth', *Interface: A Journal for and about Social Movements* 9, no. 1 (2017): 327–56.

In contrast to this one-sided view of man, and strongly inspired by feminist criticisms of *Homo economicus* (see section 3.5), degrowth takes a view of the human being as part of a complex system of relationships with manifold interests, among which self-interest and the pursuit of material prosperity are only one of many facets.[72] The French-speaking network of anti-utilitarian scholars MAUSS, which is closely linked to degrowth, argues for the right to exist in all the manifold states a human subject may exist in, including cooperativism and interdependency with others.[73] The critique of *Homo economicus* is thus twofold: on the one hand, it is a critique of the limited understanding of the human being, as found in economics and popular science, as a rational utility maximizer; on the other hand, it is a critique of the hegemony of specific 'growth subjects' that accompany, are generated by, and structure growth societies.

Logics of intensification, acceleration, and alienation

Anti-utilitarians rightly criticize the way that, in capitalist society, diverse human goals are reduced to the satisfaction of a constricted economic subject. The sociologist Hartmut Rosa extends this critique to argue that subjects are also embedded in, and internalize, a 'logic of intensification' which expresses itself through acceleration and scarcity of time. A key condition of the modern subject is thus that the world of things, the social world, and the subject itself are in permanent change and moving ever faster, forcing every person to permanently intensify their relations and their world reach in order not to be left behind. Three dynamics drive this logic. First, there is technological acceleration, driven by the 'economic motor' of the capitalist mode of production. Second, there is the concomitant acceleration of social change by the 'social-structural motor' of functional differentiation – the emergence of ever more

---

72 Frank Adloff, *Gifts of Cooperation, Mauss and Pragmatism* (London: Routledge, 2017); Schmelzer and Eversberg, 'Mehr als Weniger'.

73 Alain Caillé, *Critique de la raison utilitaire: Manifeste du MAUSS* (Paris: La Découverte, 1989); Marcel Mauss, *The Gift: Forms and Functions of Exchange in Archaic Societies* (London: Cohen and West, 1954); D'Alisa, Demaria, and Kallis, *Degrowth: A Vocabulary for a New Era*.

numerous social subsystems with specific logics, demands, and challenges of their own (such as politics, economy, law, science, and so on), which make it possible to deal with complexity only by increasing in complexity, expertise, and differentiation in a competitive dynamic. Third, there is the pace of life itself, driven by the 'cultural motor' of 'the promise of acceleration'. This promise involves the continuous enlargement of one's world reach, and the increase of the variety of options, in one's own life, without which one's participation in society declines and becomes precarious. Standing still becomes a setback, like going up a downward-moving staircase. If we do not participate in these competitive dynamics of acceleration, we fall behind. A worker at a food packaging warehouse wears herself thin through working various side-jobs so that she can afford to travel. An office worker uses every minute off work to post Instagram stories and grow his follower count. A climate justice activist rushes from one protest camp to another, and in between writes a few articles about degrowth. We are all, in different ways, subject to these accelerating dictates of the growth society, which pertain in every sphere of life, including romantic relationships, work, and leisure time. According to Rosa, these constraints work even when the individual themself does not wish for acceleration at all: in a growth society, intensification is necessary to maintain the status quo. The logic of intensification can therefore hardly be overcome by people individually changing their lives. Structural and collective transformations are needed (as will be discussed in chapters 4 and 5).[74]

Subjective limits to growth

Aside from these broader, systemic critiques, some authors also focus on the 'subjective' limits to growth, which can show themselves either in exhaustion, general dissatisfaction, feelings of lack, or resistance to one's own work or life situation. According to Barbara Muraca, the

---

74 Rosa, *Alienation and Acceleration*; Hartmut Rosa, *Resonance: A Sociology of Our Relationship to the World* (Cambridge: Polity Press, 2019); for a similar perspective, see Luc Boltanski and Eve Chiapello, *The New Spirit of Capitalism* (London: Verso, 2006).

pressures from institutions of growth, work, and consumption push us to our limits.[75] Already in the 1970s, Ivan Illich argued that a society geared only to increasing productivity and always creating new needs will necessarily fall victim to lack, deficit, and want, since these newly created needs can never be fully satisfied.[76] The sociologist Dennis Eversberg speaks of the 'individual limits to growth'. These manifest less in the limits of human physiology (apart from the fact that death inevitably occurs after certain periods of food or sleep deprivation) than in the resistance that people mount against the imposition of intensifying their productivity in the ever-accelerating world of work and consumption.[77] In this way, different 'growth regimes' produce different kinds of limits, and, correspondingly, forms of resistance. For example, in the Fordist regime, the monotony and uniformity of work and consumption became a limit to both the willingness of people to continue to work and consume within this regime and to the possibilities of expansion. Yet the factory worker using every bathroom break allowed in the eight-hour workday to go outside for a smoke may also use this time to talk with other workers and eventually to form a union. Or, in the regime of neoliberal or flexible capitalism, a Facebook employee, who aspires to advance her career, will try to be more and more efficient, and become a 'creative' and forward-thinking worker, but will, sooner or later, face burnout. She may either abandon her career or use the resources she has built to start a cooperatively owned social media platform. Another contemporary example would be the elderly caregiver, who is required to keep a very strict schedule and note down every activity during her working hours – but she may lie about her schedule and instead have a tea or chat with the person she is caring for. In this

---

75 Barbara Muraca, 'Décroissance: A Project for a Radical Transformation of Society', *Environmental Values* 22, no. 2 (2013): 147–69.

76 Ivan Illich, *Tools for Conviviality* (London: Marion Boyars, 2001).

77 Dennis Eversberg, 'Die Erzeugung kapitalistischer Realitätsprobleme: Wachstumsregimes und ihre subjektiven Grenzen', *WSI Mitteilungen* 7 (2014): 528–35; Dennis Eversberg, 'From Democracy at Others' Expense to Externalization at Democracy's Expense: Property-Based Personhood and Citizenship Struggles in Organized and Flexible Capitalism', *Anthropological Theory* 21, no. 3 (2021): 315–40.

way, even as economic pressures are forced on us in our daily lives and limit us, we find ways to use those limits to our advantage. Thus, within the limits upon individuals within the growth regime, there are also possibilities that can be taken advantage of. Expanding on this, in chapter 6, we discuss how Ernst Bloch's thesis of utopian surplus opens up opportunities for collective resistance to the effects of the growth regime on our psyches.

Significance for degrowth: Interdependence as the human condition

Cultural criticism has been integrated in very different ways in degrowth discussions in various countries. In the French-speaking discourse on *décroissance*, alienation plays a central role, as it is influenced by the Situationists and the work of André Gorz, for example (see section 3.6). In addition, the theses of the MAUSS group have been widely received there. In German *Postwachstum* ('post-growth') discourse, the theses of Hartmut Rosa on acceleration and expansion are extremely prominent, but these have so far hardly been taken up in the international debate. In the English-speaking discourse, where degrowth has made bigger inroads only more recently, degrowth has a close affinity with authors such as E. F. Schumacher and Wendell Berry, who levelled a critique of contemporary society and sought to offer more ecological, contemplative alternatives.

We argue that cultural criticism is particularly fruitful and a necessary ingredient to an emancipatory post-capitalist politics if it builds on these various international roots and does not appear as a one-sided bourgeois critique of 'the modern way of life' that advocates manual labour, uncritically promotes a 'return to community', engages with common tropes of personal self-optimization and individuality in the face of mass culture, or fails to engage in a critique of social structures and political systems of power altogether. Certain kinds of cultural criticism are often seen as reactionary and as being against modernity, rather than being understood as seeking to move beyond modernity. Criticism of consumerism, in particular, often faces the charge that it focuses on individual action and is not sufficiently engaged with a critique of capitalist production, which drives and creates consumption in the first place (see section 3.4 immediately below). While it is true that, more broadly, criticism of consumption often appears depoliticized, individualized, and simply reactionary, we have sought to highlight critiques that offer much more. Indeed, the cultural critique of growth described here largely points to the role culture plays in driving and further intensifying the exploitation of individuals, leading to new forms of accumulation of capital. In other words, this critique highlights the fact that consumption and culture themselves should be seen as a site of capitalist domination that must be addressed collectively – in addition to and beyond addressing exploitation in the workplace or ecological degradation alone. And, because culture is so intimately tied to our lives, the cultural critique is also an entry point for many to start engaging with anti-establishment ideas – the challenge is to transform this into a cogent critique of capitalist alienation, beyond individual dissatisfaction or self-improvement.

For degrowth, then, cultural critique raises the question of what other forms of subjectivation, those that overcome growth and expansion, might look like: such as, for instance, the 'relational self', a subject that seeks to undo hierarchies and sees itself not as autonomous but as fundamentally connected with other living beings. One way of approaching this is to foreground a more precise notion of 'conviviality', forms of social organization that enable mutual dependencies, the negotiation of interpersonal relationships, and good coexistence. Alongside this, a critique of alienation opens avenues to discuss the social conditions for non-alienated relationships to the world, not by focusing on greater prosperity, individual autonomy, or expanding our world reach (more income, mobility, and so on) but by focusing on the quality of a few, stable relational axes to the world, by developing non-growth forms of flourishing, and by creating the conditions for non-alienated forms of work through democratic institutions to collectively govern our lives, our economy, and our relations with nature.[78]

---

78 On these avenues to overcome alienation, see in particular Adloff, *Gifts of Cooperation*; Rosi Braidotti, Ewa Charkiewicz, Sabine Hausler, and Saskia Wieringa, *Women, the Environment and Sustainable Development: Towards a Theoretical Synthesis* (London: Zed Books, 1994); Arturo Escobar, *Designs for the Pluriverse: Radical Interdependence, Autonomy, and the Making of Worlds*

3.4. Critique of capitalism

'Accumulate, accumulate! That is Moses and the prophets!'[79] This quotation from Marx's *Capital* concisely summarizes the thesis that capitalism – through the competitive compulsion to accumulate – is fundamentally organized around competitive expansion, growth, and intensification and can only function in this way. In classical economics, accumulation (from the Latin *accumulare*, 'to heap up'), describes the continuous process of adding value to capital. Value is created through the metabolic interaction with nature in the form of work, and then exploited by the property-owning classes who can extract surplus value by selling the finished commodity. In a competitive market system, this surplus value must largely be reinvested as capital (machinery, resources, labour), thus leading to expansion and the continued expanded reproduction of capital at ever-higher levels. As we explain further below, this process of accumulation materializes as growth, but also leads to systemic crises and 'contradictions' (ecological, financial, social, political, etc.).[80] As feminist and Global South critics emphasize, beyond the exploitation in the workplace (the 'hidden abode of production', to use Marx's famous term), capitalism is also fundamentally dependent on appropriation and the continuous colonization of a non-capitalist outside. This process of appropriating the non-capitalist 'outside', which following Rosa Luxemburg has been theorized as *Landnahme* (land grabbing), can be understood geographically (as colonialism), socially (as reproduction work, spheres of life not yet commodified), and in relation to nature.[81] The

---

(Durham, NC: Duke University Press, 2018); Schmelzer and Eversberg, 'Mehr als Weniger'; Robin Wall Kimmerer, *Braiding Sweetgrass: Indigenous Wisdom, Scientific Knowledge and the Teachings of Plants* (Minneapolis: Milkweed Editions, 2018); Hartmut, *Resonance*.

79 Marx, *Capital, Volume 1*, 621.

80 David Harvey, *Seventeen Contradictions and the End of Capitalism* (Oxford: Oxford University Press, 2014).

81 Marx, *Capital, Volume 1*, 279; Rosa Luxemburg, *The Accumulation of Capital* (London: Routledge, 2003 [1913]). For more details and literature, see sections 3.5 and 3.7.

crises resulting from this double dynamic of exploitation and appropriation inherent to the process of economic growth – so goes the core argument of the critique of capitalism – cannot be understood nor overcome without undoing the systemic logic and associated social relations of domination and exploitation of capitalist accumulation.[82]

The critique of capitalism is as old as capitalism itself. Even if, in parts of the degrowth discussion, the critique of capitalism is ignored, we consider it essential to understanding the growth society and to the possibility of changing it. The critique of growth, we argue, must also include a critique of capitalist accumulation. In the words of Elmar Altvater (who himself modified Max Horkheimer's statement about the connection between capitalism and fascism): 'They who will not speak of the accumulation of capital shall remain silent about growth.'[83]

From a degrowth perspective, growth can be analysed as a necessary consequence, but also as a condition, of capitalist accumulation. In addition to the critique of consumption and the external limits of growth, production and the mode of production must also be central to a critique of growth. This includes capitalism's tendency to enter into crises – and its continuous overcoming of them through transformations of the mode of production and further expansion to new frontiers – as well as class conflicts and the social institutions (property, corporations, banks, nation-states, the military, monopolies) involved in accumulation and growth processes. Since the limits of growth are also the limits of capitalism (which dynamically stabilizes itself through growth), it is not just economic growth that is under consideration but the capitalist system as such. For, without growth, capitalism threatens to further deteriorate into a refeudalized, miserable, unequal, and authoritarian system marked by strengthened

---

82 Jason W. Moore, *Capitalism in the Web of Life: Ecology and the Accumulation of Capital* (London: Verso, 2015); Sven Beckert, *Empire of Cotton: A Global History* (New York: Alfred A. Knopf, 2014); Rosa, Lessenich, and Dörre, *Sociology, Capitalism, Critique.*

83 Elmar Altvater, 'Wer von der Akkumulation des Kapitals nicht reden will, soll zum Wachstum schweigen', *Emanzipation* 1, no. 1 (2011): 1–21, 1.

borders and conflicts over resources. From the point of view of this criticism, degrowth necessarily also means post-capitalism and is therefore closely aligned with anti-capitalist movements and eco-socialism in particular.[84]

Continuous accumulation process

According to Marx, capitalism is a social structure and economic system which, first, is driven by capital being invested with the aim of earning more money, and in which, second, this accumulation dynamic – based on private ownership of the means of production, wage labour, and competitive markets – has a decisive influence on society. This is often explained using the formula M–C–M' (or: money–commodities–more money). Capitalists invest capital in commodities such as machinery, raw materials, and energy, but also in labour. The 'double character' of wage labour in captialism creates a product that not only has a concrete use value, but also an abstract exchange value. Based on the exchange value, the commodity is worth more than the capital invested and is sold again on markets. This means that the amount of money (M) initially used is converted into a larger amount of money (M') through a metabolic exchange with nature and commodified work (that is, wage labour) that produces commodities (C).[85] If this were the whole story, capitalism would simply involve surplus being consumed privately or spent socially – whether through building palaces or churches or holding large feasts or parades. However, because of market competition, the productive forces moving forward through

---

84 Bengi Akbulut, 'Degrowth', *Rethinking Marxism* 33, 1 (2021): 98–110; Stefania Barca, 'The Labor(s) of Degrowth', *Capitalism Nature Socialism* 30, no. 2 (2019): 207–16; Hickel, *Less Is More*; Giorgos Kallis, 'Socialism without Growth', *Capitalism Nature Socialism* 30, no. 2 (2019): 189–206; Matthias Schmelzer and Dennis Eversberg, 'Beyond Growth, Capitalism, and Industrialism? Consensus, Divisions and Currents within the Emerging Movement for Sustainable Degrowth', *Interface: A Journal for and about Social Movements* 9, no. 1 (2017): 327–56; Frederik Berend Blauwhof, 'Overcoming Accumulation: Is a Capitalist Steady-state Economy Possible?', *Ecological Economics* 84 (2012): 254–61.

85 Marx, *Capital, Volume 1*.

technological improvements, and the competitive need to accumulate capital, a large part of the profits must be reinvested into acquiring more capital. This creates a continuous accumulation process.[86] The fact that the generated surplus value is constantly reinvested in the purchase of better and more modern machines, more or cheaper materials, or in the employment of more or more productive workers is not the result of the individual greed of the capitalist. Due to the competition for market shares and advances in productivity, investing is not an arbitrary decision, but a constraint that restricts all actions of owners of capital and dominates the entire economic system.

The tremendous increase in productivity under capitalism goes back to this principle of competition – because those who lag behind in the pursuit of extra profits through better production methods, technical progress, or more efficient organization of work lose market share to the competition, lack the resources for updating their machinery to the newest standards, and thus sooner or later lose the basis of their business. The pressure on society as a whole to grow production also follows from this dynamic of accumulation. If there is no growth, average capitalists are stuck with unrealized values, unsold goods lose their exchange value, investments decline, and the entire supply chain slows or even comes to a standstill. And, since human life reproduces itself in capitalism through markets – on which provisioning basic necessities depends – every capitalist crisis is also a social crisis.[87] As we discuss below, this capitalist process of accumulation is fundamentally based on inequality, domination, and various forms of social rule. The capitalist system has to be analysed as a social relationship, including class, racial, and gender relations, the post-colonial global world system, and a form of politics comprising states and parties. And capitalism has to be analysed as a biophysical system as well.[88]

---

86 Harvey, *Seventeen Contradictions*; Eric Pineault, 'From Provocation to Challenge: Degrowth, Capitalism and the Prospect of "Socialism without Growth"; A Commentary on Giorgios Kallis', *Capitalism Nature Socialism* 30, no. 2 (2018): 1–16.

87 Pineault, 'From Provocation to Challenge'; Moore, *Capitalism in the Web of Life*.

88 Ulrich Brand and Markus Wissen, *The Imperial Mode of Living: Everyday*

Growth is the materialization of accumulation

The capitalist economy is defined by the drive towards accumulation. Economic growth is the materialization of this process – a materialization that is biophysical and ecological as much as it is social, as we explored in chapter 2. Economic growth is the consequence of the compulsion to make a profit, a process resulting from accumulation. But economic growth is also a condition of accumulation – without growth and the related biophysical and social processes there can be no accumulation.[89] Capital is necessarily excessive; it does not know boundaries; its only drive is to grow itself – which is characterized by the fact that it only refers to itself as quantity. People's needs play only a subordinate role: in exchange value–oriented production needs must be taken into account to the extent that they allow for meeting the conditions of extended production and reproduction of capital, and no more than that.[90] That is, without workers being in a sufficiently healthy state to work, and without consumers being able and having the money to consume, capitalist accumulation would fail either to be profitable or to sell commodities, each of which is an essential condition of the continued process of accumulation and the capture of surplus value.

The economy is thus driven by the pursuit of profits. Within this 'monetary production economy', growth results from two interlinked but different forms of investments, both of which aim at expanding the capacity to produce and accumulate: 'Expansion can be the simple production of more machines, materials and labour power or this expansion can be the production of new forms of machines, materials

Life and the Ecological Crisis of Capitalism (London: Verso, 2021). See also Melvin Leiman, *The Political Economy of Racism* (Chicago: Haymarket Books, 2010); and Cedric J. Robinson, *On Racial Capitalism, Black Internationalism, and Cultures of Resistance* (London: Pluto Press, 2019).

89 Eric Pineault, 'The Growth Imperative of Capitalist Society', in *Degrowth in Movement(s): Exploring Pathways for Transformation*, ed. Corinna Burkhart, Matthias Schmelzer, and Nina Treu (Winchester: Zer0, 2020), 29–43.

90 Harvey, *Seventeen Contradictions*; Frigga Haug, 'The Four-in-One Perspective: A Manifesto for a More Just Life', *Socialism and Democracy* 23, no. 1 (2009): 119–23; Maria Mies and Vandana Shiva, *Ecofeminism* (London: Zed Books, 1993).

and labour power, and the design of new, hitherto non-existent commodity forms.[91] While both extensive and intensive investments affect growth, it is in particular accumulation based on intensive investments that increases productivity and drives ever-expanding and changing consumer markets and permanently 'improving' products (for which advertisement creates the necessary demand). From the labour-centric, productivist perspective it is this latter drive which gives a historically 'progressive' direction to capitalism.

It is this logic of accumulation, driven by competition, which, following the rules of capitalism's development, brings about a permanent revolution of all conditions, has unfolded a previously unknown development of productive forces, and is expanding into ever-growing regions of the world but also into new areas of society. Many – including the productivist currents within the (Marxist) left – hope that capitalism will, through technical innovation, develop the productive forces to make a liberated, post-capitalist society possible.[92] But it is also this dynamic of accumulation that underlies the crisis-like nature of capitalism, as we explore below.

Growth as perpetual crisis

In a famous passage of *Capital*, Marx, writing about the continuous development of the means of production in agriculture and industry through innovation, technology, and the divide between city and countryside, also discussed what has later been termed the 'metabolic rift':

> Capitalist production collects the population together in great centres, and causes the urban population to achieve an ever-growing preponderance. This has two results. On the one hand it

---

91 Pineault, 'The Growth Imperative of Capitalist Society', 34. See also Hickel, *Less Is More*; Stephen A. Marglin and Juliet B. Schor, *The Golden Age of Capitalism: Reinterpreting the Postwar Experience* (Oxford: Oxford University Press, 1992).

92 Paul Mason, *Postcapitalism: A Guide to Our Future* (London: Macmillan, 2016); Aaron Bastani, *Fully Automated Luxury Communism* (London: Verso, 2019). For a critique, see George Caffentzis, 'The End of Work or the Renaissance of Slavery: A Critique of Rifkin and Negri', *Common Sense*, 24 December 1999, 20–38.

concentrates the historical motive force of society; on the other hand, it disturbs the metabolic interaction between man and the earth, i.e., it prevents the return to the soil of its constituent elements consumed by man in the form of food and clothing; hence it hinders the operation of the eternal natural condition for the lasting fertility of the soil . . . But by destroying the circumstances surrounding that metabolism . . . it compels its systematic restoration as a regulative law of social production, and in a form adequate to the full development of the human race . . . All progress in capitalist agriculture is a progress in the art, not only of robbing the worker, but of robbing the soil; all progress in increasing the fertility of the soil for a given time is a progress toward ruining the more long-lasting sources of that fertility . . . Capitalist production, therefore, only develops the techniques and the degree of combination of the social process of production by simultaneously undermining the original sources of all wealth – the soil and the worker.[93]

What this dialectic of capitalist development means ecologically has been much discussed, especially in the eco-Marxist tradition (see section 3.1).[94] Equally important, however, is the ecology of living labour, or the capitalist tendency to exploit human labour through intensification, flexibilization, and the expansion of the working day, which leads to burnout and crises of reproduction and other social crises (see sections 3.3 and 3.5).[95] The central dynamic of the accumulation process lies in the fact that due to the extreme concentration of increasingly larger amounts of capital it becomes more and more difficult to invest that capital profitably. This problem of over-accumulation occurs historically in different variants, mostly in the form of overproduction or financial crises (too many

93 Marx, *Capital, Volume 1*, 529.

94 Foster, *Marx's Ecology*; Moore, *Capitalism in the Web of Life*; Salleh, *Eco-sufficiency and Global Justice*; Saito, *Karl Marx's Eco-socialism*; James O'Connor, 'Capitalism, Nature, Socialism: A Theoretical Introduction', *Capitalism Nature Socialism* 1, no. 1 (1988): 11–38.

95 Corinna Dengler and Lisa Marie Seebacher, 'What about the Global South? Towards a Feminist Decolonial Degrowth Approach', *Ecological Economics* 157 (2019): 246–52; Rosa, Lessenich, and Dörre, *Sociology, Capitalism, Critique*.

factories produce too many goods that cannot be bought in sufficient quantities; too much capital invested in certain sectors, creating bubbles). These periodically occurring crises are often overcome through the continuous incorporation of a 'non-capitalist outside'. As feminists and theorists of colonialism and ecology have shown, following Rosa Luxemburg, capitalism is not only historically based on violent processes of appropriation (the enclosures, colonies, slavery, or 'primitive accumulation'). Appropriation has shaped the entire history of capitalism up until today. The incorporation of non-capitalist forms of life also plays an important role in the expansion of markets, such as through the commodification of decommodified activity (as when sharing rides becomes Uber). The commodity system of capitalism (M–C–M'), based on monetary exchange and labour exploitation, is fundamentally dependent on and cannot function without the appropriation of unpaid labour and energy from humans and non-human nature. For, without unpaid inputs – both from people (unpaid domestic work or neo-colonial exploitation, but also public bailouts) and the raw materials and energy of nature – production costs would rise so far that profits would fall and accumulation would come to a standstill.[96]

Capitalism can be understood as a continuous movement to overcome barriers to accumulation and thus to growth.[97] The stabilization of capitalist dynamics of crisis and the repression of class conflicts in some regions – such as through the 'imperial mode of living' in the Global North (see section 3.7) – are often connected to the relocation or externalization of crises to other regions. The appropriation of 'women, nature and colonies'[98] is often not directly visible through

---

96 Rosa, Lessenich, and Dörre, *Sociology, Capitalism, Critique*; Silvia Federici, *Caliban and the Witch: Women, the Body and Primitive Accumulation* (New York: Autonomedia, 2004); Immanuel Wallerstein, *World-Systems Analysis: An Introduction* (Durham, NC: Duke University Press, 2004); J. K. Gibson-Graham, *The End of Capitalism (as We Knew It): A Feminist Critique of Political Economy* (Oxford: Blackwell, 1996); Veronika Bennholdt-Thomsen and Maria Mies, *The Subsistence Perspective: Beyond the Globalized Economy* (London: Zed Books, 1999).

97 Harvey, *Seventeen Contradictions*.

98 Bennholdt-Thomsen and Mies, *The Subsistence Perspective*.

market mechanisms, but it is an integral part of capitalist development, being closely related to science and technology, to state and military power, and to cultural perspectives – and it is the focus of feminist and South–North criticism (see sections 3.5 and 3.7). In combination with the systemic externalization of the consequences of destructive growth (see section 3.1), this dynamic of the continuous commodification of nature generates a potentially insoluble crisis of capitalist socialization, as 'an irreparable rift in the interdependent process of *social metabolism*, a *metabolism prescribed* by the *natural laws* of *life* itself'.[99] Practically, this means that going 'through' capitalism to arrive at socialism, as accelerationists promote, is not only undesirable but also impossible, as capitalism destroys more than it can create or reorganize.[100]

Urbanization and growth

Marx had already analysed the division between country and city as foundational to the emergence of capitalism, a theme further developed in particular by urban geographers such as Henri Lefebvre, writing at the time of the Situationists and André Gorz. These thinkers were beginning to notice that capital was no longer exclusively invested within primary or secondary production (extraction of raw materials or factory production) but was increasingly shifting towards speculation on real estate. As a way to deal with the overaccumulation of capital resulting from post-Fordist globalization, investment in real estate and land became a kind of 'spatial fix' (as David Harvey termed it).[101] Today, roughly 60 per cent of the world's capital is invested in real estate.[102] As a

---

99 Marx, *Capital, Volume 3*, 949–50, emphasis added; John Bellamy Foster, Brett Clark, and Richard York, *The Ecological Rift: Capitalism's War on the Earth* (New York: NYU Press, 2011); Saito, *Karl Marx's Eco-socialism*.

100 See, for example, Alex Williams and Nick Srnicek, '#ACCELERATE MANIFESTO for an Accelerationist Politics', criticallegalthinking.com, 14 May 2013.

101 David Harvey, 'The Spatial Fix – Hegel, Von Thunen, and Marx', *Antipode* 13, no. 3 (1981): 1–12.

102 Samuel Stein, *Capital City: Gentrification and the Real Estate State* (London: Verso, 2019).

corollary, urban space is a key site for resisting the flows of capital and building alternatives, much as factory production was during the Fordist era. Urban geographers now talk about 'planetary urbanization', noting that the planet is increasingly urbanized – and areas not urbanized are restructured, through infrastructure development and the rewiring of local institutions, to provide a standing reserve for urban development. Scholars have traced how this urbanization is driven by the capture of and conflicts over urban metabolic processes, such as water and energy use, and how it is driving material growth, in particular through concrete and steel (see chapter 2). Urban geographers have documented what is called a 'growth coalition' or 'growth machine' of elites (primarily developers and politicians) who seek to spur and manage urban growth for the sole purpose of profit, functioning as a kind of 'real estate state'. This combined process is a key part of the 'treadmill of production', which refers to an infrastructural web of urban development, construction, production, and consumption that works together to further capitalist accumulation (for example, through suburbanization, malls, large useless megaprojects, gentrification, highways, and so on). As a corollary, many now claim that, even as urbanization has become a key driver of capitalist development, it is also a unique site of resistance to capitalism, through the development of municipalist politics, blocking the growth coalition from achieving its profits and building alternative urban coalitions of working-class, diverse, and ecologically-oriented communities.[103]

Only recently have these questions been more deeply taken up by degrowth scholars: concepts such as the 'growth machine', the 'treadmill of production', and 'urban metabolism' are especially useful for a

103 Marx, *Capital, Volume 3*, 949; Henri Lefebvre, *The Production of Space* (Oxford: Blackwell, 1991); Stein, *Capital City*; David Harvey, *Rebel Cities: From the Right to the City to the Urban Revolution* (London: Verso, 2012); Neil Brenner, ed., *Implosions/Explosions: Towards a Study of Planetary Urbanisation* (Berlin: Jovis, 2014); Nik Heynen, Maria Kaika, and Erik Swyngedouw, eds., *In the Nature of Cities: Urban Political Ecology and the Politics of Urban Metabolism*, vol. 3 (Abingdon: Taylor & Francis, 2006); Kenneth A. Gould, David N. Pellow, and Allan Schnaiberg, *Treadmill of Production: Injustice and Unsustainability in the Global Economy* (Abingdon: Routledge, 2015).

degrowth analysis, and more work can be done here to integrate them within a degrowth framework. Increasingly, the question of urbanization and housing has been explored within degrowth literature, with debates emerging on what kind of human settlements are more appropriate for a degrowth society, and the role of urbanization in driving growth.[104]

Dépense

The concept of *dépense* (in French, 'spending' or 'expenditure'), introduced by the French writer and philosopher Georges Bataille, has been taken up in the degrowth discussion to articulate a specific critique of capitalism. *Dépense* describes the usual practice in non-capitalist societies of spending the socially produced surplus as unproductive expenditure – for example, throwing a feast using the year's surplus harvest – instead of reinvesting it. The term illustrates that the commitment to the productive reinvestment of added value is a specific feature of capitalist societies – anthropologically, however, it is a historical exception. Almost all societies see the collective, ritual, or individual expenditure of surplus – at collective celebrations, ceremonies, or in displaying collective or personal wealth through jewellery, expensive clothing, gardens, parks, and so on. The term *dépense* thus adds two ideas to the criticism of capitalism. First, it opens up the possibility of dealing with overproduction – a feature present in most societies as abundance to be spent collectively but solved in a very destructive way in capitalist societies through endless reinvestment. Second, it illustrates, through pointing to the expenditure of surplus in all human societies, that the logic of scarcity within capitalism is not a universal truth, but a historically contingent phenomenon. That is, it embraces the possibility that collective festivals, spending on art, or more generally democratically deciding how to dispense with the societal surplus could be not merely

104 See, for example, Anitra Nelson and François Schneider, eds., *Housing for Degrowth: Principles, Models, Challenges and Opportunities* (Abingdon, UK: Routledge, 2018); and Samuel Alexander and Brendan Gleeson, *Degrowth in the Suburbs: A Radical Urban Imaginary* (Singapore: Springer, 2018).

a luxury, but a common good. For example, societies could decide to leave fossil fuels in the ground and therefore unused, and invest resources and labour in the recultivation of large areas of land, transforming these into natural carbon sinks. By thus removing money and resources from circulation, capital would be removed from the accumulation process – a necessary prerequisite for undoing the endless accumulation that drives growth. Thus, the idea of *dépense* both connects critiques of capitalism and the degrowth discourse more generally, and it offers a way to go beyond a purely productivist conception of the economy (see chapter 5).[105]

Capitalism and scarcity

Prominent degrowth thinkers have also advanced new ways to think about the intersection between capitalism, scarcity, and abundance. First, it is theorized that capitalism brings about a generalized scarcity within daily life through the enclosure of the commons and the technocratic management and regulation of common space. For example, the enclosure of grazing land and forests in early capitalist Europe led to a condition of scarcity for peasants, forcing a move to the city and integrating people into a 'cash nexus' (Marx). This process of creating scarcity through enclosures has since been replicated in colonized and industrializing countries such as China, as well as increasingly through land grabbing in, for example, the Amazon region, Africa, and the Pacific – for the purpose of expanding industrial plantation agriculture or resource extraction for fossil or green capitalism.[106] In industrialized countries, the working class lives in a daily reality where it is now nearly impossible *not* to rely solely on capitalist production. For example, space is highly regulated and any alternative use of public space, such as for gardening or informal vending, becomes coded as 'loitering' or otherwise criminalized. Alternatively,

---

105 Kallis, *Degrowth*; Onofrio Romano, 'Dépense', in *Degrowth: A Vocabulary for a New Era*, ed. Giacomo D'Alisa, Federico Demaria, and Giorgos Kallis (London: Routledge, 2014), 86–9; Kallis, *Limits*.

106 Federici, *Caliban and the Witch*; Moore, *Capitalism in the Web of Life*.

in early industrialized countries, through a highly regularized tax and welfare system, informal, untaxed production (e.g., creating and selling craftwork for extra income) is controlled out of existence. Even as it imposes scarcity in this way, capitalism also creates a synthetic, manufactured abundance, where the sheer quantity of available goods and services gives an impression of prosperity and plentifulness – but this abundance is privatized in the household and for those individuals that can afford it, and when it is not sold, as with food waste, it is disposed of.[107]

Degrowth scholars such as Giorgos Kallis have argued that, in fact, this simultaneous scarcity and abundance is inherent to a growth-based system. Kallis shows how Thomas Malthus, who is often interpreted as arguing for population control to overcome economic limits, actually invoked the threat of limits to advocate for growth, arguing that scarcity is a *natural fact*, and that only a growth-based economy could overcome it. In this way, Malthus was one of the first 'apostles of growth'. Since then, both neoclassical economists and elites sought to further cement the idea that growth is needed to overcome natural scarcity as common sense. But scarcity is not a natural fact. Rather, scarcity, as well as the social hierarchies that limit autonomy and self-determination, are imposed by a capitalist system of production. As a corollary, degrowth is not about imposing limits on society according to natural scarcity, but about regaining autonomy to collectively create public abundance, and also deliberate and set limits. And this – collectively setting limits – is a key prerequisite for the formation of autonomous, democratic governance, as the Greek philosopher Cornelius Castoriadis argues in his work. Indeed, it is precisely capitalism – through alienating us from each other and from the abundance of the earth – which undemocratically imposes limits on us and makes it impossible for us to set our own. Thus, just as degrowth is about the collective reappropriation and *dépense* of social surplus, it is also about the rejection of natural scarcity, the undoing of imposed limits set on us by capitalism

107 Aaron Vansintjan, 'Urbanisation as the Death of Politics: Sketches of Degrowth Municipalism', in Nelson and Schneider, *Housing for Degrowth*, 196–209.

and hierarchy, deliberating collective limits, and thus about creating a self-determined post-scarcity society.[108]

Significance for degrowth: The role of capitalism in growth

The relationship between the critique of capitalism and the critique of growth is ambivalent and complicated, characterized by mutual scepticism. Parts of the degrowth spectrum seem to be afraid of talking too explicitly about capitalism or, consequentially, to make explicit whether degrowth should actually also mean post-capitalism.[109] More substantially, proponents of degrowth argue that the rejection of capitalism does not by itself imply the rejection of growth. After all, not only was real existing socialism a decidedly growth-oriented, productivist, and technocratic project, but also many of today's proposals for socialism or post-capitalism fall short of an emancipatory growth critique.[110] Nevertheless, a survey of degrowth conference-goers has shown that, by and large, most participants are critical of capitalism and see degrowth as a post-capitalist proposal – a trend that seems to be reinforced by recent publications.[111] Equally, within the broader

---

108 Ulrich Brand et al., 'From Planetary to Societal Boundaries: An Argument for Collectively Defined Self-limitation', *Sustainability: Science, Practice and Policy* 17, no. 1 (2021): 265–92; Kallis, *Limits*; Cornelius Castoriadis, *Philosophy, Politics, Autonomy: Essays in Political Philosophy* (New York: Oxford University Press, 1991); Jason Hickel, 'Degrowth: A Theory of Radical Abundance', *Real-World Economics Review* 87 (2019): 54–68; Viviana Asara, Emanuele Profumi, and Giorgos Kallis, 'Degrowth, Democracy and Autonomy', *Environmental Values* 22, no. 2 (2013): 217–39; Murray Bookchin, *Post-scarcity Anarchism* (Berkeley, CA: Ramparts Press, 1971); Rosemary-Claire Collard, Jessica Dempsey, and Juanita Sundberg, 'A Manifesto for Abundant Futures', *Annals of the Association of American Geographers* 105, no. 2 (2015): 322–30.

109 As an example, see Raworth, *Doughnut Economics*; and Jackson, *Prosperity without Growth*.

110 André Gorz, *Paths to Paradise: On the Liberation from Work* (London: Pluto Press, 1985); Latouche, *Farewell to Growth*; Giorgos Kallis, 'Socialism without Growth'; Pineault, 'From Provocation to Challenge'.

111 Schmelzer and Eversberg, 'Beyond Growth'; Hickel, *Less Is More*; Kallis et al., *The Case for Degrowth*; Corinna Burkhart, Matthias Schmelzer, and Nina Treu, eds., *Degrowth in Movement(s): Exploring Pathways for Transformation*

sustainability and post-growth debate, proponents of degrowth are often more amenable to a critique of capitalism than steady-state economy or post-growth proponents. Indeed, degrowth is often proposed as a more radical critique of the current society than steady-state economics or other social-ecological alternatives.[112]

On the other hand, scholars and activists critical of capitalism have been sceptical about degrowth. Degrowth has repeatedly been accused of formulating only a superficial critique of capitalism, of misjudging the actual drivers of growth, or of advancing individualizing appeals for renunciation. And, of course, sometimes these critiques are warranted. For example, a tendency to focus mainly on consumption, alternative indicators beyond GDP, or policy reforms can risk losing sight of the role that capitalist accumulation has in driving the growth process. The critique of capitalism presented in this section highlights that a criticism focusing solely on the spheres of circulation, consumption, or credit as central drivers of growth bypasses the actual problem: growth comes from the realization of capital. However, often, the anti-capitalist critique of degrowth does not really engage with the core arguments and proposals of degrowth, simply brushing aside what could become a fruitful encounter. In particular, a degrowth-inspired critique of capitalist growth as the materialization of accumulation could deepen widely held understandings of capitalism by focusing on otherwise neglected aspects, such as the material dimension of growth, social metabolism, appropriation, consumer society, artificial scarcity, or *dépense*.[113]

Criticism of capitalism offers manifold starting points for the degrowth discussion, even if many approaches critical of capitalism pay too little attention to ecological questions and global justice, and

---

(Winchester: Zer0, 2020); Ekaterina Chertkovskaya, Alexander Paulsson, and Stefania Barca, *Towards a Political Economy of Degrowth* (London: Rowman and Littlefield International, 2019).

112 Barbara Muraca and Matthias Schmelzer, 'Sustainable Degrowth: Historical Roots of the Search for Alternatives to Growth in Three Regions', in *History of the Future of Economic Growth: Historical Roots of Current Debates on Sustainable Degrowth*, ed. Iris Borowy and Matthias Schmelzer (London: Routledge, 2017), 174–97.

113 Brand and Wissen, *The Imperial Mode of Living*.

are often characterized by an uncritical attitude towards production, technology, and imperial modes of living in the industrialized core that depend on global exploitation. The key question that arises from a degrowth perspective in relation to capitalism – namely, does a reduction in growth necessarily mean overcoming capitalism?[114] – has been much discussed and answered in many different directions. Historical experience shows that phases of stagnation or declining GDP, if they are regional or temporary, do not immediately bring an end to the capitalist economy. Rather, they dramatically aggravate social and political crises and show tendencies towards a crisis-like monopoly capitalism, increasing inequality, processes of accumulation through appropriation, and the refeudalization of social relations.[115] The question – of whether a 'post-growth capitalism', one fundamentally changed by radical reforms and which has brought growth to heel, is possible, or whether degrowth necessarily points beyond capitalism – will probably continue to be a controversial debate.[116] Nevertheless, the critique of capitalism is necessary to understand what we are up against. As Eric Pineault puts it:

> A critical theory of accumulation captures the social dimension of capitalism: unequal income distribution, alienating labour processes, exploitation, class domination. A critical theory of growth captures capitalism's appearance in the material world and the socio-ecological contradictions its expansive nature implies.[117]

Together, they make it possible to understand how these contradictions tend to find growth-based answers. Degrowth's ecological materialism enables a critical debate about the biophysical scale and form of an emancipatory and post-capitalist society, and degrowth's critique of capitalism, having evolved somewhat on its own, offers a unique contribution to the debate on post-capitalism.

114 Kallis, 'Socialism without Growth'.
115 Rosa, Lessenich, and Dörre, *Sociology, Capitalism, Critique*; Piketty, *Capital in the Twenty-First Century*.
116 Jackson, *Prosperity without Growth*.
117 Pineault, 'The Growth Imperative of Capitalist Society', 41.

3.5. Feminist critique

The feminist critique of growth is based on the thesis that, in a capitalist economy geared towards economic growth and productivity, the vital reproductive work of society – which is largely carried out by women, in particular Indigenous and Black women, and women of colour – remains fundamentally unacknowledged, invisible, devalued, and precarious. This economic system is therefore essentially a patriarchal one. Reproductive work is the basis of every human society, including capitalist society. Reproductive or care work is understood to mean all those activities that directly serve the maintenance and well-being of people, ranging from accompanying children and the elderly to cooking, housework, caring activities, and, in some definitions, gardening or repair work for personal needs, caring for nature, or subsistence farming. These activities comprise between 30 and 70 per cent of the economic output of a country, depending on the method of calculation. In a patriarchal economic system, reproductive work is in a permanent crisis because it is structurally devalued and poorly or not at all remunerated. This crisis is necessarily linked to the crisis-like development of the human–nature relationship. The permanent crisis of reproductive work can only be overcome by a different economic system that values, centres, and promotes care work. This is the prerequisite and goal of gender justice – and centring care has become a key cornerstone of degrowth.[118]

Eco-feminism and feminist economics

Since at least the 1980s, there has been a rich debate within feminist circles critical of growth. Yet, though feminists critical of capitalism

---

118 Gender justice involves an intersectional approach; in other words, it also takes into account the embeddedness of various forms of discrimination such as classism, (hetero-)sexism, racism, disability, and others. See 'Kimberlé Crenshaw on Intersectionality', Newstatesman.com, 2 April 2014; and bell hooks, *Feminist Theory: From Margin to Centre*, 3rd ed. (New York: Routledge, 2014 [1984]).

have long discussed the problems of a society based on growth in their analyses and proposals and continue to do so, these discussions were not always included or acknowledged in degrowth discourse. In lists of the intellectual 'fathers' of the degrowth discussion, the 'mothers' often have not been mentioned at all, or only marginally.[119] This has only changed in the last few years, and feminist arguments are increasingly integrated into the degrowth discussion, in great part thanks to feminist interventions in publications and at international degrowth conferences. Not all feminist currents are compatible with degrowth ideas – many forms of liberal feminism ignore ecological questions or capitalism – but two theoretical currents of feminist critique are particularly central to degrowth: first, eco-feminism, which makes clear the connection between capitalism, patriarchy, and the exploitation of nature on a systemic level; and second, feminist economics, which criticizes the construction of the genderless *Homo economicus* as a central figure of economics and rejects the calculation of GDP, which does not include unpaid domestic work.[120]

119 For example, see the book series edited by Serge Latouche, Précurseur·ses de la décroissance; Serge Latouche, *Les précurseurs de la décroissance: Une anthologie* (Paris: Le Passager Clandestin, 2016); Cédric Biagini, David Murray, and Pierre Thiesset, eds., *Aux origines de la décroissance: Cinquante penseurs* (Paris: L'Echappée, 2017); Federico Demaria et al., 'What Is Degrowth? From an Activist Slogan to a Social Movement', *Environmental Values* 22, no. 2 (2013): 191–215.

120 Stefania Barca, *Forces of Reproduction: Notes for a Counter-Hegemonic Anthropocene* (Cambridge: Cambridge University Press, 2020); Dengler and Speebacher, 'What about the Global South?'; Anna Saave and Barbara Muraca, 'Rethinking Labour/Work in a Degrowth Society', in *The Palgrave Handbook of Environmental Labour Studies*, ed. Nora Räthzel, Dimitris Stevis, and David Uzzell (Cham: Springer, 2021), 743–67; Mies and Shiva, *Ecofeminism*; Ariel Salleh, *Ecofeminism as Politics: Nature, Marx and the Postmodern* (London: Zed Books, 2017); Marianne A. Ferber and Julie A. Nelson, eds., *Beyond Economic Man: Feminist Theory and Economics* (Chicago: University of Chicago Press, 1993); Waring, *Counting for Nothing*; Gibson-Graham, *The End of Capitalism*.

The iceberg model

What we usually see of an iceberg is only the tip that is above water, while 90 per cent is usually invisible to the observer underwater. Feminist economists have long argued that the capitalist market functions like an iceberg. What is usually identified as 'the economy' – commodities, labour, and investment – is in fact only the tip of the iceberg, beneath which lies an economy that is invisible, reproducing and sustaining life, and which makes the market economy possible in the first place (see Figure 3.2). All the activities that take place underwater, so to speak, are invisible to economics and its tools of measurement – and thus also to how economic policies are made and how the public evaluates different kinds of labour – but nevertheless form a foundation without which the top could not exist at all.[121] GDP measures only money flows – the tip of the iceberg – and thus simply ignores most economic activity. The irrationality of this system has long been discussed, for example with reference to the 'housewife paradox': in theory, if a man were to marry his domestic helper, and from then on she were to run his household unpaid, GDP would be reduced. Her labour – like that of all non-market services, including those of nature – would now be 'free', invisible, and 'count for nothing'.[122] The market-focused perspective of the economy denies the fundamental dependence of all economic activities upon the sphere of reproduction, which is largely done by women (and increasingly in some rich countries by precariously employed migrants) and nature – who thus come to be seen as an unlimited resource. One possibility of escaping this injustice is represented by the campaign for 'wages for housework' – in other words, the monetary remuneration of reproductive activities as demanded by the International Feminist Collective in 1972. This demand is also being discussed further in the context of degrowth.[123]

---

121 Bennholdt-Thomsen and Mies, *The Subsistence Perspective*.

122 This is from the title of Marilyn Waring's famous book *Counting for Nothing: What Men Value and What Women Are Worth*.

123 See 'Feminism(s) and Degrowth: A Midsummer Night's Dream', degrowth. info, 12 May 2018; Silvia Federici and Arlen Austin, *Wages for Housework: The New York Committee 1972–1977* (Brooklyn: Autonomedia, 2017).

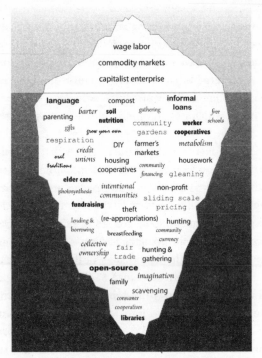

Figure 3.2. The iceberg model of the economy.
Source: Community Economies Institute.

Only by suppressing a large part of economic activities from economics is it possible to use the figure of *Homo economicus* as the basic figure of economics. *Homo economicus* is conceptualized as an independent, rationally acting, selfish, healthy, and genderless middle-aged person, maximizing their own benefit. Because economics starts from this extremely straitened conception of human beings, large parts of economics legitimize competition-based growth as the only reasonable goal of economic activity.[124]

Exclusively considering the tip of the iceberg leads to 'capitalocentrism',

---

124 Ferber and Nelson, *Beyond Economic Man*; Raworth, *Doughnut Economics*.

which makes the inherent logic of all other economic forms – giving, bartering, lending, mutual aid, and so on – invisible. Thus, the idea that 'capitalism' is an all-encompassing system is often reconstructed and tacitly supported even by those critical of capitalism, while diverse economies remain ignored. A gender-equitable society – and thus also a degrowth economy – would need to promote non-capitalist economic activity and develop what J. K. Gibson-Graham calls a 'community economy'.[125]

Gendered exploitation

Any non-capitalist or 'community' economy, however, would be in constant danger of being eaten up by the expansion of the logic of profit and commodification. This is a central finding of feminist Marxist economic research, based on Rosa Luxemburg's work (see also section 3.4). In order to gain a profit, capitalists must constantly appropriate ever more free resources – in the form of so-called 'primitive accumulation' and unpaid reproductive work.[126] This 'non-capitalist outside' of free (or cheap) resources can be found in (still) non-capitalist subsistence societies, primarily in the Global South, and in subsistence activities within capitalist societies, such as education, care, homemaking, and gardening – which are connoted as 'feminine' and are largely unpaid. On the one hand, unpaid reproductive work forms the continuous free basis of capitalist production. On the other hand, capitalist production is designed for continuous expansion and is therefore constantly trying to commercialize reproduction work in order to open up new sectors, as is the case, for example, in the privatization of nursing homes and health care.[127]

Exploitation is justified through the framing of production and reproduction as a binary, one side of which is seen as more valuable.[128] The result is a discursive hierarchy, in which 'reproductive' activities

125 J. K. Gibson-Graham, *A Postcapitalist Politics* (Minneapolis: University of Minnesota Press, 2006).

126 Bennholdt-Thomsen and Mies, *The Subsistence Perspective*.

127 Stefania Barca, *Forces of Reproduction: Notes for a Counter-hegemonic Anthropocene* (Cambridge: Cambridge University Press, 2020).

128 Salleh, *Ecofeminism as Politics*.

(subsistence labour, the 'under-developed' world, the home, nature, and femininity) are subordinated to 'productive' activities (wage labour, Western civilization, the public sphere, and masculinity). The basis of this binary is, as feminist criticism points out, at the root of the European natural sciences. Enlightenment thinkers like Francis Bacon, for example, advocated an image of the male explorer-scientist snatching the secrets of nature (conceived as 'feminine') from her womb, and framed nature as a properly enslaved subject of Man.[129] The 'master model' of Western modernity, at the root of both global inequalities and environmental crises, was developed in the context of seemingly natural, irreconcilable, and hierarchically separated dualisms – man/woman, mind/body, civilized/savage, human/nature – that 'correspond directly to and naturalize gender, class, race and nature oppressions respectively.'[130]

When we think of the iceberg model, we can clearly see that a vast majority of 'feminized' work is actually what props up the economy and allows it to function – and yet this relationship is constantly distorted, both discursively and materially. Within a patriarchal society, it seems as if wage labour is the actually important work, while subsistence and care work are unimportant. This distinction is at the root of what has been called the 'Bielefeld subsistence approach', first formulated in the 1980s by the Bielefeld development sociologists Maria Mies, Claudia von Werlhof, and Veronika Bennholdt-Thomsen.[131] Since wage labour is centred in economic valuation, and not in subsistence, what makes life possible itself becomes distorted. As the Bielefeld theorists state with great clarity:

Without subsistence production, no commodity production, but without commodity production definitely subsistence production . . . The process of capital accumulation – the transformation of life (living work and nature) into commodities, money and steadily

129 Carolyn Merchant, *The Death of Nature: Women, Ecology, and Scientific Revolution* (San Francisco: Harper and Row, 1980).

130 Val Plumwood, *Feminism and the Mastery of Nature* (London: Routledge, 1993), 43.

131 Bennholdt-Thomsen and Mies, *The Subsistence Perspective*, 20–1.

increasing capital – is polarizing and irreversible. In other words: money and capital can grow out of life, but no new life can grow out of capital and money.[132]

This argumentation also forms an important component of the South–North critique of growth (see section 3.7). This recognition entails that work must be redesigned completely, not by automating everything, but by transforming our very understanding of work: a good life does not involve overcoming work, but rather involves overcoming and eradicating alienation in work. Working in another way is not only about having more leisure time and less hours of waged work, an idea that makes sense mainly for men because most women – especially those with children or elderly they have to care for – spend most of their 'leisure' time doing care work anyway. Working differently is about sharing all kinds of necessary work equally – from care work to maintenance of material infrastructures to the production of food.[133]

Ways out: Queer ecologies and caring economies

Since the 1990s there has been a lively debate within feminist theory about whether eco-feminist approaches are 'essentialist'. The question is whether the analysis, according to which the oppression of women and nature is connected, does not prescribe dichotomous and generalizing biological categories (such as 'woman' or 'nature') instead of transgressing them. Therefore, some theorists such as Bina Agarwal or Rosi Braidotti no longer use the term 'eco-feminism'. Some of the most important eco-feminist thinkers, such as Ariel Salleh and Veronika Bennholdt-Thomsen, underline that the eco-feminist argument grows out of Marxist theory and takes women as a 'class' – which has nothing to do with biologism but with specific social relations and a corresponding lived experience of many people socially described as 'women'. More recent growth-critical feminist approaches agree that gender is considered a social construction in turn shaped by patriarchy and argue

132 Ibid., 26.
133 Saave and Muraca, 'Rethinking Labour/Work'; see also chapter 5.

in addition for a constructivist eco-feminism that includes not only Marxist categories but also post-structural thinking – thus establishing links between eco-feminism and queer ecologies.[134]

Queer ecologies seek to reframe and trouble given relationships between nature, gender, and labour.[135] There are two key lines of argumentation. First, queer ecologies interrogate who is able to produce and reproduce, and what kind of relationships are natural. This involves questioning the imperative to procreate or expand, allowing certain activities to be non-(re)productive, as well as forging new relations with non-humans.[136] Second, within patriarchy, nature and care work are often coupled together – a binary which has historically been used to justify exploitation and inequality, as already shown by eco-feminists from the 1980s onward. This binary is also the material basis for the functioning of growth-based economies, even as they must suppress natural productivity and care work in order to be profitable. True sustainability is therefore *structurally* impossible in such an economy – as the discussion on scarcity above makes clear. A queer ecological approach is valuable as it calls into question these binaries and points to the fact that they are socially and ecologically co-constructed and not inherently natural.

A first step towards a different economic system is to dissolve the binary between the productive and reproductive spheres within the field of economics. The German Netzwerk Vorsorgendes Wirtschaften (Network of Precautionary Economics) proposes what they call a precautionary economics based on the term '(re)productivity' in order

---

134 Dengler and Speebacher, 'What about the Global South?'; Greta Gaard, 'Ecofeminism Revisited: Rejecting Essentialism and Re-placing Species in a Material Feminist Environmentalism', *Feminist Formations* 23, no. 2 (2011): 26–53.

135 See, for example, Catriona Mortimer-Sandilands and Bruce Erickson, *Queer Ecologies: Sex, Nature, Politics, Desire* (Bloomington: Indiana University Press, 2010); Matthew Gandy, 'Queer Ecology: Nature, Sexuality, and Heterotopic Alliances', *Environment and Planning D: Society and Space* 30, no. 4 (August 2012): 727–47; and Greta Gaard, 'Toward a Queer Ecofeminism', *Hypatia* 12, no. 1 (1997): 114–37.

136 See, for example, Donna J. Haraway, *Staying with the Trouble: Making Kin in the Chthulucene* (Durham, NC: Duke University Press, 2016).

to approach the economy holistically. It removes the distinction between 'productive' and 'reproductive' – human production is seen as embedded in nature's production and reproduction activities, whether within or beyond a market economy. The basis of precautionary economics is an 'ethics of care' that leads to a precautionary – future-oriented, preventive, careful – rationality that serves to sustain life.[137] Indeed, feminist economists also propose restructuring the current system towards a 'caring economy' which is not geared towards growth.[138] Thus this perspective is also close to the subsistence approach, because subsistence means nothing other than *supporting life*.

The dissolution of the binaries structuring the patriarchal logic of growth can also be understood as the 'queering' of the economy.[139] This not only focuses on the positions of those who identify as women or as nonbinary, but also of men: the construction of the man as a person who does not care (*Homo economicus*) is itself a historical one, which is intimately linked to the rise of growthism in modern societies. This 'hegemonic masculinity' (as Raewyn Connell terms it[140]) arose with the separation of productivity and reproductivity and the privileging of wage labour at the expense of subsistence labour. Thus, even patriarchy benefits certain men above others – where manhood is defined as a dominant, uncaring, seemingly independent, and strong individual, and thus the epitome of an expansionary, appropriating growth subject. More recent masculinity research has been asking to what extent 'caring' or 'ecological' masculinities can create a new understanding of masculinities and gender roles that destabilizes these binaries and could be a building block of a renegotiated economic model in which all genders can develop in many ways.[141]

---

137 Netzwerk Vorsorgendes Wirtschaften, *Wege Vorsorgenden Wirtschaftens* (Marburg: Metropolis, 2012).

138 Barca, *Forces of Reproduction*.

139 Ibid.

140 R. W. Connell, *Masculinities* (Cambridge: Polity, 2005).

141 Martin Hultman and Paul M. Pulé, *Ecological Masculinities: Theoretical Foundations and Practical Guidance* (Abingdon: Routledge, 2018); Karla Elliott, 'Caring Masculinities: Theorizing an Emerging Concept', *Men and Masculinities* 19, no. 3 (1 August 2016): 240–59; Dennis Eversberg and Matthias Schmelzer,

Significance for degrowth: Foundational,
and requires more engagement

The reception of these approaches in the more recent discussion on degrowth can be described as double-sided. On the one hand, degrowth as a whole can be understood as an approach that integrates feminist positions: the rejection of *Homo economicus* as structuring image; the demand for part-time work for all, or an upgrading of subsistence work; the criticism of capitalist logics capturing more and more areas of life; and the critique of the domination of nature through scientific reason are all widely accepted positions in degrowth discussions. The subsistence approach in particular – which is closely interwoven with the works of post-development theoreticians of the 1980s and 1990s, both in terms of content and its actual participants – forms an intellectual basis, albeit one often unnamed, for the more recent degrowth discussion. The feminist debates also had a strong influence on other critiques, such as the critique of industrialism, the further development of critique of capitalism, in particular the theory of primitive accumulation, as well as the socio-economic critique, in particular by questioning the concept of labour.

On the other hand, feminist participants in the debate have repeatedly pointed out that explicitly feminist voices were at least initially largely marginalized in the degrowth discussion. In academic literature, the feminist growth critique is often not sufficiently discussed or is even ignored. However, in recent years this has started to change, at conferences, movement events, and in publications. For degrowth, feminist perspectives are crucial, not only because of all the analytical tools they provide, but also to prevent degrowth policies from having reactionary consequences or reproducing a gendered division of labour. Both a merging of feminist voices and movements with degrowth, as well as an increase in articles and special issues on the topics of

---

'Degrowth und Männlichkeiten – Zur Geschlechtlichkeit des relationalen Postwachstumssubjekts', in *Caring Masculinities? Auf der Suche nach Transformationswegen in eine demokratische Postwachstumsgesellschaft*, ed. Andreas Heilmann and Sylka Scholz (Munich: Oekom, 2019), 173–84.

feminism and degrowth, demonstrates a growing interest in the feminist critique of growth.[142]

3.6. Critique of industrialism

Critiques of industrialism argue that, no matter the kind of ownership or social organization, the development of productive forces and technology in modern societies have become authoritarian, alienating, and restrictive of self-determination and therefore cannot automatically be regarded as desirable for an emancipatory society. 'Industrialism' refers to the overall structure of a modern industrial society based on mechanized work. With the critique of progress in productivity – the ability to produce more and more goods in ever shorter time – this critique questions the central factor by which both capitalist and socialist societies measure or have measured their success. Thus, Lenin already noted that, in the competition between capitalism and socialism, the social system that achieves the higher labour productivity will win. Critics of industrialism contend that a good life need not depend on the continued progress of productive forces. Writing beginning in the 1970s, these thinkers argued that the problem lay deeper than the competition between two hegemonic systems, and thus sought to open a conceptual third way beyond the two antagonists of the Cold War. As the social philosopher André Gorz put it: 'To speak of industrialist civilization does not mean to deny or ignore its essential capitalist character. The fact that industrialism is common to capitalism and socialism illustrates the power and scope of this concept. For even the crisis is common to capitalism and socialism.'[143]

Criticism of industrialism argues that competition-driven technological development and the associated increase in productivity

---

142 Dengler and Speebacher, 'What about the Global South?'; Corinna Dengler and Birte Strunk, 'The Monetized Economy versus Care and the Environment: Degrowth Perspectives on Reconciling an Antagonism', *Feminist Economics* 24, no. 3 (2018): 160–83; Saave and Muraca, 'Rethinking Labour/ Works'; Barca, *Forces of Reproduction*.

143 Gorz, *Paths to Paradise*, 13.

themselves act as growth drivers; that technology is not neutral and therefore cannot simply be detached from the logic of profit; and that increasing mechanization hampers the self-determination of people in the world of work and everyday life. In this sense, the goal of a degrowth society must be to overcome industrialism towards a post-industrial society that strives for a fundamentally different kind of technology, which means a profound transformation and democratization of the means of production and material infrastructures such as electricity networks, transport routes, and communication technologies (see chapter 5).

The different strands of the critique of industrialism

Criticizing modern technology and its effect on the individual and society and consumption can get you called a Luddite or accused of denying people the privileges of a modern economy. However, as argued by Peter Linebaugh, 'Luddite' shouldn't actually be an insult – the Luddites in Northern England, active in the nineteenth century, broke the cotton mills because they were against participating in alienating labour and its connection to slavery in the Americas.[144] And indeed, critiques of industrialism and technology arose with and critically analyse the industrial mode of production in the eighteenth and nineteenth centuries. In some cases, they also drew attention to the connection between contemporary industrialism and the development of urban and hierarchical civilizations based on agriculture – in China, European antiquity, and the Middle East.[145]

Criticism of industrialism is often very closely interwoven with cultural criticism of growth, and both can be linked to very different

---

144 Peter Linebaugh, *Ned Ludd and Queen Mab: Machine-Breaking, Romanticism, and the Several Commons of 1811–1812* (San Francisco: PM Press, 2012); Gavin Mueller, *Breaking Things at Work: The Luddites Are Right about Why You Hate Your Job* (London: Verso, 2021).

145 Murray Bookchin, *The Ecology of Freedom* (Oakland, CA: AK Press, 2005); Abdullah Öcalan and Klaus Happel, *Prison Writings: The Roots of Civilization* (London: Pluto Press, 2007).

political attitudes. Part of the early intellectual critique of industrialism in the Romanticism of the early nineteenth century was conservative, anti-egalitarian, and glorified the feudal class-society. At the
same time, however, there are emancipatory antecedents of degrowth
thought such as the Luddite workers' revolts that took place in
England, destroying mechanical looms as part of their labour struggle for better working conditions and wages.[146] Criticism of technology and industrialized lifestyles was also one of the central arguments
of the early socialist movements of the nineteenth century. The lifestyle movements at the beginning of the twentieth century took up
these motifs again in the design of anarcho-syndicalist and ethnic
settlement projects – some of them bearing proto-Nazi and eco-
fascist undertones.[147] This shows how important it is to combine the
critique of industrialism with the other thoroughly emancipatory
critiques discussed in this chapter.

The world wars of the twentieth century, and in particular the development of nuclear power, gave rise to new forms of technology criticism that explicitly dealt with the destructive potential of large-scale
technologies, such as Günther Anders's *Antiquated Humanity* or Hans
Jonas's *Principle of Responsibility*. This was followed by demands for
better clarity and democratic accountability regarding technology (as
was advocated in E. F. Schumacher's *Small Is Beautiful*). New formula-
tions of the critique of industrialism in the 1970s have become particularly important for discussions on degrowth. Social-philosophical
works such as Lewis Mumford's *Myth of the Machine*, Jacques Ellul's *La
Technique, ou L'enjeu de siécle*, or Ivan Illich's *Tools for Conviviality* are
often cited. Authors such as André Gorz, Peter Harper (author of
Radical Technology), or Rudolf Bahro (author of *The Alternative*)
formulated their critique of technology on a Marxist basis and broke
with the classic socialist belief in progress, according to which capitalism develops the productive forces of a liberated society. Feminist

---

146 Linebaugh, *Ned Ludd and Queen Mab*; Mueller, *Breaking Things at Work*.
147 Peter Staudenmaier, 'Fascist Ideology: The Green Wing of the Nazi Party
and Its Historical Antecedents', in *Ecofascism: Lessons from the German
Experience*, ed. Janet Biehl and Peter Staudenmaier (Edinburgh: AK Press, 1995),
36–8.

theorists such as Carolyn Merchant also expanded the critique of industrialism towards a critique of patriarchy.

Technology is not neutral

Complex technologies are not neutral. We can define a complex technology as one which requires global supply chains, large infrastructure, social hierarchies, and highly specialized expertise to operate. These favour or demand specific actions and power structures in production or use – a specific form of society. It does not matter whether this technology is put at the service of a capitalist or a socialist system – it unfolds a rationalist-utilitarian logic of its own that cannot easily be democratized. This problem can be traced back to the emergence of modern science as the basis of today's technology. The conceptualization of natural science as a mode of objective recognition, which breaks down nature into its smallest, unconnected components, if uncritically applied, is in itself a domineering and gendered process. While the critique of capitalism focuses above all on the rationality of increasing profits, critique of industrialism focuses on another instrumental rationality: scientific-experimental rationality, which forms the basis of technological interventions in the ecological relationships that support modern societies. Under this rationality, it is not just the fascination with technological possibilities that is the problem; it is that the machine is considered to be a model for society as a whole, and of human development. In this way, the 'rationality of technological thinking', as Langdon Winner calls it, in fact obscures the role of capital as an inhumane driver of social disruption, and seeks to justify it. The Silicon Valley slogan 'move fast and break things', coined by the Facebook CEO Mark Zuckerberg, takes this to the extreme: the disruptive character of technology is itself considered to be its source of both societal development and private profit. This is not to say that innovation or experimentation itself is bad – to the contrary, it is rather to point out the problems that arise if innovation and experimentation do not take into account their repercussions and externalities.[148]

---

148 Gorz, *Paths to Paradise*; Illich, *Tools for Conviviality*; Lewis Mumford,

This scientific-experimental rationality goes hand in hand with a quasi-religious belief in technical progress as a saviour as originally formulated by Francis Bacon, one of the founders of modern science in the seventeenth century.[149] Lewis Mumford has noted that technological progress had emptied the concept of progress as a whole and claimed it for itself. Technological innovation becomes an end in itself:

> Western society has accepted as incontestable a technological imperative that is as arbitrary as the most primitive taboo: not merely the duty to promote inventions and continuously bring about technological innovations, but also the duty to submit unconditionally to these innovations simply because they are offered, regardless of their consequences for man.[150]

Today, this faith continues in the work of the eco-modernists, as well as of academics who champion science and technology as the main or only solution to the many-faceted crises, thus not only often promoting 'false solutions', but also suppressing the equally important and often more effective social innovations, democratic movements, or collective actions. It is also a common position on the left, where the development of productive forces through full automation of work and an increasing output are seen as preconditions for post-scarcity socialism.[151]

'Authoritarian and Democratic Technics', *Technology and Culture* 5, no. 1 (1964): 1–8. Langdon Winner, *The Whale and the Reactor: A Search for Limits in an Age of High Technology* (Chicago: University of Chicago Press, 2010); Langdon Winner, 'Do Artefacts Have Politics?', *Daedalus* 109, no. 1 (1980): 121–36; Merchant, *The Death of Nature*; Albert Borgmann, *Technology and the Character of Contemporary Life: A Philosophical Inquiry* (Chicago: University of Chicago Press, 1987).

149 Merchant, *The Death of Nature*.

150 Lewis Mumford, *The Myth of the Machine: Technics and Human Development* (London: Secker & Warburg, 1967), 185.

151 For example, see Steven Pinker, *Enlightenment Now: The Case for Reason, Science, Humanism, and Progress* (New York: Penguin, 2018); and Bastani, *Fully Automated Luxury Communism*. For a critique, see Kallis and Bliss, 'Post-environmentalism'; and Rut Elliot Blomqvist, 'Pulling the Magical Lever: A Critical Analysis of Techno-utopian Imaginaries', unevenearth.org, 2 September 2018.

Yet another critique of technology comes from a feminist perspective. Techno-feminists argue that technology is often gendered as 'masculine' and situated outside the bounds of properly 'feminine' experience – even as women have had a crucial role in the development of many technologies, such as medicine and information technologies. Furthermore, technologies have a tendency to extend masculine control over nature and people, as they are designed through a hegemonically masculine lens (via large, highly centralized power sources), excluding participation by others (engineering culture, for example, being heavily male-dominated), and further oppressing marginalized groups (for example, in the racial biases manifested in artificial intelligence security technology). While many technologies extend control and impede autonomy, we can develop others that support caring, convivial relationships. Yet again, techno-feminists do not reject technology outright but take a critical yet hopeful look on the potential of certain technologies for changing oppressive relationships and undermining binaries. Thus, while recognizing that technology is shaped by dominant social norms such as patriarchy, techno-feminism seeks to go beyond pessimistic technophobia, which they argue forecloses potential for transformation.[152]

Finally, there is also the concern that certain complex technologies lend themselves to hierarchical, undemocratic relationships within society as a whole. For example, nuclear power plants, as they exist today, are dependent on a regime of technical experts for their management and, eventually, their decommissioning. Without sufficient decommissioning expertise, socially acceptable nuclear waste repositories, and new energy sources, nuclear power plants must keep running beyond their intended lifespan, as is the case in many Western countries today. Further, the protection of nuclear assets and the management of waste requires strong military intervention, as well as large

---

152 Thanks to Ky Brooks for feedback on this section. Judy Wajcman, *Technofeminism* (Cambridge: Polity, 2004); Tina Sikka, 'Technofeminism and Ecofeminism', in *Ecofeminism in Dialogue*, ed. Douglas A. Vakoch and Sam Mickey (Lanham, MD: Lexington Books, 2017), 107–28; Saurabh Arora et al., 'Control, Care, and Conviviality in the Politics of Technology for Sustainability', *Sustainability: Science, Practice and Policy* 16, no. 1 (2020): 247–62.

infrastructures for containing it – which must then be kept inaccessible from the public for millennia.[153] Similarly, as we explored in chapter 2, the switch from coal to oil also led to the formation of a more technocratic, dispersed energy system, as miners and dock-workers could no longer strike and block energy flows as easily.[154] In this way, considering whether a certain energy technology is desirable is not just a matter of assessing its technical ability to provide reliable power but to ask whether such a hierarchical division of labour, expertise, management, and security is amenable for a democratic society, and to what extent such an energy system necessarily restructures society towards more alienated, authoritarian, militarized, and highly centralized social systems.[155]

The technosphere as driver of growth

The massive expansion of technical systems and infrastructures, especially since the mid-twentieth century, is a major cause of ecological problems (see section 3.1). Transport routes by land, sea, and air, power stations, electricity grids, water supply and disposal systems, global trade, industrial food systems, and cable and radio networks make the growth economy possible in the first place and are based mainly on fossil fuels. But their transformation is not easy to accomplish: infrastructures are associated with high investment costs and often create decades or even centuries of path dependencies – meaning that, once built, they continue to shape how we organize society. They are integrated into complex socio-technical systems such as motorized private

153 Winner, *The Whale and the Reactor*; Mumford, 'Authoritarian and Democratic Technics'; Frank Uekoetter, 'Fukushima, Europe, and the Authoritarian Nature of Nuclear Technology', *Environmental History* 17, no. 2 (2012): 277–84; Sabu Kohso, *Radiation and Revolution* (Durham, NC: Duke University Press, 2020); Samuel Miller Macdonald, 'Is Nuclear Power Our Best Bet against Climate Change?', *Bostonreview.net*, 2021.

154 Timothy Mitchell, *Carbon Democracy: Political Power in the Age of Oil* (London: Verso, 2011).

155 Aaron Vansintjan, 'Where's the "Eco" in Eco-modernism?', Redpepper. org.uk, 2018; Mumford, 'Authoritarian and Democratic Technics'; Winner, *The Whale and the Reactor*.

transport or digitally connected means of communication. Thus, they determine large parts of everyday life. Due to the increasing complexity of technical systems, technical infrastructures themselves are becoming a driver of growth, as they require a permanent increase in complexity in a society organized according to the logic of growth – not least to deal with the problems created by exactly these systems. For example, André Gorz describes the problem of automobiles and the world they have created in a striking essay, 'The Social Ideology of the Motorcar':

> The car has made the big city uninhabitable. It has made it stinking, noisy, suffocating, dusty, so congested that nobody wants to go out in the evening anymore. Thus, since cars have killed the city, we need faster cars to escape on superhighways to suburbs that are even farther away. What an impeccable circular argument: give us more cars so that we can escape the destruction caused by cars.[156]

Another example: oil became the dominant source of energy due to its ease of transportation, but this has helped to cause unprecedented climate breakdown; as the climate gets hotter we begin to use more air conditioners, which in turn make local outdoor temperatures even hotter due to their heat pollution, causing cities like Doha – whose wealth is built on oil extraction – to plan open-air air conditioning systems to allow them to stay habitable, which depends on even more carbon emissions. You can see how this process eventually leads to a cascading series of Rube Goldberg machines meant to clean up in turn the side effects of each new complex technology.[157] The profit from further technical innovations tends to decrease with increasing complexity, which fuels ever faster innovation cycles. Digital processes and technologies accelerate this process even further – cars are now increasingly digitized and thus more difficult to repair, and automated driving will likely require that road infrastructure be digitized as well. This process leads to an increasing technical penetration and to

---

156 André Gorz, 'The Social Ideology of the Motorcar', unevenearth.org, 2018.

157 Illich, *Tools for Conviviality*.

dependencies in more and more areas of life – from life habits and mobility to the world of work, surveillance, and agriculture.[158]

The radical monopoly and the counter-productivity threshold

This technical landscape affects our lives in direct and indirect ways. Ivan Illich has pointed out that, for individuals, it has a high cost and it is close to impossible not to participate in new technological developments. This is because socio-technical systems such as automotive vehicles, computers, or smartphones become a 'radical monopoly' in industrial societies, which undermines the self-determination of people to live a life according to their ideas.[159] Social institutions become an obligation through the radical monopoly – whether explicitly, as with compulsory schooling, or implicitly, as with the use of digital means of communication. Against the notion that a degrowth society can be achieved through individual frugality, the concept of 'radical monopoly' makes it clear that this individual reduction is not possible at all – or it is only possible under the threat of partial or total exclusion from society. Thus, degrowth must aim at democratizing and overcoming these radical monopolies embedded in the productive forces of capitalist society.

Another concept introduced by Ivan Illich is the 'counter-productivity threshold'. This is the idea that, when something that seems beneficial is used too much, it may actually become counter-productive. We will give a longer quotation, because this also illustrates one of the reasons why, in the Southern European *décroissance* movement, the snail is the symbol of degrowth:

---

158 Bonaiuti, *The Great Transition*; Nelson and Schneider, *Housing for Degrowth*; Christian Kerschner et al., 'Degrowth and Technology: Towards Feasible, Viable, Appropriate and Convivial Imaginaries', *Journal of Cleaner Production* 197 (2018): 1619–36; Michael J. Albert, 'The Dangers of Decoupling: Earth System Crisis and the "Fourth Industrial Revolution"', *Global Policy* 11, no. 2 (2020): 245–54.

159 Illich, *Tools for Conviviality*; Wolfgang Sachs, *The Development Reader: A Guide to Knowledge and Power* (London: Zed Books, 1992).

The snail constructs the delicate architecture of its shell by adding ever increasing spirals one after the other, but then it abruptly stops and winds back in the reverse direction. In fact, just one additional larger spiral would make the shell sixteen times bigger. Instead of being beneficial, it would overload the snail. Any increase in the snail's productivity would only be used to offset the difficulties created by the enlargement of the shell beyond its preordained limits. Once the limit to increasing spiral size has been reached, the problems of excessive growth multiply exponentially, while the snail's biological capability, in the best of cases, can only show linear growth and increase arithmetically.[160]

Illich argues that, at the point when a beneficial technology becomes institutionalized and becomes too large, it no longer offers a service to a society. For example, if everyone in a dense city were to drive a car individually, then no one would get the benefits of driving – since there would be too much traffic on the road. This is the point where the costs deriving from a technology start to outweigh its benefits, when it becomes counter-productive. Degrowth thus aims at collectively determining forms of technology that do not fall into these irrational traps of the 'more is better' ideology of technological progress, limiting the use of those technologies that stand in the way of a good life for all.

Social ecology

Discussions in political or social ecology have, building on Marx's arguments, critically analysed societal relationships to nature, arguing that the development of modern societies can only be understood by examining the specific ways that metabolism with nature is shaped by human labour. Based on this materialist perspective, there has been not only the development of empirical analyses of 'social metabolism' itself (see

---

160 This quote from Ivan Illich (which originally appeared in 'Le genre vernaculaire', *Oeuvres complètes*, vol. 2 [Paris: Fayard, 2005]) has been translated by Ronnie Richards and appears in Serge Latouche, 'The Wisdom of the Snail', Slowfood.com, 22 September 2020. On the counter-productivity threshold, see also Liegey and Nelson, *Exploring Degrowth*.

sections 2.2 and 3.1), but also a critical theory of socio-natural condi-tions. Advocates of this perspective – also in contrast to Western social democracy and the Soviet Marxism of the early twentieth century – criticize the notion that social progress and human emancipation must necessarily include increasing and perfecting the domination of nature. In the *Dialectic of the Enlightenment*, Max Horkheimer and Theodor W. Adorno have sharpened this into a radical diagnosis of crisis, which remains central to the criticism of the green economy within degrowth: 'Any attempt to break the compulsion of nature by breaking nature only succumbs more deeply to that compulsion. That has been the trajectory of European civilization.'[161] Degrowth aims at breaking this trajectory. Another key analyst of this perspective was Murray Bookchin, who developed the theory of 'social ecology' to explain how relationships of domination and oppression between humans (along lines of class, race, gender, age, and so on) in turn shape our relationships to the natural world.[162]

Attempts to deal with dependency on nature by way of technological improvements (for example, through the exploitation of fossil fuels, nuclear energy, or, more recently, bioenergy) do not lead to the disap-pearance of nature in society. Rather, the domination of nature is 'reflected' in the dominations between people: it lives on in forms of patriarchal, racist, or class oppression, for example by women doing unpaid housework or by border regimes hindering people's freedom of movement. The mastery of nature in all its variants – above all in the techno-scientific belief in progress but also in relation to modern temporality or human–animal relations – thus becomes the central object of this critique. And, moreover, the overcoming of hierarchical society–nature relations also forms the basis for overcoming domina-tion in general.[163]

---

161 Horkheimer and Adorno, *Dialectic of Enlightenment*, 9.

162 Murray Bookchin, *The Philosophy of Social Ecology: Essays on Dialectical Naturalism* (Montreal: Black Rose Books, 1995); Bookchin, *The Ecology of Freedom*.

163 Brand and Wissen, *The Imperial Mode of Living*; Burkhart, Schmelzer, and Treu, *Degrowth in Movement(s)*; Bookchin, *The Ecology of Freedom*.

Alienation through industrial labour

An essential argument of the critique of industrialism is furthermore that atomized, mechanized, and accelerated work processes, which are necessary for an increase in productivity, lead to an alienation of people from their activities (see section 3.3). This fundamentally undermines both the individual and collective autonomy of people or societies to decide how to lead their lives. 'For a hundred years now, we have been trying to make machines work for people and to train people for lifelong service to them ... It has been shown that machines enslave people', writes Ivan Illich.[164]

A proposal to solve the problem of alienation in industrial work consists in increasing automation, so that fewer and fewer people have to toil in production.[165] The proponents of automation, however, often fail to recognize that in neoliberal capitalism, people working in the service and care industries, among others, are also clocked according to industrial models, and, even then, care professions can only be automated to a limited extent because of their different work logic. Much of the service sector, certain forms of mining and extraction, and agriculture resist automation. Further, full automation may not itself be desirable (even if it were possible). For example, a sustainable, ecological agriculture requires intricate engagement with and knowledge of local ecosystems, or many caring activities can only be automatized by losing much of what we value as human. Moreover, the promise of full automation does not provide an answer to the fundamental problems of the dominance of modern technology mentioned above, nor does it itself change the terms of ownership or the form of alienated labour, nor can it account for the resource, ecological, and global justice problems associated with full automation. Therefore, thinkers critical of industrialism emphasize the need to gain democratic control over technological developments. And while this critique is not against automation per se

---

164 Illich, *Tools for Conviviality*, 27; see also the historical arguments in Mueller, *Breaking Things at Work*.

165 Bastani, *Fully Automated Luxury Communism*; Nick Srnicek and Alex Williams, *Inventing the Future: Postcapitalism and a World without Work* (London: Verso, 2015).

– in the case of unpleasant, tedious, debilitating, or dangerous work, automation is desirable from a degrowth perspective – it also emphasizes the need to reconceptualize and transform work, so that we can see and enact the socially useful activities that sustain our lives as the fundamental form of participating in society, based on a logic of care.[166]

Significance for degrowth: Beyond appropriating technology

In their 1972 ten-point programme, the Black Panthers added a demand for 'people's community control of modern technology', thus highlighting a key prerequisite for any emancipatory society.[167] From a degrowth perspective, bringing modern technology into people's hands must be accompanied by efforts to develop different, non-authoritarian technologies. Indeed, the critique of industrialism and technology, together with the feminist critique, is the strand of degrowth critique that most decisively opposes (potential) post-capitalist projects that uncritically advocate for accelerating technological innovation – whether techno-centric Green New Deal proposals, digital post-capitalism, or accelerationism.[168] For a non-alienating and non-exploitative technique would require that the structure of the means of production, as they have developed under capitalism and bureaucratic states and within hierarchical societies, are also fundamentally transformed. Economic growth

---

166 Karina Becker, Klaus Dörre, and Yalcin Kutlu, 'Counter-Landnahme? Labour Disputes in the Care-Work Field', *Equality, Diversity and Inclusion: An International Journal* 37, no. 4 (2018): 361–75; Caffentzis, 'The End of Work'; Aaron Benanav, 'Automation and the Future of Work: Part 1', *New Left Review* 119 (2019): 5–38; Max Ajl, 'How Much Will the US Way of Life Have to Change?', unevenearth.org, 2019; Lewis Mumford, 'Authoritarian and Democratic Technics'; Winner, *The Whale and the Reactor*; Kathi Weeks, *The Problem with Work: Feminism, Marxism, Antiwork Politics, and Postwork Imaginaries* (Durham, NC: Duke University Press, 2011).

167 Black Panther Party, 'Black Panther Party Program March 29, 1972 Platform', *Black Panther Party Intercommunal News Service*, 13 May 1972.

168 Mason, *Postcapitalism*; Jeremy Rifkin, *The Third Industrial Revolution: How Lateral Power Is Transforming Energy, the Economy, and the World* (New York: Macmillan, 2011); Srnicek and Williams, *Inventing the Future*; Bastani, *Fully Automated Luxury Communism*.

is not progressive, not even in this regard.[169] A correction of the distribution of production, or even completely different ownership of production, is not sufficient. The realization that technology, infrastructure, and production facilities not only need to be appropriated but also transformed and (partially) wound down is central to degrowth.[170] Nevertheless, criticism of industrialism and technology becomes problematic when technological progress and the division of labour are generally rejected and their advantages negated. There is a danger that these critiques turn reactionary or elitist unless they are combined with other forms of critique that strongly emphasize justice. Furthermore, critiques of industrialism must come with proposals for alternative forms of economic production that are not alienating and that meet human needs and well-being.

More recently in the degrowth debate, there has been an emphasis on criteria for technological development under keywords such as 'convivial technology', 'convivial design', 'frugal innovations', 'digital commons', 'peer-to-peer' or 'soft digitalization' – practices and criteria for alternative technical paths between low tech and open digitalization. In contrast to the discussions in the 1970s, which focused primarily on the risks of modern science and technology, discussions in the field of digital commons in particular also emphasize the opportunities offered by high tech.[171] However, thinking about the possibility of decentralized production combined with global design has only just begun. Technical assessments (based on life-cycle assessments, and so on) of such approaches' suitability for degrowth are still lacking, and it is also unclear whether such visions of high-tech futures adequately respond to cultural and ecological critiques.[172] We expand on proposals

---

169 Illich, *Tools for Conviviality*.

170 Aaron Vansintjan, 'Accelerationism . . . and Degrowth? The Left's Strange Bedfellows', unevenearth.org, 7 January 2017; Mueller, *Breaking Things at Work*.

171 For an exception, see Bookchin, *Post-scarcity Anarchism*.

172 Kerschner et al., 'Degrowth and Technology'; Michael Bauwens, Vasilis Kostakis, and Alex Pazaitis, *Peer-to-Peer: The Commons Manifesto* (London: Westminster University Press, 2018); Steffen Lange and Tilman Santarius, *Smart Green World? Making Digitalization Work for Sustainability* (Abingdon: Routledge, 2020).

for convivial technologies and on the need to address this gap in chapters 5 and 7.

3.7. South–North critique

Here, we summarize forms of critique that examine the social and ecological consequences of development and growth from a global justice perspective. They focus on hierarchies, exclusions, and forms of exploitation that are fundamentally associated with capitalist and universalizing European civilization. These forms of critique argue that 'growth' and 'development' as well as even the 'economy' as a concept are twentieth-century inventions that create and maintain (neo-)colonial dependencies between regions and to enforce growth-oriented, industrialist, and capitalist lifestyles in the Global South. They also argue that since the start of European expansion in the fifteenth century, growth in the centres has been based on (neo-)colonial appropriation, extractivist exploitation of nature, and the externalization of social and ecological costs. Thus, countries in the South were reduced to the dependent role of raw material suppliers without large value-added contributions of their own, causing ever-deepening inequalities and unequal power relations. And this critique argues that these processes of appropriation and externalization are fundamental to the growth dynamics of rich societies, the balance of power within them, and the stability of the imperial mode of living. In the context of increasing ecological crises, this way of life causes systemic crises because it cannot be generalized.

The origins of decolonial thought and the criticism of Eurocentrism and the associated instrumental rationality of modernity go back centuries and emerged as a counter-movement to colonialism and modernity in the Americas in Indigenous and Afro-Caribbean thought.[173] In the centuries that followed, they responded to the

---

173 Walter D. Mignolo and Catherine E. Walsh, *On Decoloniality: Concepts, Analytics, Praxis* (Durham, NC: Duke University Press, 2018); Pablo Solón et al., *Systemic Alternatives: Vivir bien, Degrowth, Commons, Ecofeminism, Rights of*

spread of colonialism, imperialism, Western development policy, and globalization to give the 'wretched of the earth' a voice.[174] Three important streams of this discourse pertain to the growth-critical discussion, each with their own thrust that complement the argument for degrowth. First, the post-development debate, which since the 1980s has criticized the entire 'development' endeavour as destructive and misguided, and which has played a central role in the initial emergence of the degrowth movement; second, the Latin American–influenced discussions about *buen vivir* ('good living') and post-extractivism, which have developed into central sources of inspiration and allies for degrowth; third, Marxian analyses of dependency, ecologically unequal exchange, and the more recent imperial mode of living.

Post-development versus the Western ideology of progress

The post-development approach emerged in the 1980s as a fundamental critique of 'development'. It is closely associated with post-colonial, decolonial, and subaltern movements.[175] Authors such as Arturo Escobar, Gustavo Esteva, Majid Rahnema, Serge Latouche, Wolfgang Sachs, Vandana Shiva, and Gilbert Rist argued that 'development' is a construct and an ideology of the West.[176] Development was invented in the middle of the twentieth century as a guiding political concept – the second inaugural speech of US president

---

Mother Earth and Deglobalisation, trans. Karen Lang, José Carlos Solón, and Mary Louise Malig (La Paz: Fundación Solón; ATTAC France; Focus on the Global South, 2017), https://systemicalternatives.files.wordpress.com/2017/03/sa-final-ingles-pdf2.pdf.

174 Frantz Fanon, *The Wretched of the Earth* (New York: Grove, 2007).

175 Dipesh Chakrabarty, *Provincializing Europe: Postcolonial Thought and Historical Difference* (Princeton, NJ: Princeton University Press, 2008); Walter Rodney, *How Europe Underdeveloped Africa* (London: Bogle-L'Ouverture Publications, 1972); Vijay Prashad, *The Poorer Nations: A Possible History of the Global South* (London: Verso, 2013).

176 Wolfgang Sachs, ed., *The Development Dictionary: A Guide to Knowledge as Power* (London: Zed, 1992).

Harry S. Truman in 1949 is often mentioned here – in order to promise people in the 'under-developed' regions integration into the capitalist world economy and its associated improvements in living
standards. This promise of 'development' was motivated above all by
the intention to provide legitimacy for late and post-colonial strategies of domination from the North towards people in the South. The
universal goal – of an industrial mass consumer society characterized by capitalist wage labour – implied by 'development' is, however,
never attainable for all due to the structure of the global world economy based on the division of labour and due to ecological limitations
(see sections 3.1, 3.4, and 3.5). It is also undesirable, since it undermines the livelihoods of many.[177]

Post-development calls into question the growth-based idea of
progress: that Europe has worked its way up to the top of a universally
recognized and desirable path of development by its own efforts,
through rationality, civilization, and liberal values.[178] Post-development
scholars point out that the growth and prosperity of the Global North
cannot be understood without colonialism, exploitation, and dispossession in the South. Post-development also places today's development
policy in its historical context, namely, the efforts beginning with the
Enlightenment to 'improve' the colonized areas and the people characterized as 'primitive', those who would later be devalued by 'race theories', through interventions from outside.[179] In contrast to ecological
approaches, which are quite prominent in the degrowth discussion and
which focus on the industrialization of the nineteenth and twentieth
centuries, post-development thinkers focus on the destructive side of
the Enlightenment and modernity in the context of colonialism starting in the centuries before. From a post-development perspective,

---

177 Arturo Escobar, *Encountering Development: The Making and Unmaking
of the Third World* (Princeton, NJ: Princeton University Press, 2011); Latouche,
Farewell to Growth; Mies and Shiva, *Ecofeminism*; Majid Rahnema and Victoria
Bawtree, eds., *The Post-development Reader* (London: Zed, 1997); Sachs, *The
Development Dictionary*; Sachs, *The Development Reader*.

178 For a contemporary example of this argumentation, see Pinker,
Enlightenment Now.

179 Escobar, *Encountering Development*.

alternatives to development are found primarily in the traditions and practices of subsistence of local communities and in movements of the Global South that oppose development ideologies. Following *The Red Deal: Indigenous Action to Save Our Earth*: 'We need a revolution of values that recenters relationships to one another and the earth over profits.'[180] This revolution in values has as its protagonists autonomous movements such as the Zapatistas, Indigenous struggles for self-determination, Afro-diasporic struggles, peasant movements such as La Via Campesina and the Movimento dos Trabalhadores Rurais Sem Terra (Landless Workers Movement) in Brazil, and movements opposing environmental distribution conflicts. As we discuss below, much of the degrowth discussion has highlighted the importance of supporting such movements for the purpose of building international solidarity against the growth regime and for an alliance of various alternatives to development.[181]

Buen vivir *and post-extractivism*

The concept and practice of *buen vivir* originated in the Andes, especially in Ecuador and Bolivia, but also in Peru and Colombia. It was formulated in the last two decades as a political framework based on traditional knowledge. With a strong anchoring in the world views, perspectives, and experiences of Indigenous groups, it stands for the inseparability and interdependence of people and nature and for a life

---

180 The Red Nation, *The Red Deal: Indigenous Action to Save Our Earth* (Brooklyn, NY: Common Notions, 2020), 26.

181 Susan Paulson, ed., 'Degrowth: Culture, Power and Change', special issue, *Journal of Political Ecology* 24, no. 1 (2017): 425–666; Martínez-Alier, 'Environmental Justice and Economic Degrowth'; Beatriz Rodríguez-Labajos et al., 'Not So Natural an Alliance? Degrowth and Environmental Justice Movements in the Global South', *Ecological Economics* 157 (2019): 175–84; Jonathan Otto, 'Finding Common Ground: Exploring Synergies between Degrowth and Environmental Justice in Chiapas, Mexico', *Journal of Political Ecology* 24, no. 1 (2017): 491–503; Bengi Akbulut et al., 'Who Promotes Sustainability? Five Theses on the Relationships between the Degrowth and the Environmental Justice Movements', *Ecological Economics* 165 (2019): 106418. See also Max Ajl, *A People's Green New Deal* (London: Pluto Press, 2021).

in balance: 'What counts in the concept of "good living" is the human individual, integrated in their community, who cultivates harmonious relationships with nature and strives, in their personal life as well as in the community, to build a sustainable, dignified life for all.'[182] Well-known proponents are Eduardo Gudynas, Maristella Svampa, Alberto Acosta, and Pablo Solón. Similar to post-development, *buen vivir* (in Kichwa, *sumak kawsay*, or in Aymara, *suma qamaña*) criticizes both capitalist and socialist forms of development because of their social and ecological destruction. Based on centuries of the experience of coloni-alism, this critique is directed against capitalist civilization with its basic assumptions of progress, competition, improvement, rationaliza-tion, productivity or efficiency, its anthropocentrism separating nature and people, and its deeply rooted patriarchy. Other non-Western concepts with a similar perspective – such as *ubuntu* (in South Africa), ecological *swaraj* and radical ecological democracy (in India), and other environmental justice movements of the poor – are also seen as partners of the degrowth movement. This diversity is being framed as a 'pluriverse' of visions and cosmologies – in this sense, degrowth is only one of many proposals for human flourishing beyond development.[183]

As a concept, *buen vivir* is politically contested, just like degrowth. It has been taken up in the constitutions of Ecuador and Bolivia; however, this has come with concerns of appropriation and co-optation of the Indigenous worldviews and movements that inspired the creation of the *buen vivir* framework. Still, its core is still practised:

> The 'good life' as the sum of experiences – many of them experiences of resistance in the truly long darkness of the colonial era and its consequences still visible today – is a vision still lived in many

---

182 Alberto Acosta, *Buen vivir: Vom Recht auf ein gutes Leben*, trans. Birte Pedersen (Munich: Oekom, 2015), 16.

183 Alberto Acosta and Ulrich Brand, *Salidas del laberinto capitalista: Decrecimiento y postextractivismo* (Quito: Fundación Rosa Luxemburg, 2017); Martínez-Alier, 'Environmental Justice and Economic Degrowth'; Burkhart, Schmelzer, and Treu, *Degrowth in Movement(s)*; Kothari et al., *Pluriverse*; Pablo Solón, 'Vivir bien: Old Cosmovisions and New Paradigms', Great Transition Initiative, February 2018, greattransition.org.

Indigenous communities. These are communities that have not been
fully absorbed by capitalist modernity and have managed to continue
to exist on its fringes. Their communal knowledge forms the basis for
ideas of another world and for the change that is necessary to achieve
it.[184]

In close connection with *buen vivir*, the struggles of the last twenty
years have led to the development of the concept of post-extractivism,
which is directed against neo-extractivism in Latin America.
Extractivism is an economic model where a country is dependent on
large-scale extraction of its resources and exports to the Global North,
while not being able to diversify its economy and being subject to
unequal trade relations. Neo-extractivism describes a variant of the
classical commodity-based economic model of many Latin American
countries, which has been advanced by left-wing governments since the
1990s and in which successful development and social programmes
have been financed by intensifying the exploitation of natural resources
and the resource revenues generated as a result. While left-wing governments seek to soften hardship through social programmes, the ecological and social consequences of the extraction of fossil and mineral
resources – as well as the spread of monocultures or the transformation
of rainforest into rapidly degrading pasture land — continue to exist.
Affected communities, social movements, and intellectuals condensed
their criticism of this dynamic into the concept of post-extractivism: a
fundamental critique both of the 'commodity consensus', as Maristella
Svampa calls it, of neo-extractivism and of neoliberalism, and a vision
which seeks to push for the conditions for a good life, without continuing relations of extraction.[185] Neo-extractivism is criticized as an ideology and practice that is linked to colonial looting (see section 3.4),
which goes hand in hand with the hierarchical view of nature as an

184 Acosta, *Buen vivir*, 15.
185 Maristella Svampa, 'Commodities Consensus: Neoextractivism and
Enclosure of the Commons in Latin America', *South Atlantic Quarterly* 114, no. 1
(1 January 2015): 65–82; Alberto Acosta and Ulrich Brand, *Radikale Alternativen:
Warum man den Kapitalismus nur mit vereinten Kräften überwinden kann*
(Munich: Oekom, 2018).

object of exploitation (as discussed in sections 3.1 and 3.6). The post-extractivist critique is particularly relevant in thinking about the global resource needs for solar panels, batteries, electric cars, bioenergy, and renewable fuels – all key ingredients of any green growth regime, all of which are sourced largely from the Global South.[186]

In addition, there is a growing critique of 'green capitalism' and the valorization of nature, a critique strongly inspired by social movements and struggles, which in recent times has also turned against recent attempts to 'solve' the climate crisis at the expense of people in the Global South. For example, attempts to maintain the way of life of rich countries by cultivating agro-fuels in the South lead to land use conflicts and thus promote the purchase of land in the South by investors and corporations (land grabbing). And the current practice of 'balancing' carbon dioxide emissions in the Global North with 'offsets' in the Global South (for instance, by planting monoculture forests or by creating forest reserves inaccessible to Indigenous communities) contributes to perpetuating neo-colonial inequalities and driving people out of their territories, while nonetheless failing to protect the climate. According to this criticism, the 'green economy' is a project of domination and control that does not overcome inequality and extractivism and that only offers fictitious solutions for ecological crises.[187] Through Joan Martínez-Alier and his colleagues at the Autonomous University of Barcelona, research on socio-ecological struggles in the Global South has been closely linked to degrowth research. The university is home to Research & Degrowth, one of the largest research networks on degrowth, and at the same time works on environmental conflicts in the Global South (through projects like the Environmental Justice Atlas, created by the organization EJOLT).[188] As Alberto Acosta and

---

186 Thea Riofrancos, *Resource Radicals: From Petro-nationalism to Post-extractivism in Ecuador* (Durham, NC: Duke University Press, 2020).

187 Barbara Unmüßig, Thomas Fatheuer, and Lili Fuhr, *Critique of the Green Economy: Toward Social and Environmental Equity* (Berlin: Heinrich Böll Foundation, 2018); Jesse Goldstein, *Planetary Improvement: Cleantech Entrepreneurship and the Contradictions of Green Capitalism* (Cambridge, MA: MIT Press, 2018).

188 Martínez-Alier, 'Environmental Justice and Economic Degrowth';

Ulrich Brand argue in their book *Radical Alternatives*, which discusses both post-extractivism and degrowth, capitalism can only be overcome through multiple alliances between actors from the North and South. Positive concepts such as good living should be at the forefront of movement-building.[189]

From uneven development to the imperial mode of living

The above critiques are rooted in a broader critique of deeply unequal, colonial relationships of industrialized countries with the Global South, in great part informed by critical analysis of capitalism and imperialism. Marxist theories of uneven development and unequal exchange propose that, for capitalist development to occur, it must rely on structural under-development elsewhere. Development is grounded in the unequal valorization of the labour of Global South workers, as well as in the exploitation of resources, which are exchanged with industrialized nations at unequal terms of trade – raw materials, food, and labour are appropriated as 'cheap' inputs into the process of accumulation, while those products with a lot of added value are manufactured in the Global North. Recent studies that have quantified the drain from the Global South resulting from unequal exchange estimate this to be in the orders of magnitude of around $62 trillion over the period 1960–2018, currently accounting for up to 7 per cent of Northern GDP and 9 per cent of Southern GDP, and resulting in $152 trillion of lost growth in the Global South.[190] Furthermore, uneven development is also driven by financial institutions, which lend to poor nations at higher interest rates and impose structural adjustment when debts cannot be paid. In this way, even though national debts of industrialized nations are far higher, countries in the Global South have little choice but to cut expenses on essential services and are systematically under-developed

Akbulut et al., 'Who Promotes Sustainability?'; and see also EJOLT (ejolt.org) and Research and Degrowth (degrowth.org).

189 Acosta and Brand, *Salidas del laberinto capitalista*.

190 Jason Hickel, Dylan Sullivan, and Huzaifa Zoomkawala, 'Plunder in the Post-Colonial Era: Quantifying Drain from the Global South through Unequal Exchange, 1960–2018', *New Political Economy* 26, no. 6 (2021): 1030–47.

– a state of affairs which privileges industrialized nations as they maintain their monetary and military dominance.

These analyses show that capital accumulation and thus economic growth in the Global North emerged historically through and currently require unequal exchange with the Global South – and thus depend on the imperial and neoliberal arrangements that enable it. As the authors of *The Red Deal* put it: 'Overconsumption in the Global North . . . is directly enabled by the dispossession of Indigenous and Black life and imperial wars in the Global South.'[191] This reality has underlined the need for building alliances between countries in the South, as well as deepening internationalism more broadly and fighting to abolish Global South debts.[192]

In recent years, analyses adjacent to degrowth have taken a critical look at the mode of production and living of the countries of the Global North. The debate on climate justice, for example, has integrated the critique of uneven development with ecological approaches, through the argument that industrialized nations owe a significant 'climate debt' to Global South nations, and a reframing of uneven development as 'ecologically unequal exchange'. The latter theory posits that the condition of uneven development allows early industrialized economies to avoid impacts of ecologically harmful industries through importing natural resources and polluting commodities from poor countries.[193]

---

191 The Red Nation, *The Red Deal*, 26.

192 Utsa Patnaik and Prabhat Patnaik, *Capital and Imperialism: Theory, History, and the Present* (New York: NYU Press, 2021); Rodney, *How Europe Underdeveloped Africa*; Raj Patel and Jason W. Moore, *A History of the World in Seven Cheap Things: A Guide to Capitalism, Nature, and the Future of the Planet* (Berkeley: University of California Press, 2017); Alexander Anievas and Kerem Nişancıoğlu, *How the West Came to Rule* (London: Pluto Press, 2015).

193 Arghiri Emmanuel, *Unequal Exchange: A Study of the Imperialism of Trade* (New York: Monthly Review Press, 1972); Amir Amin, *Unequal Development: An Essay on the Social Formations of Peripheral Capitalism*, trans. Brian Pierce (New York: Monthly Review Press, 1976); J. Timmons Roberts and Bradley C. Parks, 'Ecologically Unequal Exchange, Ecological Debt, and Climate Justice: The History and Implications of Three Related Ideas for a New Social Movement', *International Journal of Comparative Sociology* 50, nos. 3–4 (2009): 385–409.

In a similar vein, the sociologist Stephan Lessenich argues that lifestyles characterized by freedom and endless possibilities were made possible through the externalization of social and ecological costs, both historically (through colonialism, climate debt, and so on) and today – some are *Living Well at Others' Expense*. Externalization is a necessary, indispensable structural feature of the modern world system. Global capitalism is not only – as feminist and Marxist critics argue – dependent on the continuous incorporation of an 'outside' (cheap labour, land, care activities, and raw materials) but also on the *outsourcing* of costs.[194] Global power asymmetries and exploitative relationships underlying externalization are stabilized by the 'externalization habitus' of majorities in the rich countries: through socially generalized practices of 'not wanting to know', the externalization processes and the associated structural violence are systematically repressed, split off, and projected onto others. According to Lessenich, externalization fundamentally reverses and perverts Kant's categorical imperative, which had characterized the self-conception of the Enlightenment: always act in such a way that your actions could be generalisable for all people. Externalization is based on exclusiveness – and thus on enclosing public wealth. This exclusive prosperity, which for many citizens of the industrialized core also includes the privilege of almost unlimited global mobility, is defended by militarized border regimes. Freedom of movement and thus also life chances are asymmetrically, exclusively, and selectively denied to those who live outside the externalization societies and have lost out in the 'birth lottery'. However, through climate change and increasing movements of flight and migration, today the externalization societies in the capitalist core are being confronted with the consequences of their externalization – and, unfortunately, reacting with increasingly reactionary and fascistic measures.[195]

The political scientists Ulrich Brand and Markus Wissen present a related analysis, with somewhat different emphases, with their concept

---

194 Stephan Lessenich, *Living Well at Others' Expense: The Hidden Costs of Western Prosperity* (London: Polity, 2019).

195 Ibid.

of the 'imperial mode of living'. Using a neo-Gramscian approach to hegemony, a materialist theory of the state and an understanding of everyday habits from Pierre Bourdieu, they analyse the global and ecological dimension of a specific way of life that has become the norm for many people in the Global North – such as driving a car, flying on vacation, eating a lot of meat, or consumer goods and other amenities. The core idea is that everyday life in the capitalist centres is essentially made possible through the (violent) shaping of socio-ecological relations in the Global South, and that includes the more or less unlimited access to labour power, natural resources, and pollution sinks on a global scale. The concept of the 'imperial mode of living' is very broad and focuses on how certain norms of production, distribution, and consumption – how we live, work, eat, and travel – became embedded in the political, economic, and everyday practices of the population in the Global North and increasingly also in the emerging countries in the South. This way of life is a paradox that on the one hand brings about and exacerbates various crises (climate change, biodiversity loss, impoverishment, social polarization), but on the other hand stabilizes social conditions in the core – where the benefits of this mode of living are concentrated – through class compromises. Furthermore, the term 'imperial' should make it clear that this is tied to imperial structures (military intervention, extractivism, the arms industry, international institutions, monetary hegemony, and enforced borders) which further aggravate crises such as mass migration or the unequal application of climate policy. Brand and Wissen argue for radical alternatives in the form of a 'solidarity mode of living'.[196]

Significance for degrowth: Global solidarity and interdependence

The various strands of South–North criticism each play a central role in the degrowth discussion. As we will argue below, degrowth can be

196 Brand and Wissen, *The Imperial Mode of Living*; Ulrich Brand and Markus Wissen, *Limits to Capitalist Nature: Theorizing and Overcoming the Imperial Mode of Living* (London: Rowman & Littlefield, 2018); Miriam Lang, 'The Migration Crisis and the Imperial Mode of Living', unevenearth.org, 2018.

understood as a project for global ecological justice – and in this, the South–North critique is essential. However, as with all forms of criticism, some pitfalls must be avoided. In general – similar to the praise of community in the cultural critique, which can, for example, become a justification for cuts in public services – the rejection of forms of state organization or social welfare, as advocated by post-extractivism, may tend to promote a cynical legitimation of neoliberalism. Likewise, an uncritical attitude towards local communities and cultural traditions in parts of the post-development discourse could legitimize traditional forms of rule – sometimes hierarchical and oppressive. These are important points, not least because similar criticisms can also be made of the degrowth perspective as a whole. At the same time, in emphasizing the hierarchical and exploitative relationships between centres and peripheries, it is important not to lose sight of a class analysis superimposed onto this relationship and not to homogenize entire societies or the sphere of consumption as central categories of analysis. The South–North critique can also, similarly, lead to cultural relativism – which cannot account for cross-cutting ethical commitments to human and collective rights and which may not adequately interrogate politics of nationhood or 'blood and soil'.[197] Indeed, Alain de Benoist, a French ethno-nationalist thinker of the New Right, has used the terms 'pluriverse' and 'ethnopluralism' to describe his own ideology of ethnically separate, isolated nations. To safeguard against this, degrowth-adjacent advocates for *buen vivir* and the 'pluriverse' have highlighted shared commitments to diversity, tolerance of difference, interdependence, and a rejection of ethnic nationalist arguments.[198]

It follows for degrowth that the necessary fundamental changes are driven primarily by global democratization processes and alliances with social movements from the Global South, as well as the search for and demand for the right *not* to be living or compelled to live at the expense of others.[199] Serge Latouche, who himself has formulated a

197 Aram Ziai, ed., *Exploring Post-development: Theory and Practice, Problems and Perspectives* (Abingdon: Routledge, 2007). For a critique of 'folk politics' on the left, see also Srnicek and Williams, *Inventing the Future.*

198 Escobar, *Designs for the Pluriverse*; Kothari et al., *Pluriverse.*

199 ILA Kollektiv, *At the Expense of Others: How the Imperial Mode of Living*

radical critique of the Westernization of the world and of Western civilization in general, played a key role in bringing together post-development ideas with the ecological perspective of Georgescu-Roegen. Together, these perspectives formed the early core of the discourse on *décroissance*. As an antithesis to a single, all-encompassing 'civilized world' based on patriarchal, Western, and capitalist principles, the above-mentioned concept of the 'pluriverse' is at the forefront of recent attempts to bring together different growth-critical perspectives from around the world. These 'alternatives to development' from the Global South can be allies of degrowth for the development of a variety of forms of society and life, of worlds and people that coexist in and with the planet through 'radical interdependence'.[200]

3.8. Growth critique outside of the degrowth debate

Degrowth can be understood as the convergence of seven forms of growth critique – the ecological, socio-economic, cultural, anti-capitalist, feminist, anti-industrialist, and South–North critique. Running through these various critiques of growth is the attempt to push back against the economic as a sphere of supposedly independent rationality and against economic calculation as the main basis for decision-making. This necessarily requires a more complex, interconnected, and diverse world – which involves deliberation and weighing our conflicting values and needs as a society. We would no longer ask the question 'Does this meet the bottom line

---

Prevents a Good Life for All (Munich: Oekom, 2017); Lessenich, *Living Well at Others' Expense*.

200 Acosta and Brand, *Salidas del laberinto capitalista*; Martínez-Alier, 'Environmental Justice and Economic Degrowth'; Solón et al., *Systemic Alternatives*; D'Alisa, Demaria, and Kallis, *Degrowth: A Vocabulary for a New Era*; Latouche, *Farewell to Growth*; Escobar, *Designs for the Pluriverse*; Kothari et al., *Pluriverse*; Padini Nirmal and Dianne Rocheleau, 'Decolonizing Degrowth in the Post-Development Convergence: Questions, Experiences, and Proposals from Two Indigenous Territories', *Environment and Planning E: Nature and Space* 2, no. 3 (2019): 465–92; Burkhart, Schmelzer, and Treu, *Degrowth in Movement(s)*.

(i.e., profit)?', but ask instead, 'Does this meet our needs, values and democratic decisions?'

In the next two chapters, we show how these different strands of critique have been woven together into degrowth's central principles, the proposals that have been developed to respond to the issues raised in the critiques, and the strategies that can help us reach them. But before moving on, there is some unfinished business. In the beginning of this chapter, we mentioned some common critiques of degrowth, which claim it is anti-modern, primitivist, or implicitly deriving from a position of middle-class privilege. In the remainder of this chapter, we deal more directly with forms of growth criticism that are *not* part of the degrowth debate. We briefly discuss various conservative, nationalist, capitalist, privileged, and reactionary growth critiques. We have already mentioned some of them throughout the preceding sections; however, taking a moment to explore them more fully can help us sharpen our understanding of pitfalls, of challenges, and of what an emancipatory degrowth perspective may look like.

Conservative critiques of growth

Believe it or not, several conservative critiques of growth have been put forward. Most prominently, Meinhard Miegel, the founder of a conservative think tank and one of the advisors of Germany's neoliberal privatization of old age pensions, has argued that people in industrial countries are living beyond their means, and that due to aging populations, saturated markets, and lifestyle environmental damage, the future stagnation or even reduction of the economy is the inevitable fate of modern industrial societies. To adjust, he is in favour of a culture of modesty and ecology, but also for curtailing the welfare state, which, from his perspective, is excessive and should be replaced with a culture of volunteerism, charity, and a renewed emphasis on the family. In this way, criticism of growth and a call for 'prosperity without growth' becomes a justificatory instrument and lever for social cuts, privatization, and the rollback of gender relations. In essence, it recycles the neoliberal argument for austerity, now with a green layer of paint: we can no longer afford our luxuries, so we have to tighten our belts *in order to preserve the existing social order.*[201]

A conservative criticism of growth remains uncommon since conservatives seek to reinforce the status quo and therefore ultimately want to protect economic growth – an integral component of capitalist hegemony today. Indeed, austerity is usually implemented for the sake of economic growth, not against it. So far, Miegel's proposals have had little impact on national debates. Nevertheless, it is important to mention because it shows that a critique of growth is not in itself forward-thinking. And indeed, it is possible that such a proposal may eventually be embraced by conservative governments that acknowledge impending ecological breakdown and a changed economic reality but that take advantage of this moment to maintain, and deepen, social hierarchies.

Needless to say, in the degrowth scene, such views are rejected. As degrowth fundamentally seeks to rewire our social system to one built around care, equality, and collective well-being, such a proposal runs counter to everything that degrowth stands for. The only thing that they share is an acknowledgement of current economic conditions (secular stagnation) and the need to address the social and cultural roots of ecological crises – but, even there, Miegel's own proposal is limited in its essentially conservative, regressive wish to preserve social hierarchies rather than to disassemble them.

Green fascism

In August 2019, a gunman in El Paso, Texas, shot forty-six people, killing twenty-three, most of them people of colour. As with the Christchurch shooter in New Zealand in March 2019 and other eco-fascist statements, his manifesto was replete with references to blood-and-soil environmentalism, in which he opposed immigration and cultural mixing on the grounds that 'white' land should be

---

201 Meinhard Miegel, *Exit: Wohlstand ohne Wachstum* (Berlin: Propyläen, 2010); for a critique, see Barbara Muraca, *Gut leben: Eine Gesellschaft jenseits des Wachstums* (Berlin: Wagenbach, 2014).

protected and saved from over-exploitation by immigrants. This white supremacist belief provides the basic ideological pillar for much of the New Right and 'alt right' today. And in this context of the regionalist, ethnopluralist strand of the New Right, some crossover between degrowth ideas and green fascism has been documented. The intellectual leader of the New Right in France, Alain de Benoist, published a book as early as 2007 whose title, *Demain, la décroissance!*, was identical to the title of the ground-breaking edition of Georgescu-Roegen's works in the 1970s. De Benoist articulated his ethno-pluralistic bioregionalism with terms similar to degrowth notions such as 'decolonization of the imaginary', first coined by one of the doyens of the early French *décroissance* movement, Serge Latouche, whom he befriended and published, or 'pluriverse', 'relocalization of production', or 'autonomous micro-societies'. The vision, however, was one of bioregionalist green fascism – as summarized by Andreas Malm and the Zetkin Collective, 'each race in its own habitat; no mixing and dilution; conservation of differences as against the homogenising forces of global capitalism'.[202]

Similar initiatives can be observed in other countries. Björn Höcke, a politician from the Alternative for Germany (AfD), the largest far-right party in Germany, argued in 2014 that 'by the middle of the twenty-first century we will have reached the carrying capacity of our planet . . . We must consider what a post-growth economy looks like . . . We must find an economic form that reconciles ecology and economy, and that is only possible if we overcome this kind of capitalism'.[203] In 2014 in Switzerland, the initiative Ecopop put forward a proposal to the national referendum to limit immigration for ecological reasons, which they called 'Stopping overpopulation – to safeguard the natural basis

202 Andreas Malm and the Zetkin Collective, *White Skin, Black Fuel: On the Danger of Fossil Fascism* (London: Verso, 2021), 137. For critical analyses, see Tamir Bar-On, *Rethinking the French New Right: Alternatives to Modernity* (Abingdon: Routledge, 2013); Razmig Keucheyan, 'Alan de Benoist, du néofascisme à l'extrême droite "respectable": Enquête sur une success story intellectuelle', *Revue du Crieur* 1 (2017): 128–43; Muraca, *Gut leben*.
203 Critically discussed and cited in Eversberg, 'Gefährliches Werben', our translation.

for life'. Thankfully, the proposal did not pass, and yet it was surprisingly popular. In Italy, parts of the *decrescita* movement have cooperated with the growth-critical Five-Star Movement, which claims to be neither right nor left and in 2018 became coalition partner of the rightwing extremist and racist Lega.

What brings all of these strains together is what we could call green fascism. It is the next logical step for conservatives or the formerly climate-denialist right who recognize the reality of climate change but nevertheless wish to maintain the present hierarchies between men and women, whites and persons of colour, industrialized countries and the Global South, and social classes. 'Fascism' is an often-misused word but here we refer to it as a form of capitalism that uses the power of the state, populist movements, and violent militias to mobilize the nation and seek to further deepen existing social and racial hierarchies and divisions. Thus, green fascists wish to strengthen borders and limit immigration, and simultaneously to reorganize society towards more green, ecological livelihoods – while further solidifying present hierarchies. Another term for this vision would be 'climate apartheid' or 'green nationalism'.[204]

While there are different strands of green fascism – some wish for a return to a romanticized pastoral past where white people can live as one with nature, while others advocate for modernist interventions such as geo-engineering, smart agriculture, and massive border walls – they share an obsession with ethnicity, conservative values, and, often, critiques of overpopulation.[205]

As should be clear, degrowth is fundamentally at odds with these ideas and movements – in fact, they stand for the very opposite of what degrowth strives to achieve. While ideals of localism, ecological living, and criticism of globalization and growth are shared across the degrowth spectrum, degrowth's core thrust – its focus on global justice – runs directly counter to green fascism, and most degrowth

---

204 For a detailed analysis of this, see Malm and the Zetkin Collective, *White Skin, Black Fuel*.

205 Jesse Goldstein, 'The Eco-fascism of the El Paso Shooter Haunts the Techno-optimism of the Left', Societyandspace.org, 2019.

advocates reject all social hierarchies, are committed to open borders and freedom of movement, and reject any kind of future of 'climate apartheid'. Degrowth is a proposal for a society that ends the privileges green fascism violently defends in the name of the nation. As the populist right gains more power, and as climate change denialism becomes less viable as a political strategy, there is a danger that different critiques of growth become further absorbed by the right. For this reason, degrowth proponents must be clear in their principles, oppose all efforts (also from within the degrowth spectrum) to create links to green fascist arguments and movements, and reject any form of blood-and-soil politics – just as it rejects any capitalist growth-driven ideology.[206]

Anti-modernism

On Earth Day in 2020, the renowned documentarian Michael Moore launched and produced a film slated to bust 'big green' myths, directed by little-known filmmaker Jeff Gibbs. *Planet of the Humans* aimed its ire at solar power, forms of bioenergy, and 'green' corporations and NGOs. It sought to argue that green capitalism is not possible because of its 'addiction to growth' – we would agree, on that count – but then went on to hint that overpopulation was the real problem and, further, sought to dispel any belief in alternative sources of energy as being able to replace fossil fuels. Taking advantage of Michael Moore's platform, the film did well immediately on its release, with five million views on YouTube in its first week.

Planet of the Humans does not offer any deeper critique of capitalism and in large part focuses on lifestyle choices such as living in an 'eco-house', adopting a plant-based diet, or ending population growth. As a result, viewers are left only with the rejection of existing technologies and are offered lifestylism as an alternative – a message which can only lead to

---

206 Andrea Vetter and Matthias Schmelzer, 'The Emancipatory Project of Degrowth', in *Post-Growth Geographies – Spatial Relations of Diverse and Alternative Economies*, ed. Bastian Lange et al. (Bielefeld: Transcript, 2021), 99–106.

despair or a rejection of society as a whole.[207] This kind of techno-scepticism is part of a wider discourse in environmental movements that tends to reject all technologies wholesale, while not offering any alternatives except for the wholesale rejection of modernity or civilization more generally. This is seen as the 'anti-modern' or 'anti-civ' form of environmentalism, which argues that it is civilization itself which must be destroyed – an argument that leads to its own misanthropic conclusions.

Degrowth moves past this critique in several ways. While there is a shared acknowledgement of the limits of green capitalism, growth, and renewable energy in a growth-based economy, as well as a critique of industrialist, patriarchal, and structurally racist civilization, degrowth is by no means anti-modern or anti-civilizational. Indeed, as discussed in the next chapter, degrowth firmly criticizes specific aspects of our modern civilization while underlining the role of people's struggles in guaranteeing and achieving equality *despite* its harmful, alienating, and unsustainable elements. In other words, a degrowth perspective seeks to move beyond capitalist modernity through reconfiguring current power relations, rather than escaping it or absolving oneself of the responsibility to help reshape it.

Environmentalism of the rich

This leads us to a last criticism of growth – mainly a critique of consumption – which we can call 'middle-class environmentalism' or 'the environmentalism of the rich'.[208] We have all been told to buy recycled toilet paper, fly less, and eat organic if we want to save the environment. Alternatively, we are told that more efficient cars, carbon-neutral cruise ships, and nuclear fusion power plants will solve the problems we currently face – the problem is not capitalism but whether we can adequately harness technology and markets to address the environmental impacts of growth.

---

207 Gert Van Hecken and Vijay Kolinjivadi, 'Planet of the Dehumanized', unevenearth.org, 2020.
208 Peter Dauvergne, *Environmentalism of the Rich* (Cambridge, MA: MIT Press, 2016).

Middle-class environmentalism blames unsustainable growth on overconsumption and insufficient technological innovation, and either advocates for individual lifestyle changes and changes in consumption or for technological solutions to the problem. In this way, middle-class environmentalism does not see collective political action as an option, nor does it offer any kind of alternatives for working-class people who often have little choices in what they consume – and in many ways have *too little*. The environmentalism of the rich also does not offer much for the people of the Global South, who continue to face the burdens of unequal exchange, externalization, and an economic dependency on consumption in the North, and who are often excluded from affordable access to green technologies reserved for industrialized nations.[209]

Degrowth proponents do not accept these critiques of growth, first, because degrowth advocates for an ecological society that includes everyone, not just the privileged middle class of the industrialized countries, and secondly, because it stresses the need for collective and political action, rather than largely apolitical emphases on technological solutions or individual consumption choices.

3.9. Why degrowth is different

Although some interpret degrowth as an essentially conservative argument because of its linguistic proximity and certain superficial similarities to regressive critiques of growth, upon closer inspection there are fundamental differences. In its ecological critique of growth, degrowth is based on scientific, empirical evidence of the impossibility of infinite growth and, further, well-documented evidence that decoupling environmental impacts from growth is highly unlikely. While some of the conservative, privileged, and regressive critiques discussed in this chapter may also refer to these findings and propose changes to the way of living that are less material- or energy-intensive, that does not mean degrowth shares other similarities. In fact, the core of degrowth, with

---

209 For a thorough critique see Brand and Wissen, *The Imperial Mode of Living*; and Dauvergne, *Environmentalism of the Rich*.

its emphasis on ecological justice, a critique of all forms of exploitation and hierarchies, and a vision of solidarity, points to the very opposite of conservative, anti-modern, or regressive growth critiques. This call for equality and a good life for all goes hand in hand with critiques of global injustice, the imperial mode of living, and the imperialism that makes this possible.

Degrowth's strength is its holistic view. Degrowth relies not on a single strand of growth critique but has, from its very inception, braided the seven emancipatory strands discussed in this chapter together into a cohesive, well-developed, and broad critique of growth – one which includes feminist, anti-capitalist, and South–North critiques, among others. Finally, degrowth's vision, proposals, and strategies, to which we turn in the next chapters, fundamentally contradict anything resembling these regressive growth critiques. They can never be allies, but must be debunked, excoriated in public debates, and countered in society if degrowth is to become a reality.

It remains extremely important for degrowth to sharpen its own arguments in the face of criticism. To do so, it must continue to critically examine anti-modern, racist, and conservative critiques of growth, understand them, and seek to distinguish itself from them clearly. For this reason, we hope that our proposal to understand degrowth as the conjunction of the seven strands of criticism discussed in this chapter will provide some inspiration.

4

Degrowth visions

Imagine you go to sleep tonight and, tomorrow morning, you wake up one hundred years into the future. What would that world look like? In 1890, the artist and political theorist William Morris published a utopian novel, *News from Nowhere*, describing such a scenario. A man, William Guest, returns home from an activist meeting, goes to sleep, and finds himself in a world without private property, where work is pleasurable, and where people have as much as they need to live happy lives. There are no big cities – the countryside is fully integrated into town life. There is no money system, no government, and no prison. Everyone decides everything together.

Not all utopian visions are the same, but they can have commonalities. In the novel *The Dispossessed*, Ursula K. LeGuin imagined a planet, Anarres, without bosses, money, or centralized government, where everyone works together on a resource-scarce desert planet. The anarchist society of Anarres is high-tech but democratic, and everything is shared between everyone. In fact, the people of Anarres have decided to live on this resource-scarce desert planet, rejecting the hierarchical but much more affluent market society on a planet similar to Earth, Urras – a premise demonstrating just what autonomy and collective self-limitation might mean. LeGuin's classic science-fiction novel – written with the aspiration of putting a 'pig on the tracks . . . in a one-way future consisting only of growth' – remains an inspiration for many activists today, looking to build a better world.[1]

Many of us have our own utopia – a vision of the world as we would like it to be. Books like *News from Nowhere* and *The Dispossessed*, as well as 'near-future' science fiction like Kim Stanley Robinson's *The Ministry of the Future,* in their creativity and playfulness, help us to better imagine a world in which we would want to live, as well as how social transformation would work in practice. These are useful exercises, not just to give us hope that things could be different from the present, but also to have something towards which we can work, together. As Murray Bookchin said when talking about the importance of utopian thinking: 'Daydreams are pieces of imagination, they are bits of poetry. They are the balloons that fly up in history.'[2]

Ernst Bloch famously called utopias 'the education of desire' – they are not just far-off dreams but here with us, visible to us through glimpses and fragments in our daily experience. But, for many emancipatory thinkers, especially in the socialist tradition, utopian thought is viewed with scepticism. Memorably, Karl Marx described the utopian socialists of his time as 'those that write recipes for the cookshops of the future' – an impossible and futile task. Better, he said, to start from the contradictions within present reality and the struggles resulting from these and go from there – leading to what has been called a *Bilderverbot*, a ban on images of utopias (Theodor W. Adorno), in critical theory. In addition, it matters *who* dreams up the utopian vision. In William Morris's book, women still predominantly do the housework, while Ursula K. LeGuin also imagines an end to patriarchy and to the gendered division of labour. Utopias can be an imposition of a white and heterosexual viewpoint onto the future, or they can challenge those hierarchies and imagine a world beyond them. The tricky thing, then,

---

1 Giorgos Kallis and Hug March, 'Imaginaries of Hope: The Utopianism of Degrowth', *Annals of the Association of American Geographers* 105, no. 2 (2015): 361.

2 Murray Bookchin, 'Utopia, Not Futurism: Why Doing the Impossible Is the Most Rational Thing We Can Do', unevenearth.org, 2019; Kim Stanley Robinson, *The Ministry for the Future* (New York: Orbit, 2020). See also Kallis and March, 'Imaginaries of Hope', 360–8.

about being utopian, is that it must be principled, open, and give space for many different visions for the future.[3]

It is clear, despite the issues of utopian thinking, that *desire* for an alternative can motivate us to act to change the present. Nevertheless, when presenting utopian visions not as literature but as theoretical concepts, we must be careful not to paint an exhaustive picture, but to base it on what we know about the present, be cautious about how existing power structures shape even our visions of overcoming them, and allow plenty of room for experimentation, freedom, and continuous societal change. In this spirit, recognizing the incompleteness of our knowledge, the vulnerability of life, and the desire for co-creating the future, it is important to avoid indulging in the euphoria of expert-led planning, presenting utopia as a blueprint. Rather, degrowth visions describe steps for social transformation, not an ideal final state – not only because such a state cannot exist in the first place but also because diversity of perspectives and representation is understood as a central feature of a desirable future. Thus, degrowth does not propose a universal future but a 'pluriverse' – a world where many worlds fit.[4] No one knows what the future will look like, and, even as it is important to build on a vision that people can believe in, utopian proposals should be neither set in stone nor totalitarian and universal.

In this chapter, we argue that degrowth is not only a critique of the present but also a proposal and a vision for a better future that aims to liberate the 'social imaginary' of growth societies. Because degrowth is a contested and multivalent concept, we start by describing five different 'currents' of degrowth thought and practice. These can be thought of as currents in a turbulent stream, each of them with their own characteristics but travelling in similar directions. Following this, we find ourselves in the position to propose a definition of degrowth, which consists of three common principles. This then allows us, in the next

---

3 Karl Marx, *Capital, Volume 1*, trans. Ben Fowkes (New York: Vintage, 1976): 99; Max Horkheimer and Theodor W. Adorno, *Dialectic of Enlightenment* (London: Verso, 1996); Erik Olin Wright, *Envisioning Real Utopias* (London: Verso, 2010).

4 Ashish Kothari et al., eds., *Pluriverse: A Post-development Dictionary* (New Delhi: Tulika Books and Authorsupfront, 2019).

chapter, to describe more concrete political strategies for transformation, moving from the present into a degrowth utopia.

4.1. Degrowth currents

Not being a blueprint or a single universal set of proposals, degrowth is a concept that continues to be fought over: it is a contested vision. In this section, we attempt to identify various imaginaries or 'currents' of degrowth that are present within the degrowth spectrum, and each provides different, partly complementary and partly disputed answers to the question of what a degrowth society looks like. These currents are (1) the institution-oriented current; (2) the sufficiency-oriented current; (3) the commoning, or alternative economy current; (4) the feminist current; and (5) the post-capitalist and globalization-critical current. These are idealized distinctions – they should therefore not be understood as descriptions of homogeneous groups. The terms we use to label each current emphasize the central focus of the respective set of arguments from our point of view. Naturally, each current also covers various aspects central to other currents – institutional reforms, for example, play a role in almost all currents.[5]

Institution-oriented current

This is the current that is most likely to become a government position. Based in great part on the socio-economic and ecological critique of growth, the *institution-oriented* current aims to overcome the political fixation on growth and the transformation of previously

5 Describing these various currents is not an easy task since different authors do not usually assign themselves to a specific current of thought, and debates often show a great deal of overlap. Yet, categorization can facilitate understanding. On other proposals to structure the degrowth discussion, see Dennis Eversberg and Matthias Schmelzer, 'The Degrowth Spectrum: Convergence and Divergence within a Diverse and Conflictual Alliance', *Environmental Values* 27, no. 3 (2018): 245–67; and Fabrice Flipo, *Décroissance, ici et maintenant!* (Paris: Le Passager Clandestin, 2017).

growth-dependent and growth-driving institutions through reforms and policies of sufficiency. The basic orientation is green-liberal and those within this current primarily advocate for a mix of market instruments, eco-social taxes, and regulations, combined with radical reforms of institutions and broader policy frameworks. These policy changes aim at facilitating individual lifestyle changes, steering market activity in an ecological and more just direction, and making essential social institutions – from jobs to pensions to credit – growth-independent. Thus, ecological and heterodox economists have proposed policies such as 'ecological tax reform', redistribution, and alternative economic measurement indicators. They argue for a wide range of policy instruments that could entail a macro-economic shift away from growth and towards new conceptions of prosperity.[6] Some of the less radical post-growth proposals have already seen success, with Kate Raworth's 'doughnut economy' concept guiding the city of Amsterdam's new long-term sustainability policy, and with a conference on post-growth organized around these themes in the European Parliament in 2018. There are also, in overlap with other currents, more radical institution-oriented proposals for degrowth policies – from income maximums to work-time reductions – which we'll discuss in the next chapter.[7]

According to this current, social transformation is driven by electoral politics, governments, and national or regional administrations – as well as by non-state institutions such as companies, associations, and

6 Peter Victor, *Managing without Growth: Slower by Design, Not Disaster* (Cheltenham: Edward Elgar, 2018); Herman E. Daly, *Toward a Steady-State Economy* (San Francisco: W. H. Freeman, 1973); Rob Dietz and Daniel W. O'Neil, *Enough Is Enough: Building a Sustainable Economy in a World of Finite Resources* (New York: Routledge, 2013); Tim Jackson, *Prosperity without Growth: Economics for a Finite Planet* (London: Earthscan, 2016); Kate Raworth, *Doughnut Economics: Seven Ways to Think Like a 21st-Century Economist* (White River Junction, VT: Chelsea Green Publishing, 2017).

7 Giorgos Kallis, *Degrowth* (Newcastle upon Tyne: Agenda Publishing, 2018); Inês Cosme, Rui Santos, and Daniel W. O'Neil, 'Assessing the Degrowth Discourse: A Review and Analysis of Academic Degrowth Policy Proposals', *Journal of Cleaner Production* 149 (2017): 321–34. See also 'A Green New Deal for Europe', gndforeurope.com.

civil society. These would ideally change the basic conditions that allow for structural independence from growth in the wider economy. The transformation of institutions – such as the welfare state or the labour market – through political reforms is seen as a vehicle and central condition for a democratic transformation in society as a whole. In contrast to a naïve notion of conflict-free social change that prevails in parts of the degrowth spectrum, this current is concerned with emphasizing the necessity of political pressure and policy frameworks (see chapters 5 and 6).

Sufficiency-oriented current

Based mainly on the ecological and cultural critiques of growth and the critique of industrialism, the *sufficiency-oriented* current aims to radically reduce resource consumption through the creation of local and decommercialized subsistence economies, do-it-yourself initiatives, and 'voluntary simplicity' and thus focuses on practices outside the consumer-driven capitalist market in the here and now. In more mainstream discourse on sustainability, the term 'sufficiency' receives little attention. Sufficiency poses the question of the right measure – it is about behavioural changes in relation to collective limitation, reduction of consumption, deceleration, and the desire to have *enough*. The position of German economist and post-growth advocate Niko Paech, with his radical critique of the decoupling myth and his proposals for 'liberation from excess' and to live frugally because 'less is more' can be taken as exemplary.[8] Similar positions are also held by the Italian Movimento per Decrescita Felice and in some of the writings of Serge

---

8 Based on a scathing critique of pseudo-green lifestyles, overshooting personal emission budgets, and consumerism, as well as on analyses of markets, credit, and the division of labour as drivers of economic growth, Paech's proposal rests on three pillars: self-sufficiency through self-work in the home, garden, and neighbourhood; a regional, solidarity-based economy without long supply chains; and the reduction of the globalized capitalist economy to about half its current size. Niko Paech, *Liberation from Excess: The Road to a Post-Growth Economy* (Munich: Oekom, 2012).

Latouche.[9] Latouche in particular highlights the critique of the consumerist trap of scarcity economics, in which we can only become happier by buying more things, and contrasts it to degrowth as 'frugal abundance', a means to escape from the productivist system and the religion of growth.[10] Related concepts such as 'voluntary simplicity', 'frugal living', or the 'slow economy' are also frequently represented in international degrowth discussions and play a key role in some practical degrowth projects, often aligned with 'transition town' movements, eco-villages, and other movements for a more 'simple life'.[11]

Criticism of consumption and industrialism is particularly pronounced in this current and is often combined with a pessimistic or catastrophic assessment of ecological crises and a fundamental critique of civilization. The focus on equal ecological budgets for each person globally, individual responsibilities, and change starting here and now makes this position easy to communicate and relatable. However, by thus putting the main responsibility for ecological crises on the individual it tends to ignore the class-specific significance of consumption within the societies of the Global North and can lead to an individualization and depoliticization of the search for solutions, downplaying the importance of necessary social and structural changes. This current tends to gives primacy to ecological limits, from which everything else is derived, sometimes leading to a side-lining of social questions. In his introduction to the German translation of *Degrowth: A Vocabulary for a New Era*, Niko Paech even explicitly excludes 'questions of power and distribution' from the degrowth debate, arguing that his degrowth economy is 'not an ethical but a mathematical consequence' of the recognition of boundaries.[12]

So, while some – such as Paech – see sufficiency mainly as an individual strategy for reducing consumption, in the degrowth discussion it

---

9 Murizio Pallante, *La decrescita felice: La qualità della vita non dipende dal PIL* (Rome: Decrescita Felice, 2011).

10 Serge Latouche, *Vers une société d'abondance frugale* (Paris: Fayard, 2011).

11 Samuel Alexander, *Voluntary Simplicity: The Poetic Alternative to Consumer Culture* (Whanganui, NZ: Tead & Daughters, 2009).

12 Niko Paech, 'Vortwort zur deutschen Ausgabe', in *Degrowth: Handbuch für eine neue Ära*, ed. Giacomo D'Alisa, Federico Demaria, and Giorgos Kallis (Munich: Oekom, 2016), 8–12.

is generally understood as a radical social project that can only be achieved under changed political conditions, social institutions, and ownership logics.[13] Here, others talk about eco-sufficiency – understood more as a social-ecological transformation than an orientation towards individual change – undergirded by eco-feminist and internationalist principles, such as reproductive justice and climate debt.[14] Further, initiatives such as the Global Ecovillage Network and the Transition Town movement highlight the collective nature of the sufficiency approach, as they exchange resources through global networks and also engage actively in local municipal politics. One example of the value of the sufficiency approach is Can Decreix, a vineyard in Southern France, also host to the Barcelona Degrowth Summer School. Can Decreix illustrates the possibilities of frugal, convivial living through the use of alternative technologies, agro-ecology, hands-on education, and their hosting of a 'museum of useless things'. While most people may not be able to live this way due to work and life constraints, and while such efforts do not directly challenge structural systems, Can Decreix and similar initiatives like ecovillages make it easier to imagine that post-capitalist ways of living – an 'alternative normality' – are both possible and desirable (see section 6.1).[15]

Commoning or alternative economy current

The *commoning* or *alternative economy* current focuses more strongly on the construction of alternative infrastructures, cooperatives based on solidarity, and non-capitalist forms of collective production and

---

13 For a critique of sufficiency-oriented positions from a degrowth perspective, see Corinna Dengler and Matthias Schmelzer, 'Anmerkungen zu Niko Paechs Postwachstumsökonomie: Plädoyer für weniger Individualethik, mehr Kapitalismuskritik und eine intersektionale Gerechtigkeitsperspektive', *Zeitschrift für Wirtschafts- und Unternehmensethik* 22 (2021): 191–5.

14 Ariel Salleh, *Eco-sufficiency and Global Justice: Women Write Political Ecology* (London: Pluto Press, 2009); Ricardo Mastini, 'A Sufficiency Vision for an Ecologically Constrained World', Greeneuropeanjournal.eu, 3 August 2018.

15 Corinna Burkhart, *Who Says What Is Absurd? A Case Study on Being(s) in an Alternative Normality* (Heidelberg: VÖÖ, 2015).

livelihood: in short, 'nowtopias', a term that emphasizes the possibility of realizing utopias in the here and now.[16] This current focuses on a large number of practical experiments, which often refer to initiatives such as community-supported agriculture, commoning, solidarity/cooperative/community economies, peer-to-peer production, platform cooperatives, alternative economies, and sharing economies. A large influence here is also the solidarity economy and fair trade movements in the Global South, as well as agro-ecology and peasant struggles. With a focus on the negative impact of free trade agreements and monopoly agriculture, these movements stress sovereignty, cooperative ownership, and fair labour conditions and seek to build links with consumers and movements in the Global North to support their struggles for alternative development, for example, through initiatives such as the World Social Forum.[17]

Within this current, there are two main points of emphasis. The first, which is oriented around the commons, is particularly pronounced.[18] This not only involves opposing the continuous enclosure of the commons – from community-managed land to solidarity projects – and continuous land seizures as the central growth engines of capitalist expansion. This current also aims to strengthen and expand common property as well as governance principles and economic activities based on and brought about by commoning. Inspired by the work of the winner of the 'Nobel Prize for Economics' (which is not actually a Nobel Prize), Elinor Ostrom, this perspective aims to defend and expand commons-based alternatives beyond the market and the state – such as Wikipedia, community gardens, or alternative currencies. Central to this are

16 Chris Carlsson, *Nowtopia: How Pirate Programmers, Outlaw Bicyclists, and Vacant-Lot Gardeners Are Inventing the Future Today* (Oakland, CA: AK Press, 2008).

17 Euclides A. Mance, *Redes de colaboração solidária: Aspetos econômico-filosóficos* (Petrópolis, Brazil: Editora Vozes, 2002); Raj Patel, *Stuffed and Starved: The Hidden Battle for the World Food System* (Brooklyn: Melville House, 2012).

18 While it is widespread to speak of '*the* commons', it should be highlighted that commons are not a thing but a relationship, thus the term 'common*ing*' is often used. See David Bollier and Silke Helfrich. eds., *Patterns of Commoning* (Amherst, MA: The Commons Strategies Group, 2015).

commoning processes, in which community and responsible relationships and rules are negotiated. The core idea is that a degrowth economy should be rooted in the commoning initiatives that already exist in the multitude of alternative economies, and that the principles of commoning should be at the centre of organizing the entire society.[19]

Another emphasis is more on the commons as a path to overturning capitalism. This Marxist-inspired perspective is based on a fundamental critique of capitalist competition, barter logic, and thus the use of markets and money. The goal is a society where most forms of property are abolished, one based on an economic system without markets and in which everyone contributes according to their own means. From this perspective, the above-mentioned commons approach often cannot sufficiently challenge the demobilizing power of the state and subsequent recuperation by the capitalist economy. Take, for example, the nascent 'sharing economy' that was quickly capitalized on by Uber and Airbnb, or the cutting of federal funding for social services in the name of municipal democracy, as happened under austerity policies in the United Kingdom.[20] These perspectives tend to engage more with large-scale construction of initiatives that can build a 'counter-hegemony' to the dominant economy, where cooperatives, solidarity economy networks, and confederations of citizen initiatives would, as the slogan of the International Workers of the World goes, 'build a new world in the shell of the old'.[21] Descriptors like 'radical municipalism', 'libertarian

---

19 Michael Bauwens, Vasilis Kostakis, and Alex Pazaitis, *Peer-to-Peer: The Commons Manifesto* (London: Westminster University Press, 2018); Silke Helfrich and David Bollier, *Free, Fair, and Alive: The Insurgent Power of the Commons* (Gabriola Island, BC: New Society Publishers, 2019).

20 George Caffentzis and Silvia Federici, 'Commons against and beyond Capitalism', *Community Development Journal* 49, no. 1 (2014): 92–105.

21 Richard D. Wolff, *Democracy at Work: A Cure for Capitalism* (Chicago: Haymarket Books, 2012); Julie-Katharine Gibson-Graham, Jenny Cameron, and Stephen Healy, *Take Back the Economy: An Ethical Guide for Transforming our Communities* (Minneapolis: University of Minnesota Press, 2013); John Michael Colón et al., 'Community, Democracy, and Mutual Aid: Toward Dual Power and Beyond', The Next System Project, 2017, https://thenextsystem.org/sites/default/files/2017-07/Symbiosis_AtLargeFirst-corrected-2.pdf; Michael Hardt and Antonio Negri, *Assembly* (Oxford: Oxford University Press, 2017).

socialism', 'social anarchism', and 'autonomist Marxism' are often used to characterize this approach. It is therefore closely aligned with currents critical of capitalism and globalization but places the emphasis on local democratic commoning practices, a world 'beyond money' and scaled-up organization as key ingredients for overcoming any logic of exchange.[22]

Feminist current

The *feminist* degrowth current is neglected in many accounts, in large part because feminist arguments have had to struggle for recognition in the degrowth discourse. Nevertheless, many of the most prominent degrowth concepts were anticipated at least since the 1970s in feminist economics and critical theory, as well as in the subsistence approach (see section 3.5). The latter clarified the connections between capitalist exploitation of housewives, smallholders in the Global South, and nature, which they rightly saw as the analytical starting point of a critique of patriarchy and capitalism. In contrast to the structural *carelessness* of the growth economy, feminist proposals seek to place reproductive activities and care – which form the basis for society and life in general – at the centre of the economy and economic thinking and aim to overcome the separation between production and reproduction.[23] This requires, for example, a radical reduction in working hours for all while at the same time ensuring a fair distribution of care activities between people of all genders – in short, a 'care revolution'.[24] Here, transformation is understood as consisting of changed practices,

22 Anitra Nelson, *Beyond Money: A Postcapitalist Strategy* (London: Pluto, 2022); Friederike Habermann, *Ausgetauscht! Warum gutes Leben für alle tauschlogikfrei sein muss* (Sulzbach am Taunus: Ulrike Helmer, 2018).

23 Corinna Dengler and Birte Strunk, 'The Monetized Economy versus Care and the Environment: Degrowth Perspectives on Reconciling an Antagonism', *Feminist Economics* 24, no. 3 (2018): 160–83. See also Corinna Dengler and Lisa Marie Seebacher, 'What About the Global South? Towards a Feminist Decolonial Degrowth Approach', *Ecological Economics* 157 (2019): 246–52.

24 Frigga Haug, 'The Four-in-One Perspective: A Manifesto for a More Just Life', *Socialism and Democracy* 23, no. 1 (2009): 119–23; Gabriele Winkler, *Care Revolution: Schritte in eine solidarische Gesellschaft* (Bielefeld: Transcript, 2015).

subjectivities, epistemologies, and institutional reforms. A core argument is that a degrowth society can only be achieved by ending patriarchal structures both between societies and within relationships between people. The eco-feminist current also centres eco-sufficiency as a key principle of an alternative economic system.[25] One more concrete manifestation of this current is the Feminisms and Degrowth Alliance (FaDA), an international and diverse network publishing analyses, proposing research agendas, and organizing talks on the intersections between degrowth and radical feminist approaches. Following the coronavirus pandemic, FaDA released a statement describing the necessary transformations needed to build a healthy, caring economy, such as paid housework and the transformation of patriarchal nuclear families into caring communities – principles which are not often discussed in other degrowth currents.[26]

Post-capitalist and alter-globalization currents

Finally, there is the *post-capitalist and alter-globalization* current, characterized above all by a pronounced analysis of the growth constraints of capitalist societies and by an emphasis on its dynamics of power. From this perspective, an emancipatory degrowth society entails fundamental structural changes – from the way we work to forms of ownership – and will require social struggle to be achieved. Those advocating this approach strive to undo the domination of the market, socialize key sectors of the economy, and reduce social relations of domination.[27] The understanding of degrowth as 'socialism without growth' (in the sense of an anti-productivist socialism from below)

25 Salleh, *Eco-sufficiency and Global Justice*.

26 See the Feminisms and Degrowth Alliance, degrowth.info/en/blog/feminisms-and-degrowth-alliance-fada; Feminisms and Degrowth Alliance, 'Feminist Degrowth Reflections on COVID-19 and the Politics of Social Reproduction', Degrowth.info, 2020.

27 Ulrich Brand and Markus Wissen, *Limits to Capitalist Nature: Theorizing and Overcoming the Imperial Mode of Living* (London: Rowman & Littlefield, 2018); Valérie Fournier, 'Escaping from the Economy: The Politics of Degrowth', *International Journal of Sociology and Social Policy* 28, no. 11 (2008): 528–45.

increasingly plays a central role in the international debate on degrowth, and is linked to eco-socialist approaches.[28] This current is continuing to evolve in the degrowth literature, seeing promising development in recent years. This includes work on the history of growth within capitalism from a Marxist perspective, an important edited volume on the political economy of degrowth, and deeper engagement between degrowth, eco-socialist, and communist thinkers – in essence reviving red–green alliances such as those which emerged in the 1970s. With regard to strategy, this current focuses less on individualized solutions or changes in consumer behaviour, and only partly on nowtopias, even if the latter are seen as important areas for experimenting with non-capitalist and commons-based economies. But in contrast to commoning approaches, it is less focused on commons as self-organized solutions to collective problems than on reappropriating and socializing wealth and thus transforming the structural principles of society. This current highlights the need for systemic changes in political and economic structures such as distribution and ownership, economic democracy, and shorter working hours, as well as the necessity to restructure and dismantle certain industrial sectors – from coal to industrial agriculture to SUVs. Activists within this current advocate confrontational strategies such as direct action, which includes civil disobedience and occupations of key sites, and strong alliances with Global South struggles defending their territories.[29] Although different

28 Giorgos Kallis, 'Socialism without Growth', *Capitalism Nature Socialism* 30, no. 2 (2019): 189–206; Stan Cox, *The Green New Deal and Beyond: Ending the Climate Emergency While We Still Can* (San Francisco: City Lights Books, 2020); Gareth Dale, 'Degrowth and the Green New Deal', Theecologist.org, 28 October 2019.

29 Diego Andreucci and Salvatore Engel-Di Mauro, 'Capitalism, Socialism and the Challenge of Degrowth: Introduction to the Symposium', *Capitalism Nature Socialism* 30, no. 2 (2019): 176–88; Ekaterina Chertkovskaya, Alexander Paulsson, and Stefania Barca, *Towards a Political Economy of Degrowth* (London: Rowman and Littlefield International, 2019); Kohei Saito, *Karl Marx's Eco-socialism: Capital, Nature, and the Unfinished Critique of Political Economy* (New York: NYU Press, 2017); Corinna Burkhart, Matthias Schmelzer, and Nina Treu, eds., *Degrowth in Movement(s): Exploring Pathways for Transformation* (Winchester: Zer0, 2020); Hubert Buch-Hansen, 'The Prerequisites for a

structural levels of transformation are addressed, transformations at the personal and community level tend to be under-emphasized – the necessity of changing gender relations in private life as well as of organizing one's own subsistence and reproduction within alternative structures is sometimes neglected in favour of theorizing within existing infrastructures such as universities and activist interventions.

4.2. Defining degrowth

So, what is the core of the degrowth proposal, transcending all the different perspectives, imaginaries, and currents that we have just laid out? The different degrowth currents discussed in the foregoing section, and the various paths to get there – in all their variety and internal tensions – each emphasize important dimensions of degrowth thought. In the following, we will focus on the commonalities. We start by considering various definitions of degrowth that have thus far appeared and highlight their key elements. This then allows us to propose a definition that – based on three common principles – we hope is both open enough to incorporate the various currents and specific enough to clearly sketch the contours of a degrowth society. In unpacking the three core elements of this definition, we present key challenges that each approach towards a future society must address, and in doing so lay out the rationale behind the degrowth vision and its specificities.

Towards a definition of degrowth

Degrowth is, above all, a movement in motion, and should be considered an umbrella term for various movements and frameworks on the left. Nonetheless, there have been various attempts to define what constitutes a degrowth society. To begin with, degrowth is, by and large, defined as a proposal for a future society – a goal to work towards. An

---

early and much-quoted definition comes from the Research &
Degrowth research network, which stresses that degrowth describes a
fair reduction of production and consumption that encompasses both
human well-being and ecological sustainability:

> Sustainable degrowth may be defined as an equitable downscaling of
> production and consumption that increases human well-being and
> enhances ecological conditions at the local and global level, in the
> short and long term.[30]

A similar definition from authors in the same network further stresses
that degrowth is about industrialized countries, and that redistribution
plays a central role:

> Degrowth challenges the hegemony of growth and calls for a demo-
> cratically led redistributive downscaling of production and consump-
> tion in industrialised countries as a means to achieve environmental
> sustainability, social justice and well-being.[31]

Other definitions focus more on the process and political character of
the transformation and bring political institutions into focus. According
to Giorgos Kallis,

> Sustainable degrowth is a multi-faceted political project that aspires to
> mobilise support for a change of direction, at the macro-level of economic
> and political institutions and at the micro-level of personal values and
> aspirations. Income and material comfort is to be reduced for many
> along the way, but the goal is that this is not experienced as welfare loss.[32]

30 Francois Schneider, Giorgos Kallis, and Joan Martínez-Alier, 'Crisis or
Opportunity? Economic Degrowth for Social Equity and Ecological Sustainability',
Journal of Cleaner Production 18 (2010): 511.

31 Federico Demaria et al., 'What Is Degrowth? From an Activist Slogan to a
Social Movement', *Environmental Values* 22, no. 2 (2013): 209.

32 Giorgos Kallis, 'In Defence of Degrowth', *Ecological Economics* 70, no. 5
(2011): 878.

The loss of income and material comfort mentioned in the last sentence – often discussed as 'voluntary simplicity' or even 'revolutionary austerity', using the slogan 'living simply so that others can simply live'[33] – plays a central role in the public perception of degrowth. Economic reduction is emphasized above all in the sufficiency-oriented current. According to Niko Paech, a degrowth economy is 'an economy ... without growth of the Gross Domestic Product that has stable supply structures, albeit with a comparatively reduced level of consumption'.[34] While this definition does not contain a positive vision beyond overcoming GDP and stability, others stress that degrowth can be understood as 'a planned contraction of economic activity aimed at increasing wellbeing and equality'.[35]

These definitions focus above all on the overall goals of sustainability, justice, and independence from growth. Other approaches place greater emphasis on the fundamental transformation of society. For example, while no definition is given in the widely cited degrowth *Vocabulary*, the editors emphasize that degrowth is not only about *less* but also, and above all, about something *different*. Degrowth stands for a society with a lower social metabolism but, more importantly, a social metabolism with a *different* structure and that fulfils *new* tasks. Degrowth does not require the same to be done on a smaller scale. 'The objective is not to make an elephant leaner, but to turn an elephant into a snail.'[36] A more recent definition – from an article providing a comprehensive overview of recent research on degrowth – emphasizes this aspect of the 'other political-economic system' and focuses on the reduction of material and energy throughputs instead of the reduction of economic performance that had been emphasized in earlier

33 Alexander, *Voluntary Simplicity*; Giorgos Kallis, 'The Left Should Embrace Degrowth', Newint.org, 5 November 2015.

34 Niko Paech, 'Grundzüge einer Postwachstumsökonomie', Postwachstumsoekonomie.de, 2009, our translation.

35 Matthias Schmelzer, 'The Growth Paradigm: History, Hegemony, and the Contested Making of Economic Growthmanship', *Ecological Economics* 118 (2015): 262–71, 264.

36 Giacomo D'Alisa, Federico Demaria, and Giorgos Kallis, *Degrowth: A Vocabulary for a New Era* (London: Routledge, 2014), 4.

definitions: 'the degrowth hypothesis is that it is possible to organize a transition and live well under a different political-economic system that has a radically smaller resource throughput'.[37] Likewise, the book *Degrowth in Movement(s)* emphasizes the transformative character of degrowth, as well as the necessity of a fundamental change to growth-oriented culture and growth-dependent capitalism:

> Degrowth proposes as an alternative a radically democratic reorgan-isation of the political and economic structures of industrialised societies, aiming at drastic reductions in resource and energy throughput while furthering a good life for all . . . Degrowth requires fundamental changes in everyday social practices as well as a profound cultural, social and economic transformation that over-comes the capitalist mode of production.[38]

These definitions appear largely similar but each emphasizes different aspects. While some focus on material consumption and sufficiency, others focus on economic growth more generally understood, while others still are focused instead on social transformation, or the end of capitalism more specifically. What brings them together is the proposal for a radical transition, a politicization of metabolism itself, a focus on justice, and a critique of the present economy.

In a wide-spanning analysis of different definitions of degrowth, Timothée Parrique describes three kinds of definitions which help in identifying our own: the environmentalist definition, which character-izes degrowth as *decline*; the revolutionary definition, where degrowth is seen as *emancipation*; and the utopian definition, where degrowth is seen as a *destination*. In emphasizing these different aspects, each kind of definition also conflicts with various currents of degrowth. For example, while some definitions highlight *less* material comfort, others frame degrowth as an increase in well-being. Limiting degrowth as a process only relevant to industrialized countries, on the other hand,

---

37 Giorgos Kallis et al., 'Research on Degrowth', *Annual Review of Environment and Resources* 43 (2018): 291–316, 291.

38 Burkhart, Schmelzer, and Treu, *Degrowth in Movement(s)*, 144.

fails to acknowledge the relevance of degrowth for the Global South, as represented in the critiques of globalization and the imperial mode of living, which cut across North–South divisions. Thus, a more nuanced definition would account for the turbulence among the different degrowth currents highlighted above.

Balancing these three types of definitions, Parrique argues that 'degrowth includes a utopia (*espérance*) to be reached via a decrease (*décroissance*), itself made possible by a disbelief (*décroyance*)'.[39] This broad definition encapsulates degrowth as both critique and proposal, while highlighting the role of downscaling in the degrowth proposal. However, it is not as clear as to the contents of the proposal: How are decrease and utopia to be balanced? Beyond utopia as a central pillar of degrowth, what specific role does justice have in the definition? In the following, we bring together different aspects of these definitions and, balancing between degrowth currents, propose our own. This definition, we argue, is framed to go to the root of various crises we face today.

Common degrowth principles for a concrete utopia

A degrowth society, we propose, is one which, in a democratic process of transformation:

1. enables *global ecological justice* – in other words, it transforms and reduces its material metabolism, and thus also production and consumption, in such a way that its way of life is ecologically sustainable in the long term and globally just;
2. strengthens *social justice* and *self-determination* and strives for a *good life* for all under the conditions of this changed metabolism; and
3. redesigns its institutions and infrastructure so that they are *not dependent on growth and continuous expansion* for their functioning.

---

39 Timothée Parrique, *The Political Economy of Degrowth: Economics and Finance* (Clermont: Université Clermont Auvergne, 2019), 233.

These three principles take into consideration the core concerns shared across the degrowth spectrum, and they can also help us to evaluate different degrowth approaches according to how strongly they emphasize or neglect each of these points. We think all three are important.

Global ecological justice

A degrowth society is a society that, through a democratic process of transformation, enables *global ecological justice* – by transforming its material metabolism, and thus also production and consumption, in such a way that its way of life is ecologically sustainable and globally just, which necessarily includes a reduction in production and consumption among the affluent. This first dimension of the degrowth definition addresses the challenge of ecological crises and global justice. Degrowth, we argue, is fundamentally about global ecological justice, or in other words, the vision of an ecologically sustainable and socially more equal world. We are talking about a world in which, on the one hand, the ecological carrying capacity of the planet is not exceeded and, on the other hand, material standards of living converge globally to enable good living for all.[40]

This condition for degrowth has three key presuppositions. First, it requires major *lifestyle changes* for the wealthiest globally, and this includes in particular those in the Global North. Second, enabling global ecological justice depends on *systemic changes* that lead to a transformation beyond growth. Third, it also means that the transformation by the North should not displace problems to the South. We deal with each presupposition below.

First, achieving global ecological justice will require a planned contraction of economic activity to a globally equitable level and a deprivileging of those people who currently externalize the costs of their mode of living to others – humans and non-humans – elsewhere or in the

---

40 In this sense, degrowth has many similarities with the proposal of the 'doughnut economy', which describes a safe place of humanity that avoids both the degradation of the planet and the depravation of man (Raworth, *Doughnut Economics*). See also Jason Hickel, *Less Is More: How Degrowth Will Save the World* (London: William Heinemann, 2020); Max Ajl, *A People's Green New Deal* (London: Pluto Press, 2021).

future. And that means that the more affluent, who are responsible for most environmental impacts, would need to accept 'far-reaching lifestyle changes [that] complement technological advancements'.[41] A central element of a degrowth society is therefore that the material metabolism with nature, and therefore also economic production in different societies, is aligned with a long-term, ecologically sustainable, and globally generalisable level. Degrowth, in this sense, aims to replace the imperial mode of living with a solidarity-based one, to overcome the externalization society, and to foster sustainable lifestyles that end overconsumption by the affluent (which is environmentally unsustainable) and the poverty and need of the dispossessed (which is socially unsustainable).[42] Degrowth has been criticized that it focuses on consumption and renunciation and its demands are thus directed against the working class in the Global North, who need more rather than less.[43] However, this critique misses what degrowth is about. Degrowth explicitly aims at improving the living conditions for everyone – including those in the Global North who struggle to get along, who have to juggle three jobs to afford rent and cannot pay for health care. Degrowth, however, claims that this can be achieved without increasing overall economic output (which would be unsustainable and globally unjust) by tackling inequalities and guaranteeing public abundance. Indeed, degrowth is about challenging the very system in which working class well-being depends on accumulation – and shows how this can be changed. It's not a politics of less, but a politics of enough for all.

So, one might wonder, if the main goal is global ecological justice and a reduction of the biophysical size of the economy, why all this talk about *economic* growth? Though degrowth is often misunderstood in

41 Thomas Wiedmann et al., 'Scientists' Warning on Affluence', *Nature Communications* 11, no. 3107 (2020): 1.

42 Ibid.; Brand and Wissen, *Limits to Capitalist Nature*; ILA Kollektiv, *At the Expense of Others: How the Imperial Mode of Living Prevents a Good Life for All* (Munich: Oekom, 2017); Stephan Lessenich, *Living Well at Others' Expense: The Hidden Costs of Western Prosperity* (London: Polity, 2019).

43 Matthew T. Huber, "Ecological Politics for the Working Class", *Catalyst* 3, no. 1 (2019), catalyst-journal.com. See also Matthew T. Huber, *Climate Change as Class War: Building Socialism on a Warming Planet* (London: Verso, 2022).

this way, economic contraction is *not* its goal, and neither should degrowth be understood as the opposite of growth. Reductions in production and consumption are, rather, a consequence of the fact that it is impossible to sufficiently decouple material throughput and emissions from growth (for evidence, see chapters 2 and 3). These are, therefore, merely a necessary corollary of the transformation towards a globally just society.[44]

Still, while degrowth aims at reducing the social-ecological metabolism of Global North economies to a sustainable and globally just level, it is not indifferent about economic growth. On the contrary, for a wealth of reasons the question of economic growth is absolutely central to the degrowth discussion. One of these is that because, as the ecological growth critique shows, an absolute decoupling of resource consumption and emissions from economic growth is unlikely, and therefore reducing the consumption of nature also implies a (less pronounced, due to economy-wide efficiency improvements) reduction in economic output, also measured in GDP.[45] Let us put it another way: because degrowth aims for global ecological justice, and because it is not possible to sustain economic growth to meet that goal, degrowth also requires the transformation to an economy that does not depend on growth to meet well-being. This has profound repercussions, leading to the second presupposition.

The second presupposition – that degrowth also requires systemic change beyond growth and capitalism – is one of the key consequences of the demand for global ecological justice, and explains why many in the degrowth community are critical of capitalism and seek to move beyond it. As discussed in chapters 2 and 3, the question of whether an economy is expanding or not is anything but ancillary: since capitalist societies stabilize dynamically through growth and because the logic of growth is deeply inscribed in the material, social, and mental infrastructures of growth societies, it would be grossly negligent to remain agnostic about the growth question and, by extension, but also not

---

44 Giorgos Kallis et al., *The Case for Degrowth* (Cambridge: Polity, 2020).

45 Jackson, *Prosperity without Growth*; Kallis, *Degrowth*; see also section 3.1 in this book.

exclusively, about capitalism.[46] Rather, degrowth confronts head-on not only the ideology of growth, but also addresses the question of transforming social and economic structures so that they ensure stability, democracy, and a good life for all under conditions of a declining economic output.

The third presupposition – that this transformation must not unequally fall on the shoulders of the poor and, in particular, the Global South, but rather create the conditions for global justice – follows from the first two. Many proposals for sustainability transitions in the North, which rely mainly on green investments, green technology, and renewable energies, do in fact imply increasing extraction of key materials from the Global South, through vast demands for land to create biofuels or hydrogen, or dangerous negative emission technologies. From a degrowth perspective, a just transition in the North cannot depend on increasing extraction, exploitation, and pollution in the Global South. Rather, global ecological justice amounts to a radical redistribution of wealth, resources, and emission rights globally, resulting in the need to decrease the biophysical size of the economies of industrialized countries – or the amount of stuff that is moved through these economies and the energy needed for this. Today, this includes a serious assessment of the role of green technologies in driving mining conflicts and land grabbing in the South.[47] The importance of the global justice perspective for degrowth (and thus how wrong-headed the critics are who claim that degrowth wants the poor to stay poor) can be seen from the declaration adopted during the first international Degrowth Conference in Paris in 2008. It introduces degrowth as a concept aimed at '"right-sizing" the global and national economies'. Specifically, it states:

> At the global level, 'right-sizing' means reducing the global ecological footprint (including the carbon footprint) to a sustainable level.

---

46 Kallis, *Degrowth*; see also chapter 3.

47 Ajl, *A People's Green New Deal*; Martín Arboleda, *Planetary Mine: Territories of Extraction under Late Capitalism* (London: Verso, 2020); Madeleine Fairbarn, *Fields of Gold: Financing the Global Land Rush* (Ithaca, NY: Cornell University Press, 2020).

In countries where the per capita footprint is greater than the sustainable global level, right-sizing implies a reduction to this level within
a reasonable time-frame. In countries where severe poverty remains,
right-sizing implies increasing consumption by those in poverty as
quickly as possible, in a sustainable way, to a level adequate for a
decent life, following locally determined poverty-reduction paths
rather than externally imposed development policies.[48]

In other words, degrowth in the North also necessitates 'right-sizing'
the relationship between the North and South. As Jamie Tyberg and
Erica Jung put it, the 'contradiction between the material overdevelop-
ment of the Global North and the extreme overexploitation of the
Global South indicates that, for the latter to end, the former must end
first'.[49]

It is therefore no wonder that degrowth proponents, who call for a
reduction of production in early industrialized countries, also offer
themselves as allies of environmental justice movements from the
Global South.[50] Inspired by the principles of environmental justice, as
they guide the grassroots movements of the poor in the Global South,
degrowth follows the principles of 'cap and share', 'contraction and
convergence', and 'reparations'.[51] A sustainable level of consumption
requires addressing not only the extremely unequal consumption
between different world regions and countries, but also their historical
trajectory. This means that all existing and remaining wealth, resources,
raw materials, and emissions budgets would be distributed fairly, both

48 Research and Degrowth, 'Degrowth Declaration of the Paris 2008
Conference', *Journal of Cleaner Production* 18, no. 6 (April 2010): 523–4.

49 Jamie Tyberg and Erica Jung, *Degrowth and Revolutionary Organizing*
(New York: Rosa Luxemburg Foundation, 2021).

50 Hickel, *Less Is More*; Ashish Kothari et al., eds., *Pluriverse: A Post-
development Dictionary* (New Delhi: Tulika Books and Authorsupfront, 2019);
Joan Martínez-Alier, 'Environmental Justice and Economic Degrowth: An
Alliance between Two Movements', *Capitalism Nature Socialism* 23, no. 1 (2012):
51–73.

51 Joan Martínez-Alier, 'Environmental Justice and Economic Degrowth: An
Alliance between Two Movements', *Capitalism Nature Socialism* 23, no. 1 (2012):
51–73; Kallis, *Degrowth*.

between countries and regions of the world and within them. The 'ecological debt' of the industrialized countries as well as the consequences of colonialism and centuries of exploitation must also be taken into account, resulting in reparations.[52] However, as argued recently by Olúfẹ́mi O. Táíwò, reparations can also be understood as a constructive programme of 'worldmaking' that aims at undoing the currently racialized and unequal global economy and systems of power, whose advantages accrue among the privileged, and at creating systems that work to the benefit of those currently disadvantaged.[53] Building on this, degrowth can be interpreted as part of this future-oriented project of building a better social order that addresses the specific challenges for the Global North arising from the imperial mode of living. Global justice therefore also means standing up to the repressions of border regimes and against racism, which serve to defend the imperial mode of living for islands of prosperity in the capitalist core. In addition to combating the forces driving people to flee their home – protecting the right to remain – this must also include global freedom of movement – the right to move.[54]

52 Ajl, *A People's Green New Deal*, 15, 64, 147; Alberto Acosta and Ulrich Brand, *Salidas del laberinto capitalista: Derecimiento y postextractivismo* (Quito: Fundación Rosa Luxemburg, 2017); ILA Kollektiv, *At the Expense of Others*; Barbara Unmüßig, Thomas Fatheuer, and Lili Fuhr, *Critique of the Green Economy: Toward Social and Environmental Equity* (Berlin: Heinrich Böll Foundation, 2018).

53 This also means that the burdens of the global transformation – for example in terms of climate policies around mitigation, adaptation, loss and damage, or resettlement – should be distributed to the Global North and racially advantaged populations and the benefits to the Global South and Black and Indigenous populations. Olúfẹ́mi O. Táíwò, *Reconsidering Reparations: Worldmaking in the Case of Climate Crisis* (New York: Oxford University Press, 2022).

54 Lessenich, *Living Well at Others' Expense*; Burkhart, Schmelzer, and Treu, *Degrowth in Movement(s)*.

Social justice, self-determination, and a good life

The second challenge degrowth addresses is how to achieve such a transformation to a society with a much smaller metabolism and thus (due to the likely impossibility of decoupling) also a smaller economy while, at the same time, strengthening social justice and self-determination and striving for a good life for all. To achieve this, it must be asked: Under what conditions can the economic, social, and cultural rights and achievements that have been fought for in the last centuries be maintained and expanded – while the material metabolism radically declines and the economy degrows? This is not a trivial question. As we discussed in the analysis of the history of growth, 'the mansion of modern freedoms stands on an ever-expanding base of fossil fuel use' and, we would add to this pertinent formulation of Dipesh Chakrabarty, on a base of economic growth.[55] Historically, many of the emancipatory achievements people have temporarily gained in some modern nation-states – from modern democracy to workers' rights, universal health care systems or the welfare state – were attained through social struggles within the context of a growth society and the 'great acceleration', and thus are intimately bound up with these. We only know modernity as a process of expansion. Is it possible to transform this 'mansion of modern freedoms', social rights, and welfare achievements in a way that does not depend on economic growth?

Understanding how interwoven many 'modern' social rights and emancipatory achievements are with economic growth, the imperial mode of living, and the use of fossil resources makes clear the complexity and scale of overcoming expansionary modernity and moving towards what might with some caveats be called a 'degrowth modernity'. Proposals for a degrowth society thus cannot avoid addressing the necessity of fundamental societal transformations, with all its repercussions. This implies asking: How can we produce the material basis necessary for a good life for all beyond growth, acceleration, and competition? In answering this question, the

---

55 Dipesh Chakrabarty, 'The Climate of History: Four Theses', *Critical Inquiry* 35, no. 2 (2009): 208; see also chapters 2 and 3 in this book.

degrowth movement has focused on three dimensions: social justice, democracy, and well-being independent of growth.

First, degrowth is about *social justice*.[56] The question of how a society could offer 'basic material security' for all people is not necessarily dependent on the distribution of monetary wealth but on the fulfilment of basic needs.[57] For degrowth proponents, need-based provisioning of key goods and services does not necessarily depend on centralized bureaucracies but can also be ensured via democratically managed or commons-based infrastructure. Social justice also means undoing broader structures of domination such as class society, racism, colonialism, (hetero-)sexism, ableism and other forms of exclusion.[58]

Second, degrowth aims at strengthening collective *self-determination* beyond growth. In addition to the right to share in the 'output', there is also the right to have an equal 'input' in shaping social and economic conditions. Most degrowth approaches therefore attach great importance to the further development of democracy, autonomy, and collective self-determination. Derived from the work of the Greek-French philosopher Cornelius Castoriadis, 'self-determination' is understood here as the self-administration of society, in which institutions and structures such as municipal energy suppliers, public banks, educational institutions, and transport systems are designed to be transparent and controllable, as well as permanently subject to questioning, critical review, and further development. Autonomy necessarily also implies collective self-limitation wherein individuals,

---

56 The fact that the International Degrowth Conferences bear the subtitle 'For Ecological Sustainability and Social Justice' shows how central the latter is as a core demand in the international debate. Thus, unlike other sustainability approaches such as steady-state economics, degrowth focuses more on social justice than on meeting ecological limits. Cosme, Santos, and O'Neil, 'Assessing the Degrowth Discourse'; Kallis et al., 'Research on Degrowth'.

57 Claudio Cattaneo and Aaron Vansintjan, *A Wealth of Possibilities: Alternatives to Growth* (Brussels: Green European Foundation, 2016); Vincent Liegey et al., *Un projet de décroissance: Manifeste pour une dotation inconditionelly d'autonomie* (Paris: Les Éditions Utopia, 2013).

58 Acosta and Brand, *Salidas del laberinto capitalista*; Brand and Wissen, *Limits to Capitalist Nature*; Burkhart, Schmelzer, and Treu, *Degrowth in Movement(s)*.

collectives, and entire societies set rules, values, and norms.[59]
Self-determination of one's own living conditions also means
self-determination over one's own work. The counter-image to the
alienation through work in bureaucratized and industrialized contexts
– as analysed in the cultural and industrialist critique (sections 3.3
and 3.6) – is the 'post-work society', in which various paid and unpaid,
productive and reproductive, activities stand side by side on an equal
footing, or a commons-based society driven by a solidarity economy.[60] An important feature of self-determination is also that it requires
relational freedom; that is, it can only be realized in and through
interdependent networks of relationships (see section 3.5). This can
be understood through the concepts of 'power-over' and 'power-to':
we can conceive of power in the negative sense of having power over
someone, or in the positive sense of having the freedom to make
choices. But, as the feminist Amy Allen has pointed out, there is also
'power-with', which is the power of solidarity, to collaborate and
deliberate with others.[61] In this sense, and perhaps counter-intuitively
for many of those in positions of power and privilege, inter-dependence is a basic requirement for freedom. Even though, in the degrowth
debate, proposals for expanding self-determination and democracy
are very common and visible, the concrete form of the democratization process is still unclear. There is still much to be discussed and
clarified here.

59 Cornelius Castoriadis, *Le contenu du socialisme* (Paris: Éditions Seuil,
1979); Cornelius Castoriadis, *Le monde morcelé: Les carrefours du labyrinthe III*
(Paris: Éditions Seuil, 1990); Giorgos Kallis, *Limits: Why Malthus Was Wrong and
Why Environmentalists Should Care* (Stanford, CA: Stanford University Press,
2019); Barbara Muraca, *Gut leben: Eine Gesellschaft jenseits des Wachstums*
(Berlin: Wagenbach, 2014); Viviana Asara, Emanuele Profumi, and Giorgos
Kallis, 'Degrowth, Democracy and Autonomy', *Environmental Values* 22, no. 2
(2013): 217–39.

60 Kathi Weeks, *The Problem with Work: Feminism, Marxism, Antiwork
Politics, and Postwork Imaginaries* (Durham, NC: Duke University Press, 2011);
Stefania Barca, *Forces of Reproduction: Notes for a Counter-hegemonic
Anthropocene* (Cambridge: Cambridge University Press, 2020).

61 Amy Allen, 'Rethinking Power', *Hypatia* 13, no. 1 (1998): 21–40. Thanks to
Corinna Dengler for this reference.

Third, degrowth strives to create the conditions of a *good life for all* in a comprehensive sense, searching for a holistic understanding of prosperity, of which material comfort is only one part. Inspired by Latin American concept of *buen vivir*, which was developed on the basis of Indigenous cosmologies in the 2000s, prosperity must be detached from the sphere of economic quantifiability.[62] These other understandings of prosperity include embracing the complexity of human beings as relational beings, overcoming the separation of production and reproduction, and giving more space to needs that are not oriented towards increase and optimization – such as an abundance of time and stable and meaningful relationships.[63] Some concepts that are central to these discussions are resonance, conviviality, and time prosperity. Resonance is a counter-concept to acceleration and alienation and offers a yard-stick for meaningful and good self-world relationships – instead of constantly expanding individual world reach by increasing the number of accessible goods, experiences, and encounters, the focus is on establishing fewer, but stable, axes of resonance.[64] The concept of conviviality, which goes back to Ivan Illich and has since been revived, states that a good life depends not just on social justice, but also on a thriving coexistence and collective self-determination in everyday life. It means an attitude of social interaction, which is not defined by consumption and goods but by mutual respect and appreciation of social relationships (see also section 3.3).[65] Finally, the concept of time

62 Alberto Acosta, *Buen vivir: Vom Recht auf ein gutes Leben*, trans. Birte Pedersen (Munich: Oekom, 2015); Kothari et al., *Pluriverse*.

63 Barca, *Forces of Reproduction*.

64 To provide a glimpse of what this could feel like, Hartmut Rosa refers to, for example, intensive friendships and experiences of 'flow' while doing a satisfying activity, or encounters with nature in which the self feels connected to the world in a 'responsive relationship'. Hartmut Rosa, *Resonance: A Sociology of Our Relationship to the World* (Cambridge: Polity Press, 2019), chapter 4; see also Tim Jackson, *Post Growth: Life after Capitalism* (Cambridge: Polity, 2021), chapter 6.

65 Frank Adloff, *Gifts of Cooperation, Mauss and Pragmatism* (London: Routledge, 2017); Les Convivialistes, *Convivialist Manifesto: A Declaration of Independence* (Duisburg: Käte Hamburger Kolleg and Centre for Global Cooperation Research, 2014).

prosperity points out that in accelerated societies time becomes a scarce resource and that struggles for more self-determined time beyond the dictates of markets, consumption, and competition must supplement struggles for higher wages for the poorest (and less income and wealth for the richest).[66] Through these approaches, degrowth debates have attempted to develop new forms of prosperity beyond a work- and consumption-centred mode of living – concepts that resonate with what has recently been described as 'alternative hedonism.'[67]

Growth independence

A degrowth society is a society that, through a democratic process, transforms its institutions and infrastructures so that they are *not dependent on growth and continuous expansion* for their functioning. This is the third dimension of the degrowth vision. It is based on the various forms of growth critique that show how fundamentally today's societies are intertwined with growth and the expansion of their material, institutional, and social infrastructures. Degrowth aims to overcome all structural dependencies on growth, intensification, acceleration, and escalation. Thus degrowth does not shy away from one of the most fundamental dilemmas of our time: even as growth is not sustainable, non- or zero growth under current conditions is disastrous.[68]

There are four main kinds of growth dependencies: material infrastructures and technical systems; social institutions; mental infrastructures; and, finally, the economic system. At all these levels, there are institutions and infrastructures that are growth-dependent, that, in other words, are in a fundamental crisis without continuous expansion,

---

66 Konzeptwerk Neue Ökonomie, *Zeitwohlstand: Wie wir anders arbeiten, nachhaltig wirtschaften und besser leben* (Munich: Oekom, 2013); Hartmut Rosa, *Social Acceleration: A New Theory of Modernity* (New York: Columbia University Press, 2015); Giorgos Kallis et al., ' "Friday Off": Reducing Working Hours in Europe', *Sustainability* 5, no. 4 (2013): 1545–67.

67 Kate Soper, *Post-Growth Living: For an Alternative Hedonism* (London: Verso, 2020).

68 Hartmut Rosa, Stephan Lessenich, and Klaus Dörre, *Sociology, Capitalism, Critique* (London: Verso, 2015); Jackson, *Prosperity without Growth*.

intensification, and acceleration; and there are institutions and infra-structures – often the same ones – that drive growth, generating more expansion.

For example, the social institution of schooling in its current form is dependent on growth in so far as it is financed by tax revenues and historically emerged from bourgeois efforts to formalize education. Without redistribution, schools decline in times of recession, to which governments often react with budget cuts and austerity meas-ures. The school is also central to the production of the mental infra-structures of the competitive and performance-oriented growth subject. In a degrowth society, however, it could also – on the basis of growth-independent financing or supply – develop into a free space in which empowering education, cooperative autonomy, and demo-cratic learning are at the centre. There is already a kernel of this possibility within the existing schooling systems, which could be extended. As this example shows, the four levels are interwoven, although we will discuss them separately below.

First – as the critique of industrialism emphasizes – material infra-structures (the automobile with all its infrastructure, container ship-ping, energy and heat networks, deep-sea drilling for oil, distribution and disposal structures for waste, and so on) as well as large-scale, highly complex mega-projects and systems (for example, the aviation industry, nuclear power, global digital means of communication, genet-ically modified life) create path dependencies and growth imperatives. These will continue to require – not least due to their increasing complexity – material, energetic, and technological expansion in the future.[69] The material reality of infrastructures (road, energy, or supply networks) is more difficult to change than institutions or mentalities and follows other temporalities; individualizing demands or simply thinking and acting differently have their limits. From a degrowth perspective, it is necessary to repoliticize technological and infrastruc-tural developments, by slowing them down with moratoria (for

---

69 Mauro Bonaiuti, *The Great Transition* (London: Routledge, 2014); see also Steffen Lange and Tilman Santarius, *Smart Green World? Making Digitalization Work for Sustainability* (Abingdon: Routledge, 2020).

example, on mega-projects) and by replacing them with or transforming them into convivial and growth-independent techniques and procedures.[70] For example, geoengineering processes aimed at combating climate change by growing biomass over large areas, burning it, and pressing the released CO_2 into the soil (BECCS) create technologically growth-oriented path dependencies and often require globally hierarchical and undemocratic forms of management. In contrast, biodiversity regions, reforestation projects carried out by local communities, regenerative farming, or cargo bike cooperatives not only make sense in terms of climate policy, but also create independence from growth and strengthen collective autonomy. We will discuss more policies in chapter 5.

Second, a large number of social institutions are directly or indirectly dependent on economic growth. Key social, political, and economic institutions – labour, goods, and financial markets, pension and health care provision, public services, stable governments – are each in their own specific ways fundamentally and existentially dependent on continuous economic growth.[71] That is why in every economic crisis, when growth falters – such as the 2007 financial crisis or the aftermath of the COVID-19 lockdowns – these institutions are put under immense pressure, often causing rising unemployment, supply chain problems, cuts in pensions and other public services, and rising public debt.[72] A prerequisite for a degrowth society would therefore be to restructure all relevant social institutions in such a way that they can function without economic growth, or to create new growth-independent institutions that can fulfil the functions of the existing ones. Many

70 Ivan Illich, *Tools for Conviviality* (London: Marion Boyars, 2001); Christian Kerschner et al., 'Degrowth and Technology: Towards Feasible, Viable, Appropriate and Convivial Imaginaries', *Journal of Cleaner Production* 197 (2018): 1619–36; Unmüßig, Fatheuer, and Fuhr, *Critique of the Green Economy*.

71 Kallis, *Degrowth*; Irmi Seidl and Angelika Zahrnt, *Postwachstumsgesellschaft: Neue Konzepte für die Zukunft* (Marburg: Metropolis, 2010); Jackson, *Prosperity without Growth*.

72 On the effects of these two crises, see Adam Tooze, *Crashed: How a Decade of Financial Crises Changed the World* (London: Penguin UK, 2018); Adam Tooze, *Shutdown: How Covid Shook the World's Economy* (London: Penguin UK, 2021).

of the core political demands of the degrowth debate lie precisely in this area.

Third, in addition to built and institutional infrastructures, 'mental infrastructures' – the mostly unquestioned cultural patterns and attitudes, the 'motorways in our heads' – are also subject to a logic of increase and acceleration.[73] This ranges from the 'myth of growth' (Tim Jackson) that 'more' is always 'better', to logics inscribed in patterns of work and consumption to competition-based subjectivities (such as those of the 'entrepreneurial self') to hierarchical human– nature relationships associated with the imperial mode of living.[74] Degrowth thinkers are thus concerned with liberating the imaginary – in other words, with liberating socially accepted and widely shared ideas, convictions, and values, the self-understanding of a society that holds it together and legitimizes its structures, institutions, and practices.[75] On the one hand, this requires an examination of alternative concepts of prosperity that make it possible to overcome the hegemony of the growth paradigm, to make concrete utopias imaginable through the 'education of desire'.[76] On the other hand, the liberation of the imaginary also requires other modes of subjectivation – other ways of understanding and positioning oneself in the world and in relation to others – based on relationality, conviviality, and resonance.[77] The discussion

73 Harald Welzer, *Mental Infrastructures: How Growth Entered the World and Our Souls*, trans. John Hayduska (Berlin: Heinrich Böll Foundation, 2011).

74 Jackson, *Post Growth*; Brand and Wissen, *Limits to Capitalist Nature*; Dennis Eversberg, 'Growth Regimes and Visions of the Good Life: Why Capitalism Will Not Deliver', in *The Good Life beyond Growth: New Perspectives*, ed. Harmut Rosa and Christoph Henning (New York: Routledge, 2018), 95–106; Frank Trentmann, *Empire of Things: How We Became a World of Consumers, from the Fifteenth Century to the Twenty-First* (New York: Harper Perennial, 2017).

75 Cornelius Castoriadis, *The Imaginary Institution of Society* (Cambridge, MA: MIT Press, 1998); Serge Latouche, *Farewell to Growth*, trans. David Macey (Cambridge: Polity Press, 2009).

76 Barbara Muraca, 'Concrete Utopia as Education of Desire: The Role of Social Experiments in the Transformation of the Social Imaginary', paper presented at the International Conference of the European Society for Ecological Economics, 2015, University of Leeds, UK.

77 Adloff, *Gifts of Cooperation*; Rosa, *Resonance*.

about limiting or abolishing advertising has also been one of the core demands of degrowth discourse from the outset.[78]

Fourth, the basic structures of the economy are dependent on growth. On the one hand, the dependence of the economy on growth is located in sub-elements of the economic system: in the fact that unemployment rises without growth; in the debt-based monetary system, or in debt in general, which actually involves claims dependent on the future expansion of value and therefore on growth; in international competition between companies or states, which forces them to invest continuously in production and thereby to promote the extended reproduction of capital; or in the compulsion of companies to expand, which is caused by the division of labour, competitive improvements in productivity, and the financing by profit-oriented investment capital or shareholders.[79] Other analyses, based primarily on the critique of capitalism, but also on South–North and feminist growth critiques, point out that the functioning of capitalism itself is structurally dependent on growth and that capitalist societies can only stabilize themselves dynamically – that is, through growth. Therefore, they argue, a better future beyond growth is necessarily post-capitalist. From this perspective, questions about non-capitalist forms of economic activity such as commoning and participatory planning or other post-capitalist utopias come to the fore.[80]

78 Denis Bayon, Fabrice Flipo, and François Schneider, *La décroissance: Dix questions pour comprendre et débattre* (Paris: Editions La Découverte, 2010); Latouche, *Farewell to Growth*.

79 Eric Pineault, 'From Provocation to Challenge: Degrowth, Capitalism and the Prospect of "Socialism without Growth"; A Commentary on Giorgios Kallis', *Capitalism Nature Socialism* 30, no. 2 (2018): 1–16; Kallis, *Degrowth*.

80 D'Alisa, Demaria, and Kallis, *Degrowth: A Vocabulary for a New Era*; Helfrich and Bollier, *Free, Fair, and Alive*; Burkhart, Schmelzer, and Treu, *Degrowth in Movement(s)*; Pineault, 'From Provocation to Challenge'; Ariel Salleh, *Ecofeminism as Politics: Nature, Marx and the Postmodern* (London: Zed Books, 2017); Julie Katherine Gibson-Graham, *A Postcapitalist Politics* (Minneapolis: University of Minnesota Press, 2006).

4.3. Why degrowth is desirable

We have argued that degrowth is a vision for a radically different society and economy that, though comprising different currents, shares
many common principles. However, while imagining a different society
may in itself be a productive exercise, the key question remains: How
do we make it real? The sociologist Erik Olin Wright has developed
three criteria for evaluating social alternatives: *desirability*, *viability*,
and *achievability*.[81] In this chapter, we have been concerned primarily
with the *desirability* of a degrowth society – as represented in the three
core principles that we argue constitute degrowth, which incorporate
the critiques of growth discussed in the first half of the book into a
comprehensive vision for a future society. While degrowth is quite
strong in presenting the necessity for change (critique) and thus the
desirability of the degrowth vision, the questions of *viability* and *achievability* are just as important: How do we know whether it will work, and
how can we get there? These are questions we explore in the following
two chapters. In chapter 5, we discuss the kinds of policies that would
make degrowth a viable proposal, giving a coherent picture of how a
degrowth society could look like and function. In chapter 6, which
focuses on transformation, we present a theory of change that can link
the required bottom-up social movements with the large-scale policy
changes needed to make degrowth concrete. Though the scale of the
challenge is immense, we believe our proposal offers broad outlines for
ways in which the degrowth imaginary can be made concrete.

---

81 Wright, *Envisioning Real Utopias*.

5

Pathways to degrowth

The true test of whether a utopia is worth fighting for is whether it could actually work. Indeed, this is one of the most common dismissals of utopianism when people are presented with it: 'That's a very nice idea, but it will never happen.' Because, as we are often told, though capitalism may have its faults, it is the only system that is proven to work.

Yet while capitalism, with its engine of growth, is leading us straight to disaster, ample research suggests a degrowth system would be viable. The economics of degrowth is not a pipe dream: in fact, though there is always room for more research, there is also mounting evidence that it could actually work.[1] Degrowth, as we discussed last chapter, is only

---

1 For example, macro-economic studies refute the assertion that only growing economies can be stable and generate welfare. And they suggest that an economy with the contours outlined in degrowth debates is not just desirable but also feasible. According to these studies, economies can be stable – even if GDP decreases and production is restructured to such an extent that ecological boundaries are not crossed – when social structures and institutions are transformed. See Tim Jackson, *Prosperity without Growth: Economics for a Finite Planet* (London: Earthscan, 2016); Giorgos Kallis, *Degrowth* (Newcastle upon Tyne: Agenda Publishing, 2018); Giorgos Kallis et al., 'Research on Degrowth', *Annual Review of Environment and Resources* 43 (2018): 291–316; Steffen Lange, *Macroeconomics without Growth: Sustainable Economies in Neoclassical,*

viable if it is paired with a diverse set of policies that make it sustainable, stable, and just. The good news is that these policies would, in themselves, make life a lot better. Of course, just like there is no single, unified vision of a degrowth utopia, there is also not a single path to get there, but several paths, often crossing. And when it comes to the world of policy proposals, single solutions are often fetishized as panaceas. In contrast, we know that degrowth will require experimenting with many different policies and actions to work together – from governmental policy platforms to new economic practices.

While visions of a degrowth society might appear open-ended, unresolved, politically contested, and sometimes even contradictory, degrowth takes the various growth critiques as its starting point and is based on the three elements of a degrowth vision developed in the last chapter: the globally just reduction of social metabolism while at the same time striving for social justice, self-determination, and prioritizing the good life by means of transforming social institutions and infrastructures to become independent of growth. With this goal in sight, degrowth proponents elaborate political proposals and platforms. Serge Latouche, for example, described an 'Eight R Programme' (named after eight key concepts in French, roughly translated in English as reevaluate, reconceptualize, restructure, redistribute, relocalize, reduce, reuse, and recycle). However, there are many proposals that are not as abstract. The Research & Degrowth network developed 'Ten policy proposals for the new left' which are far more concrete. But why limit ourselves to ten? One review article by Inês Cosme et al. evaluating degrowth policy proposals found a total of twenty-seven policy tools in the literature, with proposals from the reduction of environmental impacts to the

Keynesian and Marxian Theories (Marburg: Metropolis, 2018); Peter Victor, Managing without Growth: Slower by Design, Not Disaster (Cheltenham: Edward Elgar, 2018); Daniel W. O'Neill et al., 'A Good Life for All within Planetary Boundaries', Nature Sustainability 1, no. 2 (2018): 88–95; Giorgos Kallis, Christian Kerschner, and Joan Martínez-Alier, 'The Economics of Degrowth', Ecological Economics 84 (2012): 172–80; Lukas Hardt and Daniel W. O'Neill, 'Ecological Macroeconomic Models: Assessing Current Developments', Ecological Economics 134 (2017): 198–211; Giorgos Kallis et al., 'Research on Degrowth', Annual Review of Environment and Resources 43 (2018): 291–316.

214 The Future Is Degrowth

redistribution of wealth and prioritization of well-being. Timothée Parrique, in his extensive research, found a total of 140 policy tools or 'instruments' (as opposed to policy goals or objectives) in party platforms, scientific literature, and opinion pieces related to the degrowth movement.[2]

Clearly, degrowth is characterized by a lively debate on concrete proposals for transformation. Even if many proposals differ greatly, they crystallize around a common nucleus. In their entirety, these proposals can be regarded as typical of the central thrust of degrowth policy: they are 'non-reformist reforms' (per André Gorz), or proposals for a 'revolutionary Realpolitik' (per Rosa Luxemburg) – reformist measures that increase popular power and provoke a destabilization and reorientation of growth-oriented structures. In addition, it must be noted that, often, social movements and thinkers tend to focus on one policy above others. The movement for basic income has taken this route today: becoming a central demand for transforming the economy as a whole. However, by and large, degrowth proponents prefer a diverse policy platform and tend to approach the issue more holistically. This is because focusing on a single policy tends to minimize the amount of change needed in the whole system while failing to hedge against the possible negative effects of that policy taken in isolation. For example, if a basic income were to be implemented without further policy changes, it is likely that this would further entrench class and labour divisions between citizens of a country and migrants, who cannot access such policies. It could, furthermore, actually increase unsustainable consumption – and would not solve the alienation of labour in itself. Finally, a basic income, within patriarchy, could further push women out of the sphere of wage labour, as they may spend much of their time focusing on care work and housework instead of pursuing a

---

2 Inês Cosme, Rui Santos, and Daniel W. O'Neil, 'Assessing the Degrowth Discourse: A Review and Analysis of Academic Degrowth Policy Proposals', *Journal of Cleaner Production* 149 (2017): 321–34; Timothée Parrique, *The Political Economy of Degrowth: Economics and Finance* (Clermont: Université Clermont Auvergne, 2019), chapter 8; Giorgos Kallis, 'Yes, We Can Prosper without Growth: Ten Policy Proposals for the New Left', Commondreams.org, 28 January 2015.

profession. All this changes if a basic income is combined with other degrowth policies. So, think of these degrowth proposals as a well-balanced cocktail as opposed to asking for a single policy 'on the rocks'.

In the following, we focus on some of the most characteristic policy proposals – keeping in mind that these proposals are still incomplete at this stage, that they are, rather, a tentative attempt to think economies differently. Rather than summarizing, in detail and exhaustively, each proposal that has been put forward, we group these proposals into six clusters, each having a specific trajectory that we think is particularly characteristic of the degrowth perspective: (1) the democratization of the economy, or, the strengthening of the commons, a solidarity-based economy, and economic democracy; (2) social security, redistribution, and caps on income and wealth; (3) convivial and democratic technology; (4) the redistribution and revaluation of labour; (5) the equitable dismantling and reconstruction of production; and (6) international solidarity. We also do not want to give the impression that policy alone should be the sole driver of change. That is why, in the next chapter, we take on degrowth's *achievability*: not just the kinds of policies that would make it viable but the ways in which the combination of collective action, grassroots change, and policy reforms could work together to make it a reality.

5.1. Democratization, solidarity economy, and commoning

Degrowth stands for a new post-capitalist economy. It is – to put it in a nutshell – diverse, social-ecological, democratic and participatory, cooperative, needs-oriented, open but regionally anchored, and oriented towards overcoming the distinction between production and reproduction. Since these multiple economic activities have little to do with 'the economy', as it was invented by economists in the 1930s as a sphere of market relations (see chapter 2), degrowth is sometimes associated with an 'escape from the economy' – an invitation to abandon economistic thinking.[3] Nonetheless, core degrowth policy proposals

---

3 Valérie Fournier, 'Escaping from the Economy: The Politics of Degrowth', *International Journal of Sociology and Social Policy* 28, no. 11 (2008): 528–45.

deal with the transformation of the economy, aiming above all to orient economic activities towards concrete needs and the common good, to democratize it and to shape it independently of growth, without exploiting people and nature. To make this possible, economic decisions must be seen as *political* problems. This means putting the economy in the hands of people and involving more and more people in key decisions – such as the producers in a factory, the neighbours of a farm, the users of a community-owned power plant, or the care recipients in retirement homes deciding what is produced, how to relate to the environment and other economic agents, which services are needed, and how work is organized. Seeing economic decisions as political problems also means overcoming the idea of there being a universal yard-stick to measure all activities, whether that is GDP, money, or any other indicator, or the hope of delegating efficient production to algorithms (even though they might be extremely useful as tools), and consequently to collectively deliberate about and plan societies' economic life based on a multiplicity of relevant aspects, ranging from work (alienating or empowering) to needs (necessary or not so necessary) to resources and technology (see below), and so on.

Within degrowth discourse, the economy is often thought of as *diverse*. A degrowth economy aims at enabling different economic activities, actors, and logics – from cooperative to public, from commons to planning – to coexist as an economic pluriverse.[4] This is why degrowth is also linked to the many initiatives and movements which seek to appropriate the economy from below: from collectively administered common property, to the solidarity economy and community-supported agriculture (see section 4.4). It is argued that these initiatives, which are currently under immense pressure from competition and neoliberal markets, must not only be defended, supported, and strengthened but also that degrowth policies must create the social conditions for their flourishing and expansion. Three

4 J. K. Gibson-Graham, *A Postcapitalist Politics* (Minneapolis: University of Minnesota Press, 2006); Ashish Kothari et al., eds., *Pluriverse: A Post-development Dictionary* (New Delhi: Tulika Books and Authorsupfront, 2019); Pablo Solón et al., *Systemic Alternatives: Vivir bien, Degrowth, Commons, Ecofeminism, Rights of Mother Earth and Deglobalisation* (La Paz: Fundación Solón, 2017).

concepts are particularly relevant here: the commons, the solidarity economy, and economic democracy or participatory planning.

The defence of existing commons and the expansion of production methods based on commons principles can be seen as a central component of a degrowth economy. Commoning is based neither on competition nor on exploitation and growth; the commons are those social practices through which self-organized communities govern certain goods, resources, or territories, according to self-designed rules and institutions. From the analysis of thousands of existing and historical commons, Elinor Ostrom identified a number of principles that distinguish successful commons – patterns of commoning that are highly relevant to structuring a degrowth alternative.[5] The basic idea is to manage shared resources outside of markets based on money, competition, and centralized and hierarchical states, according to participatory and democratic rules and for the benefit of all concerned. Projects such as Wikipedia (where the world's largest encyclopedia was created according to the principle of contribution rather than exchange), community-supported agriculture (where farmers manage a farm together with a group of consumers, who bear the costs jointly and in solidarity and distribute the proceeds among all), or the millions of examples of traditional commons that have existed for hundreds of years all around the world (in which communities manage their land, forests, water, and so on) show that this can work. 'Commoning' refers to the different forms of negotiation and the more permanent, autonomously managed institutions – depending on the type of goods available – that govern the access, use, management, and permanent conservation of these goods.[6]

---

5 The design principles of successful public property management were developed by Ostrom and her students and include rules in the following eight areas: define group boundaries, match rules governing commons to local needs, ensure that those affected by rules can participate in making them, ensure that authorities respect the rights of community members to make rules, develop a system to monitor the behavior of users, use sanctions for those violating rules developed by the community, provide accessible means to resolve conflict, build responsibility for governing commons at different scales (local, municipal, legal, etc.). See also Silke Helfrich and David Bollier, *Free, Fair, and Alive: The Insurgent Power of the Commons* (Gabriola Island, BC: New Society Publishers, 2019).

6 Helfrich and Bollier, *Free, Fair, and Alive*; D'Alisa, Demaria, and Kallis,

The debate over the commons has gained considerable momentum due to the omnipresence of digital data, since such data can only be fit into the private property logic necessary for capitalist exploitation processes with great technical effort. For this reason, some theorists also assume that the currently progressing digitalization of productive areas (and subsequent falling marginal costs) already bears the seed of post-capitalist relations in itself. This, they argue, must be developed through suitable political conditions.[7] More recently, crypto-technology advocates have argued that the rise of cryptocurrencies heralds the end of centralized banking by offering a democratic, decentralized alternative. However, at present, we can also observe steadily increasing efforts to contain or integrate digital commons into capitalist exploitation processes, as well as to use these same digital commons as means of surveillance, propaganda, and disinformation campaigns. This concerns both a commercial reorganization of areas of life such as private housing or car traffic through profit-oriented digital platforms (such as Airbnb and Uber) or non-profit digital networking such as the development of apps for neighbourhood assistance – both of which function as a band-aid for state failures.[8] With regard to crypto-technology, most increasingly appear to be used as means for speculation

Degrowth; Kallis, *Degrowth*; Aggelos Varvarousis and Giorgos Kallis, 'Commoning against the Crisis', in Manuel Castells et al., *Another Economy Is Possible: Culture and Economy in a Time of Crisis* (Cambridge: Polity, 2017), 128–59; Corinna Burkhart, Matthias Schmelzer, and Nina Treu, eds., *Degrowth in Movement(s): Exploring Pathways for Transformation* (Winchester: Zer0, 2020); Kallis et al., 'Research on Degrowth'.

7 Paul Mason, *Postcapitalism: A Guide to Our Future* (London: Macmillan, 2016); Jeremy Rifkin, *The Third Industrial Revolution: How Lateral Power Is Transforming Energy, the Economy, and the World* (New York: Macmillan, 2011).

8 Michael Bauwens, Vasilis Kostakis, and Alex Pazaitis, *Peer-to-Peer: The Commons Manifesto* (London: Westminster University Press, 2018); Silke van Dyk, 'Post-wage Politics and the Rise of Community Capitalism', *Work, Employment and Society* 32, no. 3 (2018): 528–45; Steffen Lange and Tilman Santarius, *Smart Green World? Making Digitalization Work for Sustainability* (Abingdon: Routledge, 2020); Lucia Argüelles, Isabelle Anguelovski, and Elizabeth Dinnie, 'Power and Privilege in Alternative Civic Practices: Examining Imaginaries of Change and Embedded Rationalities in Community Economies', *Geoforum* 86 (2017): 30–41.

on new forms of capital, involving the further enclosure of digital commons and relationships, rather than offering more democratically managed financial tools. From the perspective of degrowth, it is therefore important to defend and expand commons that are oriented towards the common good – based, for example, on the experience of the occupations of the Indignados in Spain or the solidarity clinics in Greece – and to promote the commonization of the economy (instead of the dominant forms of economic and digital management, or the enclosure of the commons through speculation on cryptocurrencies and digital spaces such as the 'metaverse').[9]

Many degrowth proponents postulate that smaller, social, and cooperatively organized forms of economic activity – especially cooperatives and other smaller companies oriented towards the common good – are more likely to be able to produce in a participatory manner and without the compulsion to achieve economic growth, since they are not forced to accumulate and compete by investors and shareholders. Accordingly, they should account for a much larger share of total production in a degrowth economy.[10] Central here is the movement of cooperative or collective enterprises, which can be described under the framework of a 'solidarity economy' and which work according to the core values of 'cooperation instead of competition' and 'purpose before profit' – ranging from small self-organized collectives all around the world to large companies such as the Venezuelan association of Cecosesola with a total of more than 20,000 members.

Some see potential for a degrowth economy in the combination of cooperative principles with digital platforms in order to counter the monopoly of commercial platform providers. Demands include reforming cooperative law to support and simplify paperwork for cooperative start-ups, as well as the right for workers to take over production sites in the event of threatened plant closures. Others argue for the development of cryptocurrencies that do not function as capital assets, and therefore

---

9   Varvarousis and Kallis, 'Commoning against the Crisis'.

10   Kallis, *Degrowth*; Niko Paech, *Liberation from Excess: The Road to a Post-growth Society* (Munich: Oekom, 2012).

resist speculation.[11] Nevertheless, the problem of a market driven by competition remains. This means that changes in wider social conditions are also important. The concept of the 'economy for the common good' aims at expanding socio-ecologically oriented entrepreneurial activity. According to this proposal, companies should submit comprehensive public-interest balances in which their activities are evaluated according to social, ecological, democratic, and economic criteria as well as other public-interest criteria, to be determined democratically. In addition to transparency, this creates the basis for giving companies with good balance sheets preferential taxes and regulations. When such a policy is combined with other regulations – such as a ban on companies driven primarily by shareholders' interests and large multinational corporations, the favouring of smaller and democratic enterprises, a different monetary order, and global trade rules based on solidarity – enterprises that least serve the democratically determined common good would continuously be pushed out of business, making space for the emergence of a non-capitalist market economy.[12]

In addition to the development of the commons and the solidarity economy, reference is repeatedly made to concepts of economic democracy and the kinds of democratic investment and management originally developed in the trade union environment.[13] This also includes what some call the 're-municipalization' of basic services

11 Sam Dallyn and Fabian Frenzel, 'The Challenge of Building a Scalable Postcapitalist Commons: The Limits of FairCoin as a Commons-Based Cryptocurrency', *Antipode* 53, no. 3 (2021): 859–83.

12 Christian Felber, *Change Everything: Creating an Economy for the Common Good* (London: Zed Books, 2019); see also Burkhart, Schmelzer, and Treu, *Degrowth in Movement(s)*, 176–87; Dagmar Embshoff, Clarita Müller-Plantenberg, and Guiliana Georgi, 'Solidarity Economy: Paths to Transformation', in *Degrowth in Movement(s): Exploring Pathways for Transformation*, ed. Corinna Burkhart, Matthias Schmelzer, and Nina Treu (Winchester: Zer0, 2020), 344; Bauwens, Kostakis, and Pazaitis, *Peer-to-Peer*.

13 Kali Akuno and Ajamu Nangwaya, eds., *Jackson Rising: The Struggle for Economic Democracy and Black Self-Determination in Jackson, Mississippi* (Ottawa: Daraja Press, 2017); Marjorie Kelly and Ted Howard, *The Making of a Democratic Economy: How to Build Prosperity for the Many, Not the Few* (Oakland, CA: Berrett-Koehler, 2019).

– that is, putting utilities such as water and electricity into the hands of municipalities, at which scale they can be more transparent and democratically run.[14] However, the debate about these alternative frameworks for society as a whole is only just developing, especially with regard to their connections to degrowth. More broadly, economic democracy aims to contain and dismantle the high concentration of economic power in a few corporations and their connections to the state. It should enable all people to participate in economic activities and decisions as they do in other political decisions. This involves both economic regulations of all kinds (such as democratic deliberation on the question of which unsustainable economic activities should be phased out and how) and the support and expansion of the solidarity economy and commons. In addition, economic democracy is about the reappropriation of private enterprises into collective forms of ownership, abolishing decision-making hierarchies in the workplace, and encouraging collective self-determination in society more broadly.[15] This could be advanced by limiting the ownership of the means of production to a certain maximum size. The larger companies get, they would be placed under more and more democratic control, and beyond a certain size they would be transferred to common ownership.[16] In addition, the principles of a participatory economy ('parecon') offer guidelines for a further deepening of the democratization processes of the economy, starting first within companies and then expanding out to the economy as a whole. The participatory economy is a comprehensive vision for an anarchist-inspired, non-hierarchical economy with participatory planning from below. It proposes that democratic assemblies and councils of producers and consumers would plan economic activities and a distribution

---

14 Satoko Kishimoto, Lavinia Steinfort, and Olivier Petitjean, eds., *The Future Is Public: Towards Democratic Ownership of Public Services* (Amsterdam: Transnational Institute, 2020).

15 Bengi Akbulut and Fikret Adaman, 'The Ecological Economics of Economic Democracy', *Ecological Economics* 176 (2020): 106750; Nadia Johanisova and Stephan Wolf, 'Economic Democracy: A Path for the Future?', *Futures* 44, no. 6 (Spring 2012): 562–70.

16 Felber, *Change Everything*.

of the economy's administrative and management tasks among all in order to counteract the emergence of a bureaucratic or managerial class with more knowledge and power.[17]

One question that often comes up when discussing these wide-ranging policies is how this would all be funded. A central starting point is that financial institutions would themselves be radically transformed. Rather than being controlled by the owners of capital, society's economic surplus would be democratically managed. This involves not only the question of democratically allocating key investments, but also collectively deciding, based on goals of well-being, how to manage pension funds and other financial institutions, the investments of banks and private companies, how to spend public money, and *dépense* (expenditure; see chapter 3).[18] This is necessary because the conversion to a sustainable, just degrowth economy would require massive investments, especially in the transition phase. For example, significant investments would be needed in institutions and infrastructures that enable a socially just life for all (ecological agriculture, decentralized renewable energies, ecological housing, collective mobility, etc.), in projects for adapting to and mitigating climate change and ecological destruction, as well as in financial transfers from the Global North to the Global South to offset historically accumulated climate debt. Since these necessary investments cannot be generated automatically and sufficiently through market mechanisms, neither today nor in the foreseeable future, a strengthening of public investments and a new democratic monetary system, including public control of central banks, are necessary.[19] This is to be supported by democratically controlled cooperative banks.[20] Restructuring banking and systems of finance also

17 Michael Albert, *Parecon: Life after Capitalism* (London: Verso, 2004).

18 Stefania Barca, 'The Labor(s) of Degrowth', *Capitalism Nature Socialism* 30, no. 2 (2019): 207–16; Jackson, *Prosperity without Growth*; Jason Hickel, *Less Is More: How Degrowth Will Save the World* (London: William Heinemann, 2020).

19 Jason Hickel, 'Degrowth and MMT: A Thought Experiment, jasonhickel .org, 10 September 2020; Stephanie Kelton, *The Deficit Myth: Modern Monetary Theory and the Birth of the People's Economy* (New York: PublicAffairs, 2020).

20 Jackson, *Prosperity without Growth*; Tim Jackson, *Post Growth: Life after Capitalism* (Cambridge: Polity, 2021); Kallis, *Degrowth*; Matthias Schmelzer and

means challenging the power of private and transnational lending agencies and financial institutions, ensuring that governments can spend freely on public infrastructure (for example, building on the proposals of modern monetary theory, or MMT, which is also at the core of radical Green New Deal proposals).[21] In line with this, and to make all of this possible, it is also important to radically shrink, reorganize, and democratically control financial markets and institutions in order to put them at the service of people and their economic interests. Giorgos Kallis and colleagues thus propose 'changing money systems by limiting the domain of general purpose money, creating positive (or public) money, forbidding private banks to create new money through loans, and supporting community currencies and time-banks'.[22]

Restructuring financial institutions is one thing, but there are also other possibilities for funding the transition. First, abandoning subsidies for and taxing harmful industries, not least the fossil fuel industry, would generate significant sources in the short term. The withdrawal of funding from the military industrial complex – which emits more greenhouse gases than most countries and drives imperial, uneven relations worldwide – would open up massive opportunities for reinvestment as well as relieve pressure on other countries to funnel resources into national defence instead of a just transition. Second, as explained in the next section, taxing extreme wealth would also raise significant amounts of funding. Third, while financial capital would eventually shrink in the aggregate, *kinds of wealth* would eventually be diversified, for example, through the promotion of local currencies and the prioritization of reproductive labour and leisure activities. As a result, though switching to a degrowth economy would initially take significant capital, eventually it would lead to an economy where capital no longer dominates and fades out – in other words, to post-capitalism.[23]

Alexis Passadakis, *Postwachstum: Krise, ökologische Grenzen, soziale Reche* (Hamburg: VSA-Verlag, 2011).

21 Ann Pettifor, *The Case for the Green New Deal* (London: Verso, 2019); Kelton, *The Deficit Myth*.

22 Giorgos Kallis et al., *The Case for Degrowth* (Cambridge: Polity Press, 2020), 82.

23 Claudio Cattaneo and Aaron Vansintjan, *A Wealth of Possibilities:*

It is clear, however, that the question of financial restructuring and funding the transition certainly requires further exploration, both through macro-economic modelling and real-world experimentation.

Beyond democratizing the economy, there is also the question of democratizing *politics*. Electoral representation is seen by many as insufficiently democratic. Our representatives have little accountability to voters once they are elected into office, and politicians are often in a revolving door with industry, being offered positions on boards and as CEOs of companies as soon as their term is over. Systems of governance are also highly discriminatory, systematically prioritizing persons with gender, class, or race privileges to leadership positions. By and large, proposals for transforming a highly corrupt and alienating political system involve either ensuring that representatives are accountable to their constituents by developing institutions that support deliberative, participatory politics or replacing electoralism altogether. Proposals include, for example, instituting citizen assemblies and women's councils; participatory budgeting and taxation; forbidding politicians to take up positions in industry following their term; or even mandating 'sortition', in which citizens are nominated and selected in lots as representatives – reducing the professionalization of politics entirely. One proposal to eliminate electoralism while still enabling a scaled-up trans-local system of governance is democratic confederalism, where local citizen assemblies nominate a recallable delegate to take part in regional and national assemblies – a system currently practised in northern Syria, inspired by Abdullah Öcalan's political philosophy.[24]

Alternatives to Growth (Brussels: Green European Foundation, 2016); Hickel, 'Degrowth and MMT'.

24 Gianpaolo Baiocchi, *Militants and Citizens: The Politics of Participatory Democracy in Porto Alegre* (Stanford, CA: Stanford University Press, 2005); Laura Roth and Kate Shea Baird, 'Municipalism and the Feminization of Politics', Roarmag.org, 2017; Barcelona En Comù, *Fearless Cities: A Guide to the Global Municipalist Movement* (Oxford: New Internationalist Publications, 2019); Claudio Cattaneo and Aaron Vansintjan, *A Wealth of Possibilities: Alternatives to Growth* (Brussels: Green European Foundation, 2016); Abdulla Öcalan, *The Political Thought of Abdullah Öcalan: Kurdistan, Woman's Revolution and Democratic Confederalism* (London: Pluto Press, 2017).

5.2. Social security, redistribution, and caps on income and wealth

In the transformation to a degrowth society, the redistribution of wealth will become fundamentally important. If the traditional and growth-based idea that redistribution is equivalent to the sharing of economic surplus no longer works, then the distribution of income and wealth becomes an explosive issue and there will need to be entirely new mechanisms for furthering equality and guaranteeing social security for all. In other words, because society will no longer be oriented towards the increase of GDP, taxation and money transfers based on the annual surplus generated by economic growth will no longer be viable as the key mechanism for the redistribution of wealth and for financing welfare states. Thus, innovative proposals to create equal access to resources, and ideas for a fundamental transformation and broadening of social security and basic services, have been core degrowth demands from the very beginning. These proposals can substantially improve living conditions for most people.

Alongside other policies that also aim at social justice, such as ecological tax reform or reduction in working hours, which are discussed in later sections, most of these proposals aim at reappropriating and socializing the resources of the rich through effective taxation and income and wealth caps and to withdraw from the market, or decommodify, the supply of goods and services necessary for a good life for all. It is therefore demanded that basic goods and services such as housing, food, water, energy, local transport, and communication, education, and health be made available to all regardless of the current rate of economic growth or individual income. This should take place largely beyond the market, for example, in the form of public access for all, municipal cooperatives, or through commoning.[25] Not coincidentally, public services have the added benefit of having much smaller

---

25 Denis Bayon, Fabrice Flipo, and François Schneider, *La décroissance: Dix questions pour comprendre et débattre* (Paris: Editions La Découverte, 2010); Vincent Liegey et al., *Un projet de décroissance: Manifeste pour une dotation inconditionelly d'autonomie* (Paris: Les Éditions Utopia, 2013).

environmental impacts than their private and individual equivalents: think buses, trains, and tramways instead of cars.[26]

Still, the most popular proposal for the radical restructuring of social security systems remains unconditional basic income. This is a recurring cash transfer for all members of society, awarded without obligation to work or threat of repression, and enough to ensure the full participation in society. Some advocates of a basic income see it explicitly as an entry-point into a degrowth society. Some have also proposed an ecological basic income, where an unconditional basic income is financed by progressively increasing taxes on ecologically harmful consumption, thereby reducing the potentially negative effects of increased ecologically harmful activity.[27]

Beyond the basic income, the French *décroissance* movement has put forward a supplementary proposal called *dotation inconditionelle d'autonomie* – an unconditional gift or endowment of autonomy, which could also be translated as 'unconditional basic services'. As an alternative or supplement to the basic income paid in money, it should grant all people – from birth to death – access to democratically determined basic goods as a social right. These include the right to housing and access to land (a certain number of square metres per person), the right to dignity (a minimum amount of locally produced food and goods for basic needs such as clothing, furniture, and bicycles), access rights to water and energy, the right to mobility (free local transport, reliable long-distance transport), and finally the right to access public services such as health, education, culture, information, childcare, care for the elderly, assistance for people with disabilities, funerals, and so on. All these rights should be guaranteed through processes of the reappropriation and democratization of existing infrastructures.[28] Since this

26 Ian Gough, *Heat, Greed and Human Need: Climate Change, Capitalism and Sustainable Wellbeing* (Cheltenham: Edward Elgar, 2017).

27 Ulrich Schachtschneider, 'How to Green a UBI', contribution to the GTI Forum 'Universal Basic Income: Has the Time Come?', greattransition.org, November 2020; Ulrich Schachtschneider, *Freiheit, Gleichheit, Gelassenheit: Mit dem Ökologischen Grundeinkommen aus der Wachstumsfalle* (Munich: Oekom, 2014).

28 Liegey et al., *Un projet de décroissance*.

would lead to the progressive demonetization of society – a democratically organized public supply beyond the market, and thus a partial exit
from 'the economy' or from money and credit as the medium of media-
tion – this proposal in particular lends itself to a degrowth vision.

Degrowth proposals also aim to radically cap the accumulation of
wealth in the hands of an affluent minority. In 2020, CEOs in the United
States were paid 351 times as much as an average worker – this was up
from just 20 times as much in the 1950s. Globally, the richest 10 per
cent own around 60 to 80 per cent of all existing wealth, leaving less
than 5 per cent for the poorest half of humanity.[29] An unequal distribution of income is not only radically undemocratic from an egalitarian
perspective, but an individual's material footprint is also closely corre-
lated to their available disposable income. Globally, according to
Oxfam, the richest 1 per cent are responsible for over twice as many
carbon emissions as humanity's poorest half. Similar – though somewhat less extreme – inequalities exist within countries.[30]

Ecological justice requires the radical equalization of income and
wealth.[31] As has been argued by Thomas Piketty, among others, curtailing the wealth of the rich might be among the most effective levers to
reducing emissions (think not only private jets, yachts, and energy-
consuming villas, but also investments), and this certainly is a precondition to making society-wide changes acceptable.[32] Thus, degrowth
not only demands a guaranteed basic provisioning or income for all
but, equally importantly, also focuses on the opposite: redistribution

29 Lucas Chancel et al., *World Inequality Report 2022* (Harvard University
Press, 2022).

30 Ibid.; Tim Gore, *Confronting Carbon Inequality: Putting Climate Justice at
the Heart of the COVID-19 Recovery* (London: Oxfam, 2020).

31 Stephanie Moser and Silke Kleinhückelkotten, 'Good Intents, but Low
Impacts: Diverging Importance of Motivational and Socioeconomic Determinants
Explaining Pro-environmental Behavior, Energy Use, and Carbon Footprint',
Environment and Behavior 50, no. 6 (2018): 626–56; Thomas Wiedmann et al.,
'Scientists' Warning on Affluence', *Nature Communications* 11, no. 3107 (2020);
Stephan Lessenich, *Living Well at Others' Expense: The Hidden Costs of Western
Prosperity* (London: Polity, 2019).

32 Thomas Piketty, 'The Illusion of Centrist Ecology', Lemonde.fr, 11 June
2019; Chancel et al., *World Inequality Report*.

aimed at taxing the rich out of existence, reappropriation, and caps on maximum income and wealth. This demand, a key component in the political repertoire of the degrowth spectrum, can be thought of as capping incomes at two, five, or ten times the basic income of society – or, during a transition phase, at x times the minimum income in a specific business or sector. In addition, degrowth also advocates fundamental changes to the way private ownership structures society. These include taxation of inheritances, since these stabilize inequalities and class hierarchies over generations. But there is also a demand to severely restrict income not dependent on labour itself but on ownership of property such as land, buildings, or intellectual property (referred to by economists as 'unearned income') or to abolish them altogether through other ownership structures.[33] In fact, as discussed in the previous section, a degrowth economy requires a very fundamental overhaul of the private property regime to create the conditions in which all have the resources to fully participate in creating welfare for all.

The goal of these proposals is to achieve – in the process of social-ecological transformation and the necessary phaseout of larger parts of the economy – a more egalitarian society, and thus a mode of living based on solidarity that does not transgress ecological boundaries globally. The decisive point in this context is that anyone who wants to achieve a degrowth economy democratically must address extreme distributional injustices and the fear of poverty. The project will only gain political legitimacy if an increase in social justice and equality can really be felt by all.

5.3. Convivial and democratic technology

From the degrowth perspective, the social-ecological transformation means not only the democratization of the economy and a

---

33 Hubert Buch-Hansen and Max Koch, 'Degrowth through Income and Wealth Caps?', *Ecological Economics* 160 (2019): 264–71; Giacomo D'Alisa and Giorgos Kallis. 'Degrowth and the State', *Ecological Economics* 169 (2020): 106486; Schmelzer and Passadakis, *Postwachstum*; Hickel, *Less Is More*.

radical redistribution of resources, but also a profound restructuring of the material-technical basis of society, as called for by the critique of industrialism and technology. A fundamental change in the productive forces of modern industrial societies requires both different technical models and changed ownership structures: as long as the primacy of economic efficiency – rather than criteria of sustainability and utility – dominates design processes and investments in technical infrastructures, this transformation will not succeed.[34] Instead of the general hostility to technology that is often assumed to be a hallmark of degrowth, degrowth is characterized by a differentiated view of technology and the democratization of technological development. The question degrowth puts at the centre is: Which technology should society use? And for what, by whom, how, and how much of it? And who decides? It is also a matter of opposing the myth of unstoppable and independent technological progress, the continuous increase of productivity, and the constant improvement of social productive forces (as it also prevails in large parts of the techno-futuristic left[35]) and about offering a democratic alternative.

How we think of technology influences technological development, the public perception of technology, and thus also research funding and the distribution of subsidies. One attempt to develop a concept of technology for the degrowth debate is the design of *convivial* technology, based on Ivan Illich's concept of 'convivial tools'.[36] While sustainability discourses in the broader sense primarily emphasize the ecological impact of technologies, the concept of convivial technology emphasizes the social and cultural effects of technological development, not only in use but also in the manufacturing process. Examples of spaces that encourage the development of convivial technology today include tool-lending libraries, repair cafés, do-it-yourself spaces, and some

34 Christian Kerschner et al., 'Degrowth and Technology: Towards Feasible, Viable, Appropriate and Convivial Imaginaries', *Journal of Cleaner Production* 197 (2018): 1619–36.

35 See, for example, Mason, *Postcapitalism*.

36 Andrea Vetter, 'The Matrix of Convivial Technology: Assessing Technologies for Degrowth', *Journal of Cleaner Production* 197 (2018): 1778–86.

ecologically and non-commercially oriented hacker spaces, maker spaces, or fab labs.[37]

The concept of convivial technology includes five central values for technoloigical development in the sense of a degrowth perspective: connectedness, accessibility, adaptability, bio-interaction, and appropriateness. *Connectedness* asks in what way a technology shapes the relationships between people, both in terms of its production and use or infrastructure. The majority of technical equipment used today, for example, contains metallic elements that are predominantly mined under exploitative conditions in the Global South. From a degrowth perspective, it is a matter of developing and promoting technologies that are produced under fair conditions, the infrastructures necessary for the operation of which do not destroy local communities, and which are organized on a decentralized and equal basis. *Accessibility* asks where, by whom, and under what circumstances a technology can be (further) developed and used. From the perspective of degrowth, this means, among other things, promoting the technological literacy of women in particular, putting publicly funded technology under open source licenses, and not preventing technological development through profit-driven patents. *Adaptability* is about the extent to which a technique can be used independently, how easily it can be extended and coupled with other techniques, and how this can be facilitated by standardizing basic components. From a degrowth perspective, this encourages longer warranty periods and guaranteed reparability, as well as control over one's own data in digital space, since internet users could then safeguard the information they share across different platforms. *Bio-interaction* means the interaction with the living world: What effects does a technology have on living organisms, whether humans, animals, or plants, as well as on entire ecosystems? Degrowth thinkers are calling for technologies to be considered over their entire life cycles, from resource procurement to disposal, and for the precautionary principle to be applied when assessing the health and environmental risks of new technologies – emphasizing caution, pausing and reviewing

---

37 Burkhart, Schmelzer, and Treu, *Degrowth in Movement(s)*, 154–65, 236–47.

before launching into new innovations that may have far-reaching and irreversible (unintended) consequences. Such technologies aim to achieve a closed-loop economy that is as complete as possible, in which all industrial raw materials are completely recycled and all degradable raw materials are returned to the ecological cycle. The fifth dimension of convivial technology, *appropriateness*, involves assessing whether a certain technology is appropriate for the task to be performed. In a degrowth society, technologies should maintain a meaningful relationship between the time and material resource input and what is to be achieved. This means, for example, moving around in a largely car-free city with public transport, (cargo) bicycles, and on foot – thus being faster, emitting less, and conserving more resources.[38]

Along these five dimensions, products and technologies can be qualitatively assessed over their entire life cycle. Instead of the most profitable technologies and innovations – driven by capitalist competition and military research – asserting themselves, which makes a continuous increase in production possible, technological development should require multidimensional evaluation. The aim is to promote convivial forms of technology as well as collective deliberation about technology. A central demand is for a comprehensive civil society assessment before the introduction of new technologies with consequences for society as a whole, as well as for a moratorium on high-risk research and technologies.[39] On the basis of these criteria, it also becomes clear why, for example, criticism of cars and individualized mobility is so widespread across the degrowth spectrum.[40] In principle, technological development in a degrowth society is not market-oriented but needs-oriented, which should lead to a radical change in the form and direction of the future development of society's productive forces.

---

38 Vetter, 'The Matrix of Convivial Technology'.

39 Kerschner et al., 'Degrowth and Technology'.

40 Ulrich Brand and Markus Wissen, *Limits to Capitalist Nature: Theorizing and Overcoming the Imperial Mode of Living* (London: Rowman & Littlefield, 2018); André Gorz, *Paths to Paradise: On the Liberation from Work* (London: Pluto Press, 1985).

5.4. Revalorization and redistribution of labour

Work is an important focal point of the degrowth debate, not least because all growth critiques essentially revolve around work. The main proposals in this area are: a radical reduction in working hours without lower pay groups losing income; access for all to good, non-alienated, and meaningful work; a valorization of reproductive and care work and the distribution of this work among all; collective self-determination in the workplace; and, finally, the strengthening of worker's rights and autonomy through the provision of basic services, independent of people's employment. Through this, and in combination with the other policies discussed in this chapter, degrowth aims at fundamentally transforming work – by phasing out unnecessary and destructive work, automating as much as possible those necessary activities that cannot be made empowering, making those activities that sustain social life as pleasurable as possible, and giving those that do the work autonomy in their workplaces, thus continually transferring economic activities to a logic beyond the imperatives of accumulation.[41]

The degrowth perspective on work is fundamentally a question of foregrounding the entirety of work – as has been emphasized above all by feminist thinkers. This includes all socially necessary activities, which today are often seen as separate from employment, including subsistence, care, and voluntary work (see section 3.5). The goal of a degrowth society is to put the reproduction of life, earthcare labour, or what Stefania Barca calls the 'forces of reproduction' at the centre of society and to think about the economy from this viewpoint: What are people's (and the planet's) needs and how can they be fulfilled? The

41 See for example Stefania Barca, 'The Labor(s) of Degrowth', *Capitalism Nature Socialism* 30, 2 (2019): 207–16; Jackson, *Post Growth*, chapter 7; Vincent Liegey and Anitra Nelson, *Exploring Degrowth: A Critical Guide* (London: Pluto Press, 2020), chapter 4; Anitra Nelson and Ferne Edwards, eds., *Food for Degrowth: Perspectives and Practices* (New York: Routledge, 2020); Anna Saave and Barbara Muraca, 'Rethinking Labour/Work in a Degrowth Society', in *The Palgrave Handbook of Environmental Labour Studies*, ed. Nora Räthzel, Dimitris Stevis, and David Uzzell (Cham: Springer International Publishing, 2021), 743–67.

foregrounding of care is intended to overcome the division of the economy into a monetized portion (paid wage labour, dominated by men, and politically and economically privileged) and a non-monetary portion (reproductive work, care activities, not paid at all or poorly paid, mostly done by women and migrants, and devalued).[42]

An obvious and much-discussed entry point towards achieving these goals is the significant reduction in working hours for all – the 'enjoyable reduction of work'.[43] One goal here is to reduce harmful and senseless activities both in terms of production and consumption – such as 'bullshit' and 'batshit' jobs.[44] Reducing working hours is a goal in and of itself, since it liberates time. But it can also ensure a balanced distribution of employment in which the economy stops growing even as productivity continues to rise. In a capitalist society, the product of an economy – conventionally measured in GDP – roughly corresponds to the number of hours worked multiplied by labour productivity. Therefore, if the GDP of an economy declines due to ecological policies, but labour productivity continues to rise due to technological progress, working hours must be reduced – otherwise the problem of unemployment will worsen massively.[45] Even if it is unclear how labour

42 Stefania Barca, *Forces of Reproduction: Notes for a Counter-Hegemonic Anthropocene* (Cambridge: Cambridge University Press, 2020); Corinna Dengler and Lisa Marie Seebacher, 'What about the Global South? Towards a Feminist Decolonial Degrowth Approach', *Ecological Economics* 157 (2019): 246–52; Matthias Neumann and Gabriele Winkler, 'Care Revolution: Care Work, the Core of the Economy', in *Degrowth in Movement(s): Exploring Pathways for Transformation*, ed. Corinna Burkhart, Matthias Schmelzer, and Nina Treu (Winchester: Zer0, 2020), 100–13.

43 Kate Soper, *Post-Growth Living: For an Alternative Hedonism* (London: Verso, 2020), 84.

44 Bullshit jobs are those which are considered useless but which people have to do anyway to make a living (such as telling people where to stand in line at the airport, or most jobs in advertising), while batshit jobs are those which contribute to destroying life but are necessary for the continuation of the economy, such as working on an oil rig. See David Graeber, *Bullshit Jobs: A Theory* (New York: Simon & Schuster, 2018); Bue Rübner Hansen, ' "Batshit Jobs": No-One Should Have to Destroy the Planet to Make a Living', opendemocracy.net, 2019.

45 Lange, *Macroeconomics without Growth*; Jackson, *Prosperity without Growth*.

productivity would develop in a degrowth society, many thinkers have underlined this proposal since the beginning of the growth debates and frequently refer to Keynes, who already in 1930 assumed that in the age of his grandchildren a working week of ten to fifteen hours would be normal and sufficient (see section 3.2).[46]

According to André Gorz, the radical reduction in working time can be understood as the redistribution of the surplus value that results from increases in productivity from capital to labour – in the form of free time. From a degrowth perspective, however, the extent of possible reductions in working hours has its limits, as labour productivity is very likely to increase more slowly, or even decline, due to the importance of care activities and the elimination of 'energy slaves' from fossil fuels. In the case of care activities, including paid care work, increasing productivity is either impossible or would result in a reduction in the quality of work. And in a solar-powered, resource-saving, and partly deindustrialized circular economy with sustainable farming, the demand for human labour would likely increase in some sectors.[47] On the other hand, it is argued that certain kinds of digitization may also save time and make local production more efficient, and thus increase production. In addition, because many useless jobs would ideally be regulated and reduced, such as in the advertising industry, there may also be a large transformation of the composition of labour in the economy as a whole. How the volume of working time will develop as a result is thus ultimately an open question that can only be answered empirically. It is possible that a completely different and more comprehensive understanding of the active life or 'vita activa' (Hannah Arendt) will emerge in a degrowth society.[48]

46 Miya Tokumitsu, 'The Fight for Free Time', Jacobinmag.com, 2017; Kathi Weeks, *The Problem with Work: Feminism, Marxism, Antiwork Politics, and Postwork Imaginaries* (Durham, NC: Duke University Press, 2011); André Gorz, *Critique of Economic Reason* (New York: Verso, 1989); Van Dyk, 'Post-wage Politics'.

47 Liz Carlisle et al., 'Transitioning to Sustainable Agriculture Requires Growing and Sustaining an Ecologically Skilled Workforce', *Frontiers in Sustainable Food Systems* 3 (2019): 96.

48 Gorz, *Critique of Economic Reason*; Bayon, Flipo, and Schneider, *La décroissance*; Kallis, *Degrowth*; Paech, *Liberation from Excess*; Karina Becker,

While some authors advocate a reduction in working hours without wage compensation, where the loss of wages would be compensated for by more self-work such as repairing goods, self-production, or vegetable cultivation,[49] a just degrowth approach stresses the need to combine the reduction of working hours with either an equalization of wages, increases in wages for low-income groups, or compensation of income loss with other forms of monetary and non-monetary social welfare. For example, while generally reducing working hours – the New Economics Foundation estimated that twenty-one hours per week would be enough – wages in the lower third of the income bracket could be raised to the average, while wages in upper income groups could be continually reduced.[50] Another proposal is work-sharing, where multiple people would be hired for the same position, working only two or three hours a day while keeping the same benefits. This is seen as a transitional policy that would allow people to shift to working fewer total hours while employment levels stay the same or increase.[51] In addition to the equitable redistribution of work, particularly in terms of gender, a central goal of shortening working hours is the achievement of 'time prosperity' and the expansion of free time, which can be used for activities beyond the market economy, for political self-determination, care, or for the hedonic enjoyment of a more relaxed existence beyond the treadmill of the 'work and spend' economy (see section 4.1).[52]

Klaus Dörre, and Yalcin Kutlu, 'Counter-Landnahme? Labour Disputes in the Care-Work Field', *Equality, Diversity and Inclusion: An International Journal* 37, no. 4 (2018): 361–75; Alevgul H. Sorman and Mario Giampietro, 'The Energetic Metabolism of Societies and the Degrowth Paradigm: Analyzing Biophysical Constraints and Realities', *Journal of Cleaner Production* 38 (Spring 2013): 80–93; Jackson, *Prosperity without Growth*; Bauwens, Kostakis, and Pazaitis, *Peer-to-Peer*; Lange and Santarius, *Smart Green World?*

49 See, for example, Paech, *Liberation from Excess*.

50 Schmelzer and Passadakis, *Postwachstum*; New Economics Foundation, *21 hours: The Case for a Shorter Working Week* (London: New Economics Foundation, 2010).

51 Kallis, *Degrowth*.

52 Konzeptwerk Neue Ökonomie, *Zeitwohlstand: Wie wir anders arbeiten, nachhaltig wirtschaften und besser leben* (Munich: Oekom, 2013); Aaron Benanav,

Degrowth does not aim at dispensing with work altogether. While stressing the shortening of working hours, degrowth also aims to revalue care activities and to defend and strengthen non-alienated, socially meaningful, self-determined, and dignified work as a central component of human life. The re-skilling of artisanal capabilities in many aspects of economic life, with all the social and ecological benefits this brings, is thus a core issue of degrowth.[53] Here, as noted by Kate Soper, it is important to not fall for 'a sentimental nostalgia for earlier craft-based modes of producing', which often defined traditional roles and 'encrusted' parochial social hierarchies, but to reclaim artisanal, slow, and fulfilling ways of working 'as a component of an avant-garde, post-consumerist political imaginary'.[54] So, while embracing automation where it frees humanity from dull, dangerous, and unattractive work, degrowth also focuses on making the heteronomous and care work that remains – and this will be quite a bit – as intrinsically pleasurable and self-determined as possible.[55]

While some degrowth texts argue for the 'right to laziness', as Paul Lafargue had put it already in 1880, feminist authors point to the sexist implications such a perspective often entails: not only does 'part-time work for all' already represent the current normal situation for many women, but such a policy would also free up the necessary time to make a gender-equitable division of (domestic) care work easier to

---

Automation and the Future of Work (London: Verso, 2020); Soper, *Post-Growth Living*; Kenneth A. Gould, David N. Pellow, and Allan Schnaiberg, *Treadmill of Production: Injustice and Unsustainability in the Global Economy* (London: Routledge, 2015).

53 See for example the proposals discussed in Nelson and Edwards, *Food for Degrowth*; Anitra Nelson and François Schneider, eds., *Housing for Degrowth: Principles, Models, Challenges and Opportunities* (Abingdon: Taylor & Francis Ltd, 2018); Christine Ax, *Die Könnensgesellschaft: Mit guter Arbeit aus der Krise* (Berlin: Rhombos-Verlag, 2009).

54 Soper, *Post-Growth Living*, 104.

55 André Gorz, *Farewell to the Working Class: An Essay on Post-Industrial Socialism* (London: Pluto Press, 1997); André Gorz, *Paths to Paradise: On the Liberation from Work* (London: Pluto Press, 1985); Barca, 'The Labor(s) of Degrowth'.

achieve.[56] There is, however, controversy as to how care work should be carried out in a degrowth society. Some proposed ideas include offering remuneration for care work within the (nuclear) family, distributed gender-equitably; or, instead, rethinking care work collectively, especially in the context of local communities; the idea of a 'care municipalism' as a communal and publicly understood task that also supports household work; as well as proposals to expand care work as a better paid and recognized professional occupation, to grow the care sector as we switch from a fossil fuel–based industrialized society to a decarbonized society based on human services.[57]

Already very early on in the debate, in the beginning of the 1980s, André Gorz saw the many who are indifferent to work as a possible political subject of change – in contrast to the 'class of the regularly working', whom he saw as preservers of the old order. Gorz thus identified as areas of struggle not only the division of labour and the general shortening of working hours, but also the abolition of wage dependency through more artisanal forms of non-alienated production and a basic income guaranteed to all.[58] All these policies continue to be central to the creation of the 'plenitude' of a degrowth society.[59]

5.5. Democratizing social metabolism

Degrowth also centres the politicization of social metabolism and its repercussions for policy design – and thus democratizes the process of growth. In the capitalist market economy, there is a tendency for that

56 Frigga Haug, 'The Four-in-One Perspective: A Manifesto for a More Just Life', *Socialism and Democracy* 23, no.1 (2009): 119–23; Dengler and Speebacher, 'What about the Global South?'.

57 Kallis, 'Yes, We Can Prosper'; Burkhart, Schmelzer, and Treu, *Degrowth in Movement(s)*, 84–95; Emma Dowling, 'Confronting Capital's Care Fix: Care through the Lens of Democracy', *Equality, Diversity and Inclusion: An International Journal* 37, no. 4 (Spring 2018): 332–46; Becker, Dörre, and Kutlu, 'Counter-Landnahme?'.

58 Gorz, *Paths to Paradise*, 58. See also Soper, *Post-Growth Living*, chapter 4.

59 Juliet B. Schor, *Plenitude: The New Economics of True Wealth* (Melbourne: Scribe Publications, 2010).

which generates the greatest profits to be prioritized and thus grow, which in turn makes relationships between production and consumption highly irrational, inefficient, exploitative, and oppressive. A degrowth transformation in turn means that the 'creative destruction' (per Joseph Schumpeter) and related expansion – or, to put it differently, the phasing out and simultaneous expansion of different sectors, technologies, resource-uses, or economic activities – would no longer be left to the market, competition, and prices. Rather, the social-ecological transformation of society demands that these questions are democratically and politically deliberated at regional, national, and global levels. The central demand is to repoliticize and democratize social metabolism. This also includes a democratic deliberation of what strategies for meeting needs are compatible with the demands of social justice, self-determination, and a good life for all – a discussion that can only really be made possible by eliminating anxieties around poverty and deprivation through the provision of universal basic services to all (see above). And this includes the democratic establishment of limits, within which human well-being can flourish – collective self-limitations being a hallmark of autonomy, a 'social choice, not . . . an external imperative for environmental or other reasons'.[60]

While the flourishing of some economic activities and the qualitative transformation or contraction of others certainly involves selective growth, the overall result will not be an increase in the size of the economy (even if measured in GDP).[61] This is because the aim is a fundamental socio-ecological transformation. In fact, many of the degrowth policies such as work-time reductions, centring care,

---

60 Francois Schneider, Giorgos Kallis, and Joan Martinez-Alier, 'Crisis or Opportunity? Economic Degrowth for Social Equity and Ecological Sustainability', *Journal of Cleaner Production* 18 (2010): 511–18; Kallis, *Limits*; Barbara Muraca, 'Decroissance: A Project for a Radical Transformation of Society', *Environmental Values* 22, no. 2 (2013): 147–69.

61 This is one of the key differences to most proposals for a Green New Deal, which imply that the combination of renewable build-up and fossil downscale will be economic growth. See, for example, Noam Chomsky and Robert Pollin, *Climate Crisis and the Global Green New Deal: The Political Economy of Saving the Planet* (London: Verso, 2020), 118.

conservation of nature, or curtailing accumulation will slow down GDP. But most importantly, the non-profit, regionalized, collaborative, sustainable, and solidarity economies and the commons that are continuously strengthened in the transition to degrowth tend to not only be less energy- and material-intensive, but also contribute much less (or not at all) to GDP. The provision of basic services for all (health care, food, clean water, housing, energy, free movement) would enable a kind of 'public abundance', where the material basis of life is freely given. Yet guaranteeing these services for all collectively and publicly or as commons, rather than individualized and via the market, would *decrease* material throughput, as it would reduce inefficiency, overproduction, and the private consumption of goods. For example, a functioning public transport system would make private electric cars in cities largely superfluous; food waste (currently responsible for 6 per cent of emissions globally, according to one study[62]) could be minimized radically; instead of everyone buying a washing machine, people would be able to share them; tools would be freely available in a tool lending library; and repair cafés where you learn to repair your electronics, clothes, and furniture would be widely accessible.[63] Beyond basic services, municipalities and governments could also support infrastructure that offers people a fulfilling life: playgrounds, open areas, investment in arts and culture, and local citizens' assemblies that guide political decisions. Thus, while a degrowth society would seek to meet people's basic needs with a much smaller material and energy throughput, and without relying on GDP growth, this way of post-growth living would also be more fulfilling overall, creating avenues for an 'alternative hedonism'.[64]

However, degrowth does not only promote an ecological and needs-based alternative economy, as other proposals for ecological change

---

62 J. Poore and T. Nemecek, 'Reducing Food's Environmental Impacts through Producers and Consumers', *Science* 360, no. 6392 (2018): 987–92.

63 Aaron Vansintjan, 'Public Abundance Is the Secret to the Green New Deal', Greeneuropeanjournal, 2020; Kate Aronoff et al., *A Planet to Win: Why We Need a Green New Deal* (London: Verso, 2019).

64 Soper, *Post-Growth Living*; Jackson, *Post Growth*.

often do, but also focuses on the need to actively phase out the globalized, profit-oriented, fossil fuel–based industrial economic sectors and activities that do not serve the common good and cannot be sustainably or democratically restructured. Social activity that is not fulfilling and does not advance human well-being, such as 'bullshit' and 'batshit' jobs, the arms industry and the military, advertising, lobbying, planned obsolescence, fast fashion, border security, and large parts of the financial industry, will have to be scaled down. The same goes for any economic activity that cannot be restructured socio-ecologically, such as the coal and oil and gas industries, motorized individual transport (above all in cities), or large parts of air transport and globalized trade, as well as industrial agriculture and industrial animal farming.[65]

Instead of relying on the market and hoping that green alternatives will eventually outcompete these harmful activities, degrowth proposes a wide range of political measures that aim at actively curbing and downscaling them. These include policies such as caps on resource use, moratoria, ecological tax reform, just transitions, or confrontations with private ownership structures that impede the fast scaling down of fossil resources, and they will have to result in processes of deaccumulation. An essential measure would be to set global and national ceilings for the extraction of resources, emissions, and land use, which – when broken down to specific regions – take the historical ecological and climate debt of the early industrialized countries into account and adjust for the consumption of resources, energy, and land hidden in imported goods as 'ecological rucksacks'.[66] With regard to climate change, the single most effective policy intervention is probably also one of the most simple ones, but has been conspicuously avoided by governments around the world: to cap fossil fuel extraction – in line with the core demand of the climate justice movement from the Global

---

65 Claudio Cattaneo et al., eds., 'Politics, Democracy and Degrowth', special issue, *Futures* 44, no. 6 (2012): 515–654; Fabrice Flipo, *Décroissance, ici et maintenant!* (Paris: Le Passager Clandestin, 2017); Jackson, *Prosperity without Growth*; Kallis, *Degrowth*; Nelson and Edwards, *Food for Degrowth*.

66 Burkhart, Schmelzer, and Treu, *Degrowth in Movement(s)*; Hickel, *Less Is More*; Kallis, *Degrowth*; Paech, *Liberation from Excess*.

South, 'Leave coal in the hole, oil in the soil, and gas under the grass.'[67] The aim is to rapidly scale down fossil fuel use on a fair and binding schedule to the point where the industry is largely dismantled – globally by 2050 at the latest, and in rich countries, which are responsible for the largest share of (historical) emissions, already by around 2030. Absolute caps are not only highly effective, avoiding the fallacies of empty promises and other false solutions around dubious 'net zero' targets and negative emissions, but have other beneficial effects. Rather than increasing productivity and efficiency gains resulting in rebound effects, technological development could translate into actually lowering resource use and emissions if caps are in place.[68] However, given the speed and scale of the necessary emission reductions in rich countries – which amount to effectively cutting fossil fuel use by around 10 per cent every single year – efficiency improvements and investment in renewable energy will not be enough. Wealthy countries will have to create economies relying on less energy – and this requires fundamental changes to the entire economy along the lines of degrowth policies.[69]

67 Dennis Eversberg and Matthias Schmelzer, 'The Degrowth Spectrum: Convergence and Divergence within a Diverse and Conflictual Alliance', *Environmental Values* 27, no. 3 (2018): 245–67; Joan Martínez-Alier, 'Environmental Justice and Economic Degrowth: An Alliance between Two Movements', *Capitalism Nature Socialism* 23, no. 1 (2012): 51–73.

68 Lange, *Macroeconomics without Growth*; Tilman Santarius, Hans Jakob Walnum, and Carlo Aall, *Rethinking Climate and Energy Policies: New Perspectives on the Rebound Phenomenon* (New York: Springer, 2016).

69 Lorenz T. Keyßer and Manfred Lenzen, '1.5°C Degrowth Scenarios Suggest the Need for New Mitigation Pathways', *Nature Communications* 12, no. 1 (2021): 1–16; Wiedmann et al., 'Scientists' Warning on Affluence'; Jefim Vogel et al., 'Socio-Economic Conditions for Satisfying Human Needs at Low Energy Use: An International Analysis of Social Provisioning', *Global Environmental Change* (2021): 102287; Jason Hickel, 'Quantifying National Responsibility for Climate Breakdown: An Equality-Based Attribution Approach for Carbon Dioxide Emissions in Excess of the Planetary Boundary', *Lancet Planetary Health* 4, no. 9 (2020): 399–404; Jason Hickel et al., 'Urgent Need for Post-Growth Climate Mitigation Scenarios', *Nature Energy* (2021): 1–3; Stan Cox, *The Green New Deal and Beyond: Ending the Climate Emergency While We Still Can* (San Francisco: City Lights Books, 2020).

To achieve such fundamental changes, from a degrowth perspective the excess consumption by the rich might be a good starting point – it is absurd to permit SUVs, private jets, or private space travel amid a climate emergency. Other proposals along these lines are the moratoria on newly planned carbon- and resource-intensive megaprojects or infrastructures (airports, mining, motorways, hydro-power dams, mega-malls, corporate industrial plants and warehouses, industrialized agriculture and animal farming, IT monopolies such as new infrastructure dedicated for Amazon and Google servers, and so on), but also on all non-renewable construction activities as a whole.[70] Furthermore, ecological tax reform could support the contraction of fossil-resource use by shifting taxes from labour (i.e., income) to energy and resource consumption or to environmentally harmful activities more generally.[71] For example, a gradual replacement of income tax with CO_2 or resource taxes could incentivize the transition from environmentally harmful to more environmentally friendly consumption and at the same time encourage development of sustainable companies and cooperatives.[72] However, since low-income households spend a larger portion of their income on consumption, ecological taxes should be combined with redistributive measures so that they do not place a greater burden on the poor. The revenues from ecological taxes could be paid out in equal parts to all, as discussed above. Alternatively, they could be used to finance social infrastructure or to provide tax relief for lower-income groups.[73]

'Just transitions' will be necessary for the people and regions currently employed in sectors that need to transition. Where possible, industries could be converted so that, for example, trams, heat pumps, or bicycles are produced in former car factories – a question that is obviously highly complicated and demands a considerable degree of

70 Nelson and Schneider, *Housing for Degrowth*.

71 Herman Daly and Joshua Farley, *Ecological Economics: Principles and Applications* (Washington, DC: Island Press, 2011); Jackson, *Prosperity without Growth*; Latouche, *Farewell to Growth*; Irmi Seidl and Angelika Zahrnt, *Postwachstumsgesellschaft: Neue Konzepte für die Zukunft* (Marburg: Metropolis, 2010).

72 Cattaneo and Vansintjan, *A Wealth of Possibilities*.

73 Liegey et al., *Un projet de décroissance*.

economic planning and bottom-up deliberative processes. For those who lose their previous sources of income through the dismantling of certain sectors – such as the withdrawal from coal or the liquidation of parts of the car industry – and are forced to make significant changes, social security and retraining are just as central. Regional transformation councils composed of workers, citizens, and civil society organizations could be set up to transform entire economic sectors in those regions most affected by the transition. In these processes, those employed in the (formerly) carbon-intensive industries could become key actors of the transition, not only as political stakeholders and potential allies of climate justice movements, but also through public takeovers of companies. As has been argued recently: 'Seizing control of workplaces would be necessary to repurpose them to make what we actually need and move away from ecologically destructive production.'[74]

These policies also imply the need to address the central question of ownership. The industries that cannot be converted into a low-carbon, energy-efficient, solidarity-based economy of the future account for a very large share of the global economy. To limit the overheating of the earth, for example, we cannot wait until all destructive investments have been written off, because the payback periods for mining, airports, and incineration plants are decades. So, if certain sectors are to be phased out in a relatively short period of time, this would require the loss of capital already invested in unsustainable infrastructure. In other words, we simply cannot afford to wait – capital investments must be destroyed now rather than slowly divested. For example, multinational companies own much of the oil and coal reserves that remain in the ground but that cannot be extracted if we are to limit the risks of runaway climate change (so-called 'unburnable coal'). Degrowth thus faces the challenge that certain industries must be expropriated and transferred to common ownership in order not to stand in the way of

---

74 Angry Workers, 'Climate and Class Struggle ... One Struggle, One Plight?', angryworkers.org, 8 November 2021. See also Burkhart, Schmelzer, and Treu, *Degrowth in Movement(s)*; Klaus Dörre, *Die Utopie des Sozialismus: Kompass für eine Nachhaltigkeitsrevolution* (Berlin: Matthes & Seitz Verlag, 2021).

socio-ecological change.[75] The political and geo-political consequences of this cannot be neglected. A degrowth transformation will therefore not be a smooth passage, but undoubtedly require confrontations with fossil capital and those who benefit from existing economic structures (see chapter 6).

5.6. International solidarity

'Degrowth in the wealthier world, which would reduce its material impact on the remainder of the planet, is the most effective international-ism, leaving more space for others to live'; so goes the succinct summary of a widely held view within the degrowth spectrum, as described by Max Ajl. By attempting to overcome the imperial mode of living, which is based on the neocolonial appropriation of Global South resources and the externalization of its costs of living to others, degrowth – 'a corrective prescription for the Global North' – is putting its own house in order, the reasoning goes.[76] And yes, as we have argued by framing degrowth as an ecological global justice movement, degrowth is in this sense interna-tionalist. However, as Ajl continues, 'there is a thin line between modesty and myopia, an inwards-looking ostrich syndrome, in a country marked by imperial modes of living.' Instead of confronting the complexities and conflicts of international solidarity, there might be the danger that degrowth becomes a self-sufficient but also self-centered movement of localists that would 'silence demands for climate reparations'.[77] Further, the common argument that degrowth is a movement only 'for the North' misses an opportunity to, first, challenge the undisputably *global* desire for an imperial mode of living, and second, challenge the growth impera-tives *imposed* on the Global South through, for example, structural adjustment, odious debt, or sanctions of countries that seek another path to development.

---

75 Lessenich, *Living Well at Others' Expense.*

76 Jamie Tyberg and Erica Jung, *Degrowth and Revolutionary Organizing* (New York: Rosa Luxemburg Foundation, 2021).

77 Ajl, *A People's Green New Deal*, 147.

This highlights the need not only to address issues of international social-ecological justice conceptually, but also to build active alliances with actors in and from the Global South, ranging from movements within the pluriverse of 'alternatives to development' to support for environmental justice struggles to solidarity with communities fighting for reparations and to refugees and migrants arguing: 'We are here because you destroy our countries.'[78] If, as we have argued, degrowth is at its core about global ecological justice, international solidarity is central to the degrowth agenda. And this includes not only policies of debt cancellation, support for territorially rooted struggles in the Global South, a strong commitment to ecological reparations and transfers of financial resources, renewable technology and knowledge (including patent waivers), as well as strengthening Indigenous land rights. This also includes the broader constructive programme of reparations as 'worldmaking' to create the conditions for a truly just world.[79]

International solidarity also involves protection of wilderness and the saving of land from enclosure. However, care must be taken when considering different radical proposals for conservation, many of which often rest on colonial assumptions. For example, within degrowth and among its allies, there is strong criticism of global proposals such as that of 'Half-Earth', first proposed by biologist E. O. Wilson and increasingly taken up by conservation and development groups. Half-Earth proposes to leave half of Earth's surface for nature and bereft of human settlement, thereby exacerbating highly colonial processes of dispossession of Indigenous people from their land. Indigenous people, it must be noted, are stewards of up to 65 per cent

---

78 Olaf Bernau, 'Refugee Movement: Struggling with Migration and Escape', in Burkhart, Schmelzer, and Treu, *Degrowth in Movement(s)*, 272–86; Kothari et al., *Pluriverse*.

79 Olúfẹ́mi O. Táíwò, *Reconsidering Reparations: Worldmaking in the Case of Climate Crisis* (New York: Oxford University Press, 2022); Padini Nirmal and Dianne Rocheleau, 'Decolonizing Degrowth in the Post-Development Convergence: Questions, Experiences, and Proposals from Two Indigenous Territories', *Environment and Planning E: Nature and Space* 2, no. 3 (2019): 465–92; Hickel, *Less Is More*.

of the world's landmass – though only 18 per cent of which is formally recognized as theirs.[80] Indeed, Indigenous land stewardship has been shown to be better at limiting carbon emissions and ecological degradation than most policies.[81] Further, such proposals, and similar conservation initiatives, operate through the colonial imaginary of separation between humans and nature, while degrowth largely advocates for inter-dependence between humans and non-human life forms, and decolonizing our relationship to nature. It is not humanity as a whole that is the problem – much less the world's poor living in ecologically fragile areas – but the affluent world driving the majority of extraction, production, and consumption. In terms of policy, alternatives to colonialist conservation proposals include supporting Indigenous peoples in their efforts to steward the land, advocating for land reform and the protection of peasant livelihoods globally, transforming industrial agriculture and production so that it does not rely on as much extraction and production, thereby stopping land degradation globally, and putting a stop to speculative, neo-colonial land grabs – whether carried out by private or public investment firms or conservation NGOs.[82]

One further issue with degrowth policies is that the economies of industrialized countries must not only be redesigned to be more socio-ecologically just, the effects of such policies on people in the

80 E. O. Wilson, *Half-Earth: Our Planet's Fight for Life.* (New York: W. W. Norton & Company, 2016); Eileen Crist et al., 'Protecting Half the Planet and Transforming Human Systems Are Complementary Goals', *Frontiers in Conservation Science* 2 (2021): 91; Rights and Resources Initiative, *Who Owns the World's Land? A Global Baseline of Formally Recognized Indigenous and Community Land Rights* (Washington, DC: RRI, 2015).

81 Wayne S. Walker et al., 'The Role of Forest Conversion, Degradation, and Disturbance in the Carbon Dynamics of Amazon Indigenous Territories and Protected Areas', *Proceedings of the National Academy of Sciences* 117, no. 6 (2020): 3015–25; Indigenous Environmental Network, *Indigenous Resistance against Carbon* (Washington, DC: Oil Change International, 2021). Richard Schuster et al., 'Vertebrate Biodiversity on Indigenous-Managed Lands in Australia, Brazil, and Canada Equals That in Protected Areas', *Environmental Science and Policy* 101 (2019): 1–6.

82 Bram Buscher and Robert Fletcher, *The Conservation Revolution: Radical Ideas for Saving Nature beyond the Anthropocene* (London: Verso, 2020).

Global South must also be accounted for. For example, a shift towards unconditional basic services, as well as ecological taxation and a localization of needs-oriented production, will likely lead to less consumption overall, less reliance on resource extraction from the Global South, but could possibly also heavily damage the economies of the Global South that rely on exporting resources and consumer goods, or on tourism, as was evidenced by the effects of the COVID-19 lockdown.[83]

Policies will need to be put in place to address this – not only through supporting the Global South in switching from its dependency on unequal exchange and globalized markets, but also to ensure that degrowth policies do actually lead to greater global justice through a sharing of resources, knowledge, technology, and cooperation as well as through preferential trade arrangements and reparations. Essentially, most non-industrialized countries simply cannot offer basic income or basic services because they cannot borrow money as freely as industrialized countries, and they are already subject to structural adjustment policies imposed by international lending organizations. Addressing this could involve restructuring global finance to democratize uneven economic relationships between the North and South. Of course, this would also require dismantling the ongoing colonialism of industrialized countries practised through, for example, land grabbing and extractivism (increasingly also 'green extractivism'), as well as ending military imperialism by the West.[84]

Global trade and the international economic system itself would also eventually have to be entirely transformed. The restructuring of the economy along the lines proposed by degrowth implies a 'deglobalization' of economic relations or, as has recently been argued by

---

83 The ramifications for degrowth in the Global North on the Global South, on migration, remittances, countries relying on extractive industry, and so on, is certainly understudied and should be further examined. See, however, Ajl, *A People's Green New Deal*.

84 Cattaneo and Vansintjan, *A Wealth of Possibilities*; Jamie Tyberg, *Unlearning: From Degrowth to Decolonization* (New York: Rosa Luxemburg Stiftung, 2020), rosalux-nyc.org/wp-content/files_mf/degrowth052020update. pdf; Max Ajl, *A People's Green New Deal* (London: Pluto Press, 2021).

Utsa and Prabhat Patnaik, a 'de-linking' of the Global South from neoliberal globalization and the exploitative trade and financial system dominated by the North.[85] The aim is to limit trade in goods and services that are problematic in ecological and human rights terms, largely driven by corporations taking advantage of international wage and price differentials, and often not necessary at all. While degrowth also aims to restrict the international movement of capital – a policy that could play a key role in the transition phase to stabilize international markets – it pursues the expansion of trade that is beneficial (in particular to the Global South), cultural exchange and slow travel, and the freedom of movement of people. It is therefore a matter of regionally anchored but interconnected and open economic relationships and a much more localized production.[86] Degrowth, accordingly, does not stand for cultural and nationalist isolationism, homogeneous bioregions, or competition-based economic protectionism, but for 'open localism'.[87] There is also the proposal to 'Design global, produce local', which is made increasingly possible through digital means of communication in combination with digitally controlled production. For example, open-source sharing of designs, building plans, and instructions for the production of goods enables localized production based on a global 'digital commons'.[88] At the global level, the aim is to avoid unnecessary transport and environmental costs through regionalization and to reduce regions' dependencies on the world market.

A key part of international solidarity would be the rewiring of international relations. Municipalities (including rural towns) and cities are envisioned as key actors of change – 'rebel cities' or 'solidarity cities'

---

85 Walden Bello, *Deglobalization: Ideas for a New World Economy* (Dhaka: Zed Books, 2005); Hickel, *Less Is More*; Utsa Patnaik and Prabhat Patnaik, *Capital and Imperialism: Theory, History, and the Present* (New York: NYU Press, 2021); Solón et al., *Systemic Alternatives*.

86 Kallis, *Degrowth*; Paech, *Liberation from Excess*; Ajl, *A People's Green New Deal*.

87 Liegey et al., *Un projet de décroissance*; Nelson and Schneider, *Housing for Degrowth*.

88 Bauwens, Kostakis, and Pazaitis, *Peer-to-Peer*.

would link up and work together to put forward new international alliances – a vision often labelled 'radical municipalism'.[89] This scale of politics is considered to be ideal for degrowth as it is in the municipality that people can practise face-to-face political deliberation.[90] In addition to a global environmental and climate justice policy, a major goal is to establish a fair world trade system through radical institutional reforms that would benefit peripheral regions. Possible measures mentioned in this context include global taxes on finance and capital, the creation of a democratic international monetary system (such as the one based on the international currency 'bancor' originally proposed by Keynes), equitable market access for public-interest companies, reforming or abolishing international organizations like the World Bank and the International Monetary Fund, and democratically negotiated financial and technological transfers to offset climate debt, the consequences of colonialism, and other negative consequences of capitalist modernity.[91]

5.7. Why degrowth is viable

This variety of proposals for the economy, social services, technology, work, and international solidarity aim to underpin a degrowth society with more concrete political visions. Even if these are incomplete and in a state of flux and must be further developed and experimented with – according to the Zapatista motto *preguntando caminamos*, or 'asking, we walk' – they are central for turning degrowth into a 'concrete utopia'. Following Erik Olin Wright, these policies indicate that degrowth is not only desirable, but also viable – meaning that a degrowth society could

89 Barcelona en Comù, *Fearless Cities*.

90 Viviana Asara, 'Democracy without Growth: The Political Ecology of the Indignados Movement', 2015, PhD thesis, Universitat Autònoma de Barcelona, Spain; Burkhart, Schmelzer, and Treu, *Degrowth in Movement(s)*; Murray Bookchin, *The Next Revolution: Popular Assemblies and the Promise of Direct Democracy* (London: Verso, 2015).

91 Ajl, *A People's Green New Deal*; Felber, *Change Everything*; Hickel, *Degrowth*; Solón et al., *Systemic Alternatives*.

actually work. Some questions, however, still remain unanswered: Is it achievable? Who is in a position to carry out and implement these fundamental societal transformations, under what conditions, and through which alliances? The question of transformation is discussed in the next chapter.

6

Making degrowth real

As we hope has now been established, degrowth both represents a multi-layered critique of growth and points to pathways beyond it. In the previous two chapters, we defined degrowth and outlined some policies that could take us there. But this still does not tell us *how* we can make degrowth happen: in Erik Olin Wright's terms, is it *achievable*? How would we align social movements, technological change, the economy, and our political systems? Who would make it happen?

This question is extremely difficult because the scale of the challenge is, to put it humbly, substantial. Since modern societies are fundamentally designed to expand and grow, transformation encompasses not only material but also economic, social, and mental changes – a 'prosperous way down' requires entirely new forms relating to each other, or a 'relational revolution'.[1] Such a transformation is comparable to world-system historical transitions such as the rise of capitalism or the advent of fossil fuel–powered industrialization. History shows that changes of this magnitude take place in complex processes that overlap in time

---

1 Howard T. Odum and Elisabeth C. Odum, *A Prosperous Way Down: Principles and Policies* (Boulder, CO: University Press of Colorado, 2008); Bini Adamczak, *Beziehungsweise Revolution: 1917, 1968 und kommende* (Frankfurt: Suhrkamp Verlag, 2017).

and space. These processes encompass political, social, ecological, and cultural dynamics and each have different temporalities. Some would emerge as crises in which the old order dies away while a new one emerges, others as processes of adaptation and innovation that realign the old system, and yet others as consciously manifested struggles for a new society. From a historical point of view, profound social transformations have always been marked by fierce controversies, public disputes, and, up to now, (violent) conflicts. Escalation of conflict is all the more likely when the changes proposed directly oppose the interests of the powerful.[2] Furthermore, this transformation must emerge out of conditions of a form of capitalism that has never been as all-encompassing and global as it is today – and on a dying planet, amid accelerating climate crises and mass extinction. As aptly put by the Salvage Collective, the traditional saying 'Workers of the world unite, you have nothing to lose but your chains. You have a world to win' seems to be out of touch with the biophysical reality of the planet. 'What if the world is already lost?'[3]

Degrowth is a vision of social transformation that has never been realized: a conscious, radically democratic process of transforming society to create the conditions for a good life for all, by pulling the emergency brake and stepping out of the capitalist and growth-driven megamachine. Given this immense scale of the challenge, the discussion about the degrowth transformation is only in its infancy. Before we begin to discuss it, we need to acknowledge a tension that often seems to underlie this discussion. On the one hand, degrowth is often proposed as a platform of relatively concrete top-down policy proposals, such as shortening working hours, establishing basic and maximum

---

2 Jürgen Osterhammel, *The Transformation of the World: A Global History of the Nineteenth Century* (Princeton, NJ: Princeton University Press, 2014); Immanuel Wallerstein, *World-Systems Analysis: An Introduction* (Durham, NC: Duke University Press, 2004). See also Christoph Ambach et al., 'Beyond Visions and Projects: The Need for a Debate on Strategy in the Degrowth Movement', Degrowth.info/blog, 3 October, 2018; Fabian Scheidler, *The End of the Megamachine: A Brief History of a Failing Civilization* (Winchester: Zer0, 2020).

3 The Salvage Collective, *The Tragedy of the Worker: Towards the Proletarocene* (London: Verso, 2021), 1.

incomes, or setting upper limits on resource consumption. Even if there are ways that this 'revolutionary realpolitik' can be carried out by organizations or municipalities, the idea is that these reforms should ultimately be implemented 'from above' by the state, or fought for through the state by social movements and parties. On the other hand, however, degrowth is just as equally characterized by a strong focus on bottom-up, small-scale alternatives and self-organized projects that function without or even against the state. Even if state policies can support their spread, these nowtopias tend to be projects 'from below'. And this is unique to degrowth, compared to other leftist orientations: a strong emphasis on desire-based, visionary, on-the-ground experimentation and organizing. Yet, despite the way this tension sits at the centre of the degrowth project, there have not been many proposals for how to connect these different approaches.[4] This tension – between bottom-up small-scale practices and top-down concrete policy proposals – is the starting point for our own proposal for how we can approach the transformation towards a degrowth society. Because, as has been noted before, the degrowth transformation cannot work without properly understanding, and building, those social forces and counter-hegemonic struggles that could accomplish the radical economic reforms discussed in the last chapter – and this requires actively relating bottom-up nowtopias and top-down policies.[5]

In order to better describe this strategy, we here build on some more ideas from the sociologist Erik Olin Wright, who has offered reflections

---

4 See, however, Frank Adler and Ulrich Schachtschneider, eds., *Postwachstumspolitiken: Wege zur wachstumsunabhängigen Gesellschaft* (Munich: Oekom, 2017); Corinna Burkhart, Matthias Schmelzer, and Nina Treu, eds., *Degrowth in Movement(s): Exploring Pathways for Transformation* (Winchester: Zer0, 2020); Giorgos Kallis, *Degrowth* (Newcastle upon Tyne: Agenda Publishing, 2018); and Giorgos Kallis et al., *The Case for Degrowth* (Cambridge: Polity Press, 2020).

5 Jamie Tyberg and Erica Jung, *Degrowth and Revolutionary Organizing* (New York: Rosa Luxemburg Foundation, 2021); Padini Nirmal and Dianne Rocheleau, 'Decolonizing Degrowth in the Post-Development Convergence: Questions, Experiences, and Proposals from Two Indigenous Territories', *Environment and Planning E: Nature and Space* 2, no. 3 (2019): 465–92.

on how to resolve these tensions in a unified vision.[6] Wright coined the term 'real utopias' to describe the emancipatory strategies that start within capitalism but are designed to overcome it. He distinguishes between three transformation strategies that are not mutually exclusive. *Interstitial strategies* – really-existing alternative institutions like cooperatives or community-based organizations – allow people to test changes to institutions, infrastructures, or forms of social organization in the cracks of capitalism. Through a process of metamorphosis, cumulative efforts can then bring about qualitative changes to the central dynamics and logics of the hegemonic system. *Symbiotic strategies* aim at setting up forms of cooperation between different social forces, in order to achieve concrete reforms and improvements that can eventually change the social system in the long term – this is then normally done through traditional political systems. Finally, Wright talks about *ruptural strategies*, which involve mass movements attempting to overcome the dominant social system through revolutionary confrontation and taking down or taking over the state. While a strategy of large-scale rupture ('revolution') is rarely discussed in the context of degrowth, interstitial and symbiotic strategies are often discussed, though regularly juxtaposed to each other.

In this chapter, we claim that top-down and bottom-up degrowth strategies, despite their apparent opposition, rely on each other to be successful. Top-down reforms allow the expansion and scaling up of nowtopias, while, without nowtopias, people will remain unable to imagine how radical reforms could improve their lives and thus desire and fight for their implementation. For example, the more reforms implemented to support cooperatives, the greater the number of people who will work in them. And, the more people work in cooperatives, the greater the pressure for conditions that allow cooperatives to flourish and the greater the desire for non-exploitative workplace democracy – in turn expanding the kinds of reforms that are seen as politically feasible. The two are linked through the state as an intermediary vehicle for

---

6 Erik Olin Wright, *Envisioning Real Utopias* (London: Verso, 2010). For similar takes on the question of a degrowth transformation, see Kallis et al., *The Case for Degrowth*, chapter 5.

the large-scale transformations needed. Yet, we also need ruptural strategies: organized resistance that builds up pressure for radical transformation and that eventually radically democratizes and appropriates the state at all levels. Thus, rather than putting these strategies in opposition to each other, we propose, following Wright, that the transformation towards a degrowth society requires an interplay among these three strategies, which in turn includes the construction of a counter-hegemony to the dominance of growth.

6.1. Nowtopias: Autonomous spaces and laboratories for the good life

In Catalonia, Spain, a cooperative of 2,500 members runs exchange networks, its own currency, food pantries, assemblies, financial cooperatives, a collectively-run factory, a machine working shop, and supports around forty-five people with a basic income. The Catalan Integral Cooperative, founded in 2010, is an amorphous network whose main mission is to 'antagonise Capital by building cooperative structures in the Catalan economy'.[7]

Since its foundation, it has developed several diverse, but interdependent, initiatives which have as their explicit goal to displace the state apparatus – covering health, food, education, housing, and transport. The cooperative has become an encompassing network that allows many to move much of their life outside of the dominant economic system. This involves, for example, participating in one of the many committees which decide the direction (legal, financial, technological, and so on) of the network. Involvement in the work of

---

7 On 'commons public partnerships', think of, for example, organizing many sectors of the economy the way many countries already organize voluntary fire brigades, or autonomously run childcare collectives, which are given funding and buildings to operate in by the municipality. Silke Helfrich and David Bollier, *Free, Fair, and Alive: The Insurgent Power of the Commons* (Gabriola Island, BC: New Society Publishers, 2019); George Dafermos, *The Catalan Integral Cooperative: An Organizational Study of a Post-capitalist Cooperative*, Commonstransition.org (P2P Foundation and Robin Hood Co-op), 2017.

the committee also implies receiving a basic income, partly in euros and partly in their own currency system. There is also a well-developed local exchange network, which supports autonomous, small-scale production as well as 'pantries' which are connected through an internal transportation and logistics system. The cooperative also includes many autonomous organizations, such as events spaces, cooperative housing units, and the impressive Calafou – a 'postcapitalist ecoindustrial colony' in the ruins of an abandoned industrial village in the Catalonian countryside. In 2017, Calafou was inhabited by two dozen people and, on top of that, housed a carpentry and mechanical workshop, a community kitchen, a biolab, a hack lab, a soap production facility, a music studio, a guest-house, a social centre, and a 'free shop' – each run collectively and non-hierarchically. By itself, Calafou is certainly unique. But what makes it so special is its connection to an expanding ecosystem of other similar projects through the cooperative and its many members.

This innovative project is emblematic of what Wright calls an 'interstitial strategy', as it allows its members to experiment with different ways of organizing housing, food supply, technology, currencies, and the revaluation of labour – away from an exploitative, alienating system towards one that is needs-oriented and meaning-making.

Interstitial strategies, such as this cooperative, seek to experiment with new institutions, infrastructures, or forms of organization. They are laboratories in which new social practices are intentionally developed, tried out, and practised. They emerge within and despite the old system and prefigure post-capitalist relations on a small scale.

Interstitial strategies are particularly present in the discussion on degrowth. Reference is often made to them in order to show that the principles of a degrowth society are already being implemented on a small scale today. Degrowth has thus contributed in recent years to advancing the visibility and politicization of a new wave of 'prefigurative' social movements – that is, experiments which prefigure the world we want to see, today. And degrowth has also fostered the development of policy proposals that could create conditions for the flourishing of these interstitial strategies – starting from legislative changes (as discussed in the last chapter) to collective networking efforts to advancing what have been called 'commons public partnerships'.[8]

Temporary interstitial practices such as the degrowth summer schools or climate camps or other political camps around the world offer people an experience of a communal, self-determined, and sufficient lifestyle through collective self-organization, shared care work, and the use of exclusively renewable energies and compost toilets. More permanent interstitial spaces tend to supply infrastructure suitable for degrowth for a certain social realm – be it energy supply, food cultivation, childcare, production, or services. Many of these 'nowtopias' exhibit a certain interpretative flexibility and are often mentioned in discussions about commons, solidarity economies, or the 'the economy for the common good' – as examples of autonomous spaces in which the core principles of a different society are already lived.[9] Examples often cited in this 'mosaic of alternatives'[10] are collective enterprises, community-supported agriculture, alternative media, urban gardens, childcare and alternative schooling, collective kitchens and food recuperation, housing projects and squats, occupations, municipal energy projects, time banks or regional currencies, repair cafés or open-source hardware.[11] In addition to these projects, which usually only cover a specific area of the participants' lives, there are also larger projects in which these various areas are integrated. These more complex practices can be found in many eco-villages or in 'integral cooperatives' such as the Catalan Integral Cooperative discussed above.[12] There are also individual practices that can be included in the nowtopian strategy of

---

8 Viviana Asara, 'Democracy without Growth: The Political Ecology of the Indignados Movement', 2015, PhD thesis, Universitat Autònoma de Barcelona, Spain; Giacomo D'Alisa, Federico Demaria, and Giorgos Kallis, *Degrowth: A Vocabulary for a New Era* (London: Routledge, 2014); Burkhart, Schmelzer, and Treu, *Degrowth in Movement(s)*; Helfrich and Bollier, *Free, Fair, and Alive*.

9 Christian Felber, *Change Everything: Creating an Economy for the Common Good* (London: Zed Books, 2019); Helfrich and Bollier, *Free, Fair, and Alive*.

10 Burkhart, Schmelzer, and Treu, *Degrowth in Movement(s)*.

11 See, for example, the Commons Transition Primer at primer.commonstransition.org.

12 D'Alisa, Demaria, and Kallis, *Degrowth: A Vocabulary for a New Era*; Burkhart, Schmelzer, and Treu, *Degrowth in Movement(s)*, 248–59.

creating interstitial space, which help people to create free space in their own life. These include greatly reducing one's working time, learning manual and horticultural skills, veganism, and practising food sovereignty.[13] Broader lifestyle changes are also important, such as 'voluntary simplicity', or practising a simpler, more fulfilling lifestyle and limiting consumption.[14] Strategically, these individual practices are formulated as positive models rather than as appeals for self-sacrifice and renunciation. Here, we can also speak about practices of 'time prosperity', which highlight the flourishing of free time and leisure as an underlying goal of the good life (see section 5.5).[15]

Many activists in the degrowth movement are engaged with one or more of these practices and are involved in collective nowtopias. While these are often discussed through the lens of individual renunciation and self-sacrifice when degrowth is reported on in the mainstream media, many of these projects are fundamentally oriented towards needs, based on a post-scarcity logic, and strive for collective organizing and large-scale political change.[16]

What clearly distinguishes nowtopias, however, is how they understand what constitutes political activity. There are more politically oriented and less politically oriented variations of these interstitial spaces. For example, while 'transition towns' and ecovillages are often framed in terms of setting the ground for a new system and illustrating new forms of well-being, and often push for changes to municipal policies, they are not often articulated in terms of a challenge to capital or the state. Other interstitial projects are far more radical and are thus also often referenced in the degrowth discussion. Examples of these

---

13 Burkhart, Schmelzer, and Treu, *Degrowth in Movement(s)*, 128–39, 356–67.

14 Cédric Biagini and Pierre Thiesset, eds., *La décroissance: Vivre la simplicité volontaire; Histoire et témoignages* (Montreuil: Editions L'Échappée, 2014); Niko Paech, *Liberation from Excess: The Road to a Post-growth Society* (Munich: Oekom, 2012).

15 Konzeptwerk Neue Ökonomie, *Zeitwohlstand: Wie wir anders arbeiten, nachhaltig wirtschaften und besser leben* (Munich: Oekom, 2013).

16 Dennis Eversberg and Matthias Schmelzer, 'The Degrowth Spectrum: Convergence and Divergence within a Diverse and Conflictual Alliance', *Environmental Values* 27, no. 3 (2018): 245–67; Burkhart, Schmelzer, and Treu, *Degrowth in Movement(s)*.

include the Zone à Défendre in Notre-Dame-des-Landes, France, where activists and farmers had long occupied a site for a future airport; Rojava in northern Syria, where a majority Kurdish revolutionary struggle has set up its own government system without centralized state structures and based on women's liberation; and the Zapatistas in Chiapas, Mexico, who, starting with a takeover of some villages, have organized their own non-state, decolonial system based on Indigenous and anti-capitalist values. These more revolutionary nowtopias can be seen as 'territories in resistance' which actively seek to model new forms of democratic government that are in opposition to a growth-based, highly centralized, hierarchical, and unecological social structure.[17]

Developing interstitial spaces is theoretically justified in different ways. Some thinkers – above all from the sufficiency-oriented current (see section 4.1) – stress that electoral, state-sanctioned politics cannot alone address ecological crises and that majorities cannot be won for degrowth policies. Therefore, the only possible course of action is the development of autonomous experiments that test and exemplify resilient self-sufficiency.[18]

Others consider this perspective too fatalistic. They see interstitial spaces as real laboratories, prefigurative projects, or spaces of possibility in which exemplary forms of organization are tried out, which then inspire others and radiate to society as a whole, thus bringing about structural change.[19] For example, the Catalan Integral Cooperative

17 See Vincent Liegey and Anitra Nelson, *Exploring Degrowth: A Critical Guide* (London: Pluto Press 2020), chapter 3; Dilar Dirik, 'Building Democracy without the State', Roarmag.org, 2016; S. G. and G. K., 'ZAD: The State of Play', trans. Janet Koenig, brooklynrail.org, 2018; Jeff Conant, *A Poetics of Resistance: The Revolutionary Public Relations of the Zapatista Insurgency* (Oakland, CA: AK Press, 2010); Abdullah Ocalan, *Democratic Confederalism* (London: Transmedia, 2015); Raùl Zibechi, *Territories in Resistance: A Cartography of Latin American Social Movements* (Oakland, CA: AK Press, 2012); Nirmal and Rocheleau, 'Decolonizing Degrowth'.

18 Biagini and Thiesset, *La décroissance*; Rob Hopkins, *The Power of Just Doing Stuff: How Local Action Can Change the World* (Croydon: Transition Books, 2012); Paech, *Liberation from Excess*.

19 D'Alisa, Demaria, and Kallis, *Degrowth: A Vocabulary for a New Era*; Friederike Habermann, *Ecommony: UmCARE zum Miteinander* (Sulzbach am

shows that it is feasible to build an alternative, solidarity-based system of credit; community-supported agriculture proves that food can be ecologically and socially responsible; and energy cooperatives prove that an energy revolution can be realized from below. What's more, at a global level, cooperatives are not a small phenomenon – in all their variety, there are around three million cooperatives in the world, in which more than 12 per cent of humanity is engaged and which provide jobs to 10 per cent of the employed population.[20]

Another line of reasoning, specific to the degrowth discussion, draws from – often without saying so explicitly – feminist theories that regard self-transformation as closely linked to social transformation. As is said, 'The personal is political.' Thus, philosopher Barbara Muraca writes:

> In these protected spaces we can question critically how conceptions of the good life and perceptions of needs came about. Moreover, we can uncover the extent to which they are merely an immediate expression of established values that have been imposed on individuals in the interest of preserving and reproducing prevailing social relations. After all, an important function of concrete utopias is the 'education of desire', as it is termed in utopian studies, or learning collectively about our desires and needs. In the alternative spaces of experience established through social experiments, one can learn to desire differently, better, and even more. Instead of repressing desire through a one-sided notion of voluntary simplicity, the point is rather to free oneself from the forces that limit the autonomy to demand more (in political terms). Social experiments teach us autonomy as a collective project.[21]

Taunus: Ulrike Helmer Verlag, 2016); Helfrich and Bollier, *Free, Fair, and Alive*; Bernd Sommer and Harald Welzer, *Transformationsdesign: Wege in eine zukunftsfähige Moderne* (Munich: Oekom, 2014).

20 These numbers are from the World Cooperative Monitor; see ica.coop/en/cooperatives/facts-and-figures.

21 Barbara Muraca, 'Foreword', in *Degrowth in Movement(s): Exploring Pathways for Transformation*, ed. Corinna Burkhart, Matthias Schmelzer, and Nina Treu (Winchester: Zer0, 2020), 6.

Self-transformation – with the goal of fostering 'degrowth subjectivities' – can be seen as a starting point for social transformation.[22]
Degrowth can thus also be understood as a form of reflection on
the privileges produced through the imperial mode of living,
which must be dismantled both in our everyday practices and
politically.

While there is a widely shared consensus within the degrowth
discussion that interstitial strategies must be part of a degrowth
transformation, their significance, function, and concrete forms are
controversial. Some argue that these alone are not sufficient, since
small initiatives do not, in themselves, foster the creation of a counter-hegemony, or construct added up to form a different macro-
economic system.[23] Instead of presenting real alternatives to growth,
prefigurative spaces run the risk of becoming a 'relic in the town
museum', failing to bring about transformative change and offering
only to keep capitalism and neoliberalism afloat.[24] Indeed, without a
broader counter-hegemonic framework, they could increase its resilience and even help to stabilize it. For example, if neighbours or rela-
tives start to focus on mutual aid in place of the state, the state will be
enabled to give up responsibility for supporting people with a safety
net. Moreover, there is a danger that the emphasis on local communities over nation-state solutions fails to recognize that these communities can be highly exclusive and extremely non-egalitarian, that
they are often based on self-exploitation and that not everyone can
participate in them, and that traditional commons were often

---

22 Jason Hickel, *Less Is More: How Degrowth Will Save the World* (London:
William Heinemann, 2020).

23 For a critique, see, for example, Greg Sharzer, *No Local: Why Small-Scale
Alternatives Won't Change the World* (Alresford: John Hunt Publishing, 2012);
and Nick Srnicek and Alex Williams, *Inventing the Future: Postcapitalism and a
World without Work* (London: Verso, 2015). For a response to such critiques, see,
for example, Brian Tokar, 'Think Globally, Act Locally?', opening reflections at the
Great Transition Initiative Forum, greattransition.org Initiative, November 2019;
Symbiosis Research Collective, 'How Radical Municipalism Can Go beyond the
Local', Theecologist.org, 8 June 2018.

24 Symbiosis Research Collective, 'How Radical Municipalism Can Go
beyond the Local'.

embedded in feudal power relations, patriarchal structures, and personal dependencies.[25]

Interstitial spaces are a central part of the transformation towards a degrowth society. However, they should not be exclusive but must be designed openly, collectively, and democratically, they must (self-)critically reflect on and dismantle all forms of discrimination, and they must be accompanied by radical institutional changes throughout society.[26] It is here that more radical examples of interstitial spaces, such as that of Rojava and Chiapas, can help orient us to consider how a wholly different economic and political system can be constructed, and how this can operate in resistance to the domination of capital.

6.2. Non-reformist reforms: Changing institutions and policies

Imagine how different life could be if we had not five days of work per week but three. We would have time to see family and friends, take care of our children and the elderly, cook meals for ourselves ahead of time instead of buying takeout, garden, and, perhaps, join more protests and organize with our neighbours and co-workers. Or, imagine if housing were no longer a form of investment or speculation but actually guaranteed to everyone, and no one was at risk of having to live on the street if they could no longer pay the rent increases. Or imagine living in cities with an abundance of well-functioning, reliable, and luxurious public resources to which everyone would have free access and could use collectively – from public transport (on streets freed from private cars) to fast internet connections and community cinemas.[27]

---

25 Silke van Dyk, 'Post-wage Politics and the Rise of Community Capitalism', *Work, Employment and Society* 32, no. 3 (2018): 528–45; George Caffentzis and Silvia Federici, 'Commons against and beyond Capitalism', *Community Development Journal* 49, no. 1 (2014): 92–105.

26 Kallis, *Degrowth*.

27 For such a vision, see the following book, which is forthcoming in English at Uneven Earth Press: Kai Kuhnhenn et al., *Zukunft für alle: Eine Vision für 2048: gerecht. ökologisch. Machbar* (Munich: oekom, 2020).

In addition to expanding post-capitalist nowtopias from below, degrowth has a strategic focus on the development of proposals for degrowth policies and institutions. This gradual change of laws, norms, infrastructures, and institutions, starting from and building on today's structures, can be understood as a symbiotic transformation strategy. As argued in chapter 5, these 'non-reformist reforms' do indeed start with existing structures and regulations but point beyond the capitalist, growth-oriented mode of production. The most important of these proposals – such as the reduction of working hours, radical policies of redistribution, universal basic services, ecological tax reform, or income maximums – have already been discussed in the previous sections. They are at the centre of the debate on degrowth, since only through a 'revolutionary realpolitik' can the goals of transformation towards a degrowth society be achieved. Here we briefly review the fundamental importance of such policies, and how they may realign society and work together with other strategies.

First, these proposals are central to the degrowth strategy because interstitial strategies only have a chance of initiating far-reaching social change if they are accompanied by political changes: 'If the delicate beginnings of the transformation to a degrowth society are to be given a chance of generalization and expansion into other social and economic areas, a mutual fertilization between micro-practices and macro-politics is necessary.'[28] Degrowth policies thus foster and strengthen grass-roots experiments, in turn ensuring that the scope of these autonomous economic practices expands and that they become commonly practised, rather than exclusive to some. This is needed because such experiments constantly face structural limits: lack of resources, land, and property, competitive conditions that reward ecological and social exploitation, lack of time, inequality in society.

Thus, the phaseout of the fossil fuel–, profit–, and stock market–driven sectors – as well as the increased fiscal and legal support of regional, sustainable, and cooperative forms of economic activity – helps to multiply democratic and collaborative nowtopias. An (ecological) basic income or the expansion of municipal public services gives

---

28 Adler and Schachtschneider, *Postwachstumspolitiken*, 10, our translation.

people the space and support they need to get involved in political discussions – beyond the fear and anxiety of capitalist work society – about how to transform society, which needs are legitimate, which areas of society should grow, and which should be phased out.[29] In combination with a reduction in working hours for all, these would also promote the development of a mode of living based on solidarity, in which the overarching importance of wage work is reduced, care work is revalued, gender relations become egalitarian, and in which everyone has time to collectively shape an increasing part of their lives and economies outside the market. In addition, a radical redistribution of wealth and income creates real opportunities for participation – for example, through a reform of tax and inheritance law and through the socialization and decentralized redistribution of the means of production such as the ownership of land and buildings, technology, and knowledge. This makes it possible for all people, in a society that is much more egalitarian and structured around public abundance rather than privatized wealth, to make equal use of the opportunities for self-development and participation, in turn deepening the democratization of politics and the economy, undoing the alienation that divides us from our environment and each other.[30]

Non-reformist degrowth policies, however, are not only central to promoting the generalization of a cooperative economy. They are also important in order to overcome the dependence by current institutions and infrastructures on growth and to achieve a mode of production and living based on solidarity at the level of society as a whole. As already discussed above, the vision of a degrowth society can only emerge in the interplay of various radical reforms: a stable and growth-independent society that strengthens social justice, democracy, and self-determination, and does so with a much lower material metabolism. According to Giorgos Kallis, if these reforms were implemented, they

29 David Graeber, *Bullshit Jobs: A Theory* (New York: Simon & Schuster, 2018); Vincent Liegey et al., *Un projet de décroissance: Manifeste pour une dotation inconditionelly d'autonomie* (Paris: Les Éditions Utopia, 2013).

30 Barbara Muraca, 'Decroissance: A Project for a Radical Transformation of Society', *Environmental Values* 22, 2 (2013): 147–69; Hickel, *Less Is More*; Serge Latouche, *Farewell to Growth* (Cambridge: Polity, 2010).

would require the very contours of the system to change radically to accommodate them. And reforms that, simple and common-sensical as they are, expose the irrationality of a system that makes them seem impossible and yet deems possible what in all likelihood will end in catastrophe.[31]

While these radical reforms may indeed be necessary, there is controversy over the role of the state in bringing about real, needed change. On the left, both anarchists and socialists argue for the need to democratize society, decentralize the state, and put power in the hands of the people – however, they often differ on the means to get there. Many socialists argue for taking over the state first, before letting it wither away, while anarchists argue the needed changes are impossible without the dissolution of the state. Relying on the state may seem expedient at first in order to bring about macro-level changes, but this has its limitation in that the state itself reproduces hierarchy, power structures, and violence. Nevertheless, the scale of action needed requires a powerful actor, and the state currently remains the dominant actor on the world stage, being one of the key loci of struggle for climate justice, labour, feminist, and decolonial movements alike.[32]

Today, we already have some inspiring proposals that model what a package of non-reformist reforms could look like. We have already mentioned, in chapter 4, the ten policy proposals drawn up by Research & Degrowth in 2015. In 2019, US Senators Ed Markey and Alexandria Ocasio-Cortez introduced a resolution for a 'Green New Deal', conceived as a ten-year mobilization to bring the US to 100 per cent renewable energy use, including a massive build-out of social services, in some ways along degrowth lines (though with little mention of growth as an issue to overcome, and little discussion of the need to reduce aggregate social metabolism and address unequal North–South relationships). While the motion was defeated in the US Senate, its

31 Kallis, *Degrowth*, 133.

32 This debate cannot be resolved here; see, for example, Max Koch, 'The State in the Transformation to a Sustainable Postgrowth Economy', *Environmental Politics* 29, no. 1 (2020): 115–33; Giacomo D'Alisa and Giorgos Kallis, 'Degrowth and the State', *Ecological Economics* 169 (2020): 106486.

afterlives continued to inspire progressive movements in the US and globally, as it set in motion renewed discussions on the possibilities of non-reformist reforms when introduced at the level of government. In the same year, experts and scholars, including many degrowth advocates, put together the 'Green New Deal for Europe', a proposal that does explicitly mention the need to push towards a post-growth economy, and offers ways to reduce social metabolism and expand public services and the cooperative economy. Today, different organizations, in great part inspired by the new leftist electoral surge, are proposing a 'Global Green New Deal'. Visionary platforms such as these, which may not have political currency yet, set the tone of the debate and are becoming an important site of discussion and deliberation about what kind of future we want to build, and the possibility that building it is entirely possible. Particularly valuable for an alliance would be a 'Green New Deal without Growth', which would incorporate common proposals – such as public investment for energy transition, industrial policies, the socialization of the energy sector, and the expansion of welfare – but also highlight the need to build growth-independent institutions, to radically reduce throughput, and to avoid environmental problem-shifting and new forms of extractivism in the South.[33]

Yet, as many have pointed out, these changes can only be implemented by shifting the balance of power in society and convincing people of the need for these demands to be realized.[34] And this is extremely difficult: because degrowth policies are less aligned with vested interests than even those proposed in various Green New Deal platforms, there will no doubt be an even greater opposition to them.

33 See Green New Deal for Europe, gndforeurope.com; and Global Green New Deal, globalgnd.org; Kate Aronoff et al., *A Planet to Win: Why We Need a Green New Deal* (London: Verso, 2019); Stan Cox, *The Green New Deal and Beyond: Ending the Climate Emergency While We Still Can* (San Francisco: City Lights Books, 2020); Riccardo Mastini, Giorgos Kallis, and Jason Hickel, 'A Green New Deal without Growth?', *Ecological Economics* 179, no. 1 (January 2021): 106832; Max Ajl, *A People's Green New Deal* (London: Pluto Press, 2021).

34 Aaron Vansintjan, 'Why the Green New Deal Needs Local Action to Succeed', Greeneuropeanjournal.eu, 2020.

That is why we need a counter-hegemonic strategy, as discussed below. Given the immense uphill struggle we have ahead of us, the time is now to get started.

6.3. Counter-hegemony: Building people power against the growth paradigm

In the early morning of 15 August 2015, around 1,500 people in white painter's suits – among them one of the authors of this book – set off on an unusual journey in the Rhineland in the west of Germany, an area known for its lignite coal mines, the largest source of CO_2 in Europe. Some hours later, hundreds of protesters reached their destination: the Garzweiler opencast lignite mine – despite a massive police presence, supported by around 1,000 of the energy companies' security guards carrying pepper spray and batons. The activists successfully blocked the huge excavators and halted mining that day, sending a message that there should be no more coal mining in Germany. This blockade was the first of many similar and much larger actions of civil disobedience. Ende Gelände, as it was called, meaning 'here and no further', is probably the first major action of civil disobedience to take place in close connection with the degrowth movement. Many people with no prior experience of civil disobedience took part in the action. Many had been mobilized through the degrowth summer school, which had taken place at the climate camp the week before the action. The public reactions to the protest action were – at least in part – very positive.

Ende Gelände is one of a number of similar actions around the globe – from Indigenous Pacific Islanders blocking coal shipping in Australia, to the Dakota peoples and their allies constructing a camp on their sacred land to block the North Dakota Pipeline, to peasants and landless workers in Brazil blocking and occupying farmland slated for industrial agriculture. Like these actions, which Naomi Klein characterizes with the term 'blockadia', Ende Gelände has played a pivotal role in shifting consensus in society so that, by now, large majorities agree that fossil fuels are not necessary and should be phased out. Actions of civil disobedience, often with the wider support of the public, have been vital in shifting hegemonic ideas of what is good and necessary in society.[35]

Interstitial strategies that test alternatives in civil society 'from below', and the non-reformist reforms that shift the transformation of central contours of the social system 'from above', seem to be, at first sight, contradictory, or perhaps unconnected, strategies. They can be related in two ways. On one hand, the wider adoption of nowtopias presupposes changes in society as a whole, and vice versa, as argued above. On the other hand, however, the implementation of radical reforms depends on the establishment of a *counter-hegemony* in order to enforce ruptures in certain areas of society and around key conflicts – and this counter-hegemony needs nowtopias to grow and gain strength.

What is counter-hegemony? Let us briefly revisit the concept of hegemony. As we argued in the second chapter, following Antonio Gramsci, capitalist growth societies not only stabilize themselves through the power of the state and the economic elites. They are also stabilized by the consent and consensus of the governed and subalterns, a consensus which is primarily established in civil society and the media. Thus, hegemony is the system of power and domination that prevails, not just through governments or the market but also through civil society, our way of life, and the ideas that we live by. Particularly central to this is the hegemony of the growth paradigm – the idea that growth is desirable, necessary, and essentially infinite. Any dominant ideology, including the growth paradigm at the core of capitalist ideology, depends on legitimacy and approval.[36] This is the hegemonic system we aim to dismantle.

---

35 Nick Estes, *Our History Is the Future: Standing Rock versus the Dakota Access Pipeline, and the Long Tradition of Indigenous Resistance* (London: Verso, 2019); Naomi Klein, *This Changes Everything: Capitalism vs. the Climate* (New York: Simon and Schuster, 2015).

36 Gareth Dale, 'The Growth Paradigm: A Critique', *International Socialism* 134 (2012), isj.org.uk; Matthias Schmelzer, *The Hegemony of Growth: The OECD and the Making of the Economic Growth Paradigm* (Cambridge: Cambridge University Press, 2016).

But the everyday mind is not uniform, and the promises and visions of a hegemonic imagination always point beyond it. According to Ernst Bloch, they contain a 'utopian surplus' – a common sense that a different world is possible – that can be taken up and strengthened.[37] Counter-hegemony is the flip side of hegemony. Building up a counter-hegemony that can undo the growth paradigm, re-orient our economy towards well-being, and scale down social metabolism in the interim would, conversely, also reshape our daily lives, our imaginaries, and the way we conduct politics and manage the economy. These counter-hegemonic imaginaries and movements can be strengthened in diverse ways: in nowtopias; in the development of a cooperative and solidarity economy; in what Ernst Bloch calls 'militant optimism'; in popular education; through engagement with mainstream media; by running radical candidates supported by social movements to push the debate to the left; through aspirational policies that change people's living conditions; and through a militant 'dual power' grounded in, for example, social movements, unions, strike actions, and people's assemblies – a strategy that we discuss further below.

Crucially, counter-hegemonic common sense is embedded in people's everyday experience and is therefore closely related to the mobilization of social movements and the spread of nowtopias. For one, counter-hegemonic values can be cultivated when people face the cumulative effects of a growth economy, such as cyclical crises, the brutality of elites in defending the status quo, and the destruction of nature. But this is only possible when these experiences of injustice are politicized through organized social movements, contestation, and public debate. Social movements are particularly important because they position themselves against a hegemonic consensus and can be important catalysts for making counter-hegemonic positions part of a future consensus, and they help to politicize people who may have been less active in the past. Shifts in everyday understanding also take place in the manifold commons, nowtopias, projects of the solidarity economy, and social and

---

37 Giorgos Kallis and Hug March, 'Imaginaries of Hope: The Utopianism of Degrowth', *Annals of the Association of American Geographers* 105, no. 2 (2015): 360–8.

ecological struggles – once again, especially when these are politically linked and understood as answers to the worsening crises of growth.[38] As Barbara Muraca argues, concrete utopias and interstitial spaces are central to fostering a counter-hegemonic environment, serving as 'workshops of liberation'. In the words of Giorgos Kallis, alternative economic spaces are not simply localized initiatives, but 'incubators' for counter-hegemony:

> They are *incubators*, where people perform every day the alternative world they would like to construct, its logic rendered common sense. Alternative commons are new civil society institutions that nurture new common senses. As they expand, they undo the common senses of growth and make ideas that are compatible with degrowth hegemonic, creating the conditions for a social and political force to change political institutions in the same direction.[39]

Thus, counter-hegemonic ideas, desires, and demands can be strengthened if more and more people interact with and benefit from the solidarity and cooperative economy, if these freedoms are politicized and social movements are formed around them. A 'militant optimism' (as Ernst Bloch calls it) drives these strategies forward, makes them visible, and reinforces them.[40]

In this sense, advancing visionary policies and experimenting with local alternatives form two sides of the same coin – which ought to be brought together discursively in the degrowth framework. This counter-hegemonic narrative can be made visible through interventions in the social sphere – including through developing new media, conferences and seminars, running radically progressive electoral campaigns (even if they do not win), but also including practices in public space such as adbusting (see section 3.2). The formation of think tanks, strategic engagement with mainstream media and pop culture, developing memes, infiltrating the arts, and engaging actively in the 'war of ideas'

---

38 Burkhart, Schmelzer, and Treu, *Degrowth in Movement(s)*.
39 Kallis, *Degrowth*, 138.
40 Muraca, 'Foreword', 5.

(per Gramsci) through opinion pieces can all create an environment where degrowth ideas advance in the popular consciousness.

Another way to encourage the formation of a counter-hegemonic imaginary is through popular education, engaging people in pedagogical experiences that allow them to readjust mental infrastructures, develop an understanding of being part of society and nature, and become politicized. This can be done through workshops, getting involved in nowtopias, organizing with their colleagues or neighbours, or engaging in political action such as Ende Gelände or a strike at their workplace. Each of these experiences may encourage feelings of enjoyment, empowerment, self-acceptance, mindfulness, solidarity, and finding meaning with others – thus fostering immaterial sources of satisfaction that are central to creating a new common sense around the degrowth imaginary.

Non-reformist reforms and the development of a counter-hegemonic common sense are also mutually reinforcing. First, a counter-hegemonic common sense is the prerequisite for building the political power to democratically implement non-reformist reforms. While local, grassroots initiatives and direct democracy are often put front and centre in interstitial strategies, it is also true that we do need organized majorities willing to work towards a cooperative society so that non-reformist reforms can be voted for and implemented. A central challenge here is that in many of these interstitial initiatives, and in the degrowth movement itself, those involved are often predominantly academically educated and from privileged social milieus.[41] Degrowth concepts can only reach a wider population if they become meaningful by directly relating to everyone's life, and if they are experienced as the promise of radical abundance rather than as the threat of individual renunciation.[42]

It is here that municipal-level changes can be crucial in radicalizing the sensibilities of the majority and creating the desire for more change. While national-level reforms may be initially difficult to achieve, people

---

41 Eversberg and Schmelzer, 'The Degrowth Spectrum'.
42 Aaron Vansintjan, 'Public Abundance Is the Secret to the Green New Deal', Greeneuropeanjournal, 2020.

can organize with their neighbours and at the level of the municipality for initiatives that transform daily life. This could include, for example, social and cooperative housing projects, free public transport, rent strikes, demanding a minimum wage, and resistance to neoliberal mega-projects that shift resources from citizens to transnational investors.[43]

Even at the national level, proposing aspirational, desirable policies can be seen as one way to politicize economic and social issues – they are themselves a kind of advertisement for degrowth. In this way, social-ecological tax reform, a basic and maximum income, the reduction in working hours, and other complementary measures offer new forms of freedom, well-being, and abundance that can help build the collective self-empowerment needed to further develop counter-hegemony and transform political and social institutions.

Finally, whether or not non-reformist reforms get implemented depends on the political pressure of social movements and the existence of already-existing alternatives – without both, they lack inspiration and legitimacy. As the Red Nation argues about the necessity of direct action, 'We must be straightforward about what is necessary. If we want to survive, there are no incremental or "non-disruptive" ways to reduce emissions. Reconciliation with the ruling class is out of the question.'[44] So, even if there are already some connections between the degrowth spectrum and other social movements – especially in the area of movements against extractivism, cars and aviation, and unsustainable and nonsensical megaprojects, as well as, alongside the global environmental justice movements, against the deepening of the crisis of care work or in the form of the Spanish movement of Indignados – these are to be strengthened. Degrowth perspectives should play a role in all the social struggles aimed at undoing the imperial mode of living

---

43 Kali Akuno and Ajamu Nangwaya, eds., *Jackson Rising: The Struggle for Economic Democracy and Black Self-Determination in Jackson, Mississippi* (Ottawa: Daraja Press, 2017); Vansintjan, 'Why the Green New Deal Needs Local Action to Succeed'; Vansintjan, 'Public Abundance Is the Secret to the Green New Deal'.

44 The Red Nation, *The Red Deal: Indigenous Action to Save Our Earth* (Brooklyn, NY: Common Notions: 2020), 34.

and fighting all kinds of hierarchies, discriminations, and power structures for a cooperative way of life.[45] Importantly, this also involves alliances with international movements, particularly those in the Global
South which are today some of the most militant and active: peasant
and Indigenous struggles, landless worker and informal labourer movements, movements for decolonization and post-extractivism and
against structural adjustment and imperialism.[46]

This goes beyond merely strengthening the different social movements that exist: there is also a necessity to think and act strategically
about the kinds of actions these movements might take, and how they
could be more effective. The question of organization is often neglected
in degrowth debates. How exactly will people organize? What are the
mechanisms and processes of organization that will bring about this
transformation? And how can we collectively shape – and plan –
economic life at a community and societal level?

One approach that can be useful to draw from here is that of 'dual
power'.[47] It is called 'dual' power because it represents a system of power
that operates parallel to the state and has the capacity, like the state, to
determine the direction of society. Today, dual power can be understood as the effort to build movements and organizations that have the
capacity to make demands from the state but that do not fully rely on
the state to function. This has three different components, unique, but
related to the strategies for counter-hegemony outlined above.

First, and more obviously, it requires building closer connections
and alliances among different movements, such as those for migrant,

---

45 Asara, *Democracy without Growth*; Eversberg and Schmelzer, 'The
Degrowth Spectrum'; Burkhart, Schmelzer, and Treu, *Degrowth in Movement(s)*;
Joan Martínez-Alier, 'Environmental Justice and Economic Degrowth: An
Alliance between Two Movements', *Capitalism Nature Socialism* 23, no. 1 (2012):
51–73.

46 Nirmal and Rocheleau, 'Decolonizing Degrowth'; Corinna Dengler and
Lisa Marie Seebacher, 'What about the Global South? Towards a Feminist
Decolonial Degrowth Approach', *Ecological Economics* 157 (2019): 246–52.

47 Vladimir Lenin coined this term to refer to a secondary power, outside of
the state, that emerged during the Bolshevik Revolution in Russia through the
worker- and peasant-organized soviets. See Joris Leverink, 'Dual Power',
Roarmag.org, no. 9, 2020.

labour, climate, and racial justice, as well as anti-imperialist, feminist, and anti-capitalist movements more broadly. This can be done through setting up networks of communication and resource-sharing, as well as through organizations that are able to coordinate between movements – some initial efforts have been done here already from a degrowth perspective.[48]

Second, there is also a need for organizing and for building movements that have the capacity to block or make demands from capital and the state. For example, strikes or blockades can be an effective tactic for pushing for demands, rather than merely performing such demands without power to back them up. This is needed because, first and foremost, even if politicians sympathetic to degrowth were to be elected, they would need both support and pressure from movements to push forward degrowth policies, since even such politicians would necessarily confront formidable vested interests to make the needed changes. It is also necessary because, by and large, those in power rarely care when you ask them nicely. When a strike takes away the profits of those in power, they are forced to come to the table and make a compromise. Of course, this requires dedicated, slow organizing in workplaces and where people live in order to build a critical mass of people who can build relationships of solidarity, block corporate profits, and guarantee accountability from elected representatives. Here, degrowth can rely less on the traditional male industrial working class, whose interests are often partly in line with defending the imperial mode of living (by being dependent on fossil-fuel jobs in the automotive or energy sectors, for example), and to a greater extent on new formations and struggles around precarity, patriarchy, racism, ableism, class hierarchies, ecology, and global justice – the 'multitude' of those left behind by the capitalist growth. Further, while those who primarily benefit from the imperial mode of living historically have had a privileged position in terms of making demands from the state, due to labour movements and to the character of labour in the industrialized core vis-a-vis capital, these groups no longer have the means

---

48 Burkhart, Schmelzer, and Treu, *Degrowth in Movement(s)*; Liegey and Nelson, *Exploring Degrowth*; Nirmal and Rocheleau, 'Decolonizing Degrowth'.

to make demands as they once did following the deindustrialization of early industrial nations, the shifting of industrial activities to the Global South, the spatial shift of capital from industry towards information technology and real estate, and the increased precarity of labour more generally. This indicates a need to expand militancy beyond the traditional industrial sectors and into the more precarious and often feminized and racialized service sector, care industry, as well as into communities living in the line of strategically important speculative, extractive, and toxic projects such as gentrification, mining, pipelines, and brownfield sites.[49]

Third, these movements must also have their own sources of power, rather than just the capacity to resist vested interests. A key component here is the solidarity and cooperative economy – which can funnel resources to at-risk communities and on-the-ground struggles. Another component is setting up democratic structures within movements, such as people's assemblies, councils, and confederations of movements and assemblies, so that movements are accountable to their members and are able to deliberate collectively. In linking economic democracy and direct democracy, social movements not only build the capacity to resist existing power structures, but also to chart their own future paths.[50] Thus, a dual-power orientation is one last, but crucial, component of a counter-hegemonic strategy.

49 Michael Hardt and Antonio Negri, *Multitude: War and Democracy in the Age of Empire* (New York: Penguin Books, 2005); Cinzia Arruzza, Tithi Batthacharya, and Nancy Fraser, *Feminism for the 99%: A Manifesto* (London: Verso, 2019); André Gorz, *Farewell to the Working Class: An Essay on Post-industrial Socialism* (London: Pluto Press, 1997); Gabriel Winant, 'The New Working Class', Dissentmagazine.org, 27 June 2017; Jason E. Smith, *Smart Machines and Service Work: Automation in an Age of Stagnation* (New York: Reaktion Books, 2020); Angry Workers, 'Climate and Class Struggle . . . One Struggle, One Plight?', angryworkers.org, 8 November 2021.

50 John Michael Colón et al., 'Community, Democracy, and Mutual Aid: Toward Dual Power and Beyond', Nextsystem.org, 2016; Kali Akuno and Ajamu Nangwaya, 'Build and Fight: The Program and Strategy of Cooperation Jackson', in *Jackson Rising*, 3–42; Tyberg and Jung, *Degrowth and Revolutionary Organizing*.

6.4. Confronting crises: Beyond 'degrowth by design or by disaster'

The combination and interplay of interstitial strategies, implementing non-reformist reforms, and building counter-hegemony is our humble proposal as to how we might best conceptualize the transformation to a degrowth society. A common feature in these strategies is that proponents of degrowth are not waiting for a distant future 'after the revolution' but aiming to change things here and now. Another common feature is that the diversity of approaches is not seen as a problem but as enriching and complementary.[51] But the challenges are enormous, especially in view of the increasingly acute socio-ecological crises and the growing threat from authoritarian nationalist movements, which promise false solutions to the problems of the growth society. Not only is this transformation diametrically opposed to the interests of capitalist enterprises and the richest groups and individuals, as well as to fossil capital and the fascist movements defending it – since it aims to drastically limit or abolish the possibilities for exploitation and accumulation; it also contradicts the interests of national governments, which are fundamentally geared to and existentially dependent on strengthening competitiveness and economic growth. And, finally, not only is the monopoly over the legitimate use of force – held by growth-oriented states – an enormous challenge; potential upheavals in geopolitical relations also present a serious problem. If degrowth were implemented in a single country, it would likely lead to capital flight, capital strikes, geopolitical tensions, and possibly even armed conflicts.[52]

---

51 D'Alisa, Demaria, and Kallis, *Degrowth: A Vocabulary for a New Era*; Eversberg and Schmelzer, 'The Degrowth Spectrum'; Burkhart, Schmelzer, and Treu, *Degrowth in Movement(s)*.

52 See chapter 7 for further discussion on the role of geopolitics and imperialism. See Andreas Malm and the Zetkin Collective, *White Skin, Black Fuel: On the Danger of Fossil Fascism* (London: Verso, 2021); Andreas Malm, *How to Blow Up a Pipeline* (London: Verso, 2021); Matthias Schmelzer and Alexis Passadakis, *Postwachstum: Krise, ökologische Grenzen, soziale Reche* (Hamburg: VSA-Verlag, 2011); Scheidler, *The End of the Megamachine*.

Ignoring these challenges and hurdles, fleeing from reality, is clearly not an option. It's no use sticking our heads in the sand. Nor can we fall into the naïve idea that we just have to talk to everyone nicely to get them on board: we need intentional, large-scale organization and mobilization to achieve the changes we need. The alternative is intensifying global environmental and social crises and the increasingly brutal defence of the imperial mode of living – in short, a world of eco-apartheid.

Yet, what these proposals do not, and in many ways cannot, take into account is the unpredictable: the role of crisis in bringing about change. As we write, the coronavirus pandemic has halted world trade and caused stock markets to collapse, leading to a global recession. Though many epidemiologists did predict the high probability of another pandemic, it took many by surprise and changed everything. In the Global South, governments already heavily laden with debts, previously incurred from structural adjustment, buckled once more under another weight. In the United States, the government initially barely responded, leading to hundreds of thousands of avoidable deaths. Countries like Spain and Canada instituted welfare systems functioning similarly to basic income, nationalized health care facilities, placed moratoria on evictions and froze rents, or instructed companies to produce health equipment in line with state plans. And a historical antiracist uprising broke out across the world, sparked by one of the largest protests of US history against police brutality, structural racism, and the racist 'politics of disposability' revealed by the pandemic.[53] Moments of crisis such as a pandemic are unpredictable events that fall upon us, junctures in the capitalist world-system that can lead to the rapid mobilization of social movements – and of repressive forces. Crises such as these can drastically affect our political projects and the horizons of what is possible by either expanding or curtailing them.

'Degrowth by design or by disaster' has become one of the main catchphrases to think through the role of crisis in bringing about a

---

53 Marc Lamont Hill, *We Still Here: Pandemic, Policing, Protest, and Possibility* (London: Haymarket Books, 2020); Adam Tooze, *Shutdown: How Covid Shook the World's Economy* (London: Penguin UK, 2021); Andreas Malm, *Corona, Climate, Chronic Emergency: War Communism in the Twenty-First Century* (London: Verso, 2020).

degrowth transition.[54] It suggests that downscaling will happen whether we want it or not: it could be planned and largely peaceful, or unplanned and violent. But, by now, readers should recognize that wholesale collapse is explicitly *not* what is meant by degrowth. The wider issue, however, is that this phrase also implies a dichotomy between design and disaster, against which we want to push. Amid an accelerating ecological collapse and faced with the threat of ever greater economic crises, as over-accumulation spirals to ever higher levels, the likelihood of a social-ecological transformation *without* crisis is small. The relations between 'by design' and 'by disaster' are, however, complex: in some cases, disaster can be an opportunity for design; in other cases, an opportunity for deepening repression. A transition by design is unlikely; and yet, by relying on a crisis alone, it won't happen.

In the degrowth literature, it is fair to say that the role of crisis is not well developed. Here we propose a more nuanced approach to the role of crisis in transformation, inviting our readers to think about it further. Let us begin by orienting ourselves once again according to Erik Olin Wright's three transformation strategies: interstitial, symbiotic, and ruptural – which we discussed in terms of nowtopias, non-reformist reforms, and counter-hegemony. Crisis, and its contradictory role in transformation, can also be conceptualized through this lens.

To begin with, *interstitial strategies* have a very important place in responding to crisis – and highlight the need to build up resilient communities. For example, when Hurricane Maria hit Puerto Rico in 2017, it resulted in billions in damages and the destruction of roughly 80 per cent of its agriculture. It was during this dark and frightening moment, when little aid was available, that democratically-run community centres such as Casa Pueblo in the city of Adjuntas provided solar-powered energy, food, and mutual aid to citizens. In any crisis, it is often local communities collaborating democratically based on altruism, resourcefulness, and generosity who are most effective in their response – relying on what Rebecca Solnit in *A Paradise Built in Hell* has analysed as

---

54 Peter Victor, *Managing without Growth: Slower by Design, Not Disaster* (Cheltenham: Edward Elgar, 2018).

proto-communist principles.[55] It is in these tumultuous moments that nowtopias like Casa Pueblo become especially relevant: people are drawn to them, and they in turn help shape the imaginary of what a post-crisis world could look like. Though a small organization, they had an outsized impact on local politics. Following their success, organizations like Resilient Puerto Rico started building out a distributed network of solar power for community centres around the island. Two years later, the whole island rose in protest, kicking out the corrupt governor and, in part inspired by Casa Pueblo, which by then had become well known, began organizing local assemblies in every town and city. And there are hundreds of similarly empowering examples from other crises – from the decentralized, anarchist-inspired mutual aid efforts around the Common Ground collective after Hurricane Katrina in 2005 and Occupy Sandy in 2012 in the US, to the wave of solidarity clinics in Greece providing people with health care and medicine in reaction to EU austerity measures, and, most recently, the mutual aid networks that sprang up around the world in the context of COVID-19. By setting up these alternatives now, they will be in place to support and inspire people when they are shaken out of their daily routines in moments of tremendous change. In this way, the windows of opportunity resulting from the crises can be used as options for action, further expanding bottom-up movements, and awakening the desire for transformation.[56]

Second, crises can also be an opportunity to roll out or expand *non-reformist reforms*. Naomi Klein famously showed how elites used shocks – such as the fall of the USSR or Augusto Pinochet's Washington-backed coup of Salvador Allende – to implement neoliberal reforms,

55 Rebecca Solnit, *A Paradise Built in Hell: The Extraordinary Communities That Arise in Disaster* (New York: Penguin, 2010).

56 Naomi Klein, 'The Battle for Paradise', Theintercept.com, 20 March 2018; Adele Peters, 'During Puerto Rico's Blackout, Solar Microgrids Kept the Lights On', Fastcompany.com, 24 April 2018; Jacqueline Villarrubia-Mendoza and Roberto Vélez-Vélez, 'Puerto Rico: The Shift from Mass Protests to People's Assemblies', Portside.org, 24 August 2019; Out of the Woods Collective, 'The Uses of Disaster', Communemag.com, 22 October 2018; Rhiannon Firth, 'Mutual Aid, Anarchist Preparedness and COVID-19', in *Coronavirus, Class and Mutual Aid in the United Kingdom*, ed. John Preston and Rhiannon Firth (Cham: Springer International Publishing, 2020), 57–111.

eventually siphoning wealth towards the rich and driving greater inequality.[57] Conversely, however, the left can also take advantage of crises to respond effectively and accomplish far-reaching change. The pandemic served as an eye-opening case in this regard – as argued by Tim Jackson: 'With an alacrity that was almost shocking, the coronavirus crisis revealed what capitalism has long denied: that it is possible for government to intervene in the health of society. Dramatically if necessary.'[58] Notwithstanding later changes, initially governments and companies adopted policies that were quite radical, as we noted above. In the context of a mass movement pushing for change and sympathetic political leaders, such moments could have been opportunities to execute a Green New Deal platform at the national level.[59]

Moreover, the state has a central role during these crises, often acting as guarantor of financial institutions when capital investments see sudden and rapid fluctuations and devaluations. Certain events – a pandemic, the loss of confidence in large spheres of investments – can shift the global economy from overaccumulation of capital to a sudden devaluation of it. As Patrick Bond notes, while 'uneven global development is on the degrowth horizon . . . capitalist crisis tendencies should be too.'[60] Normally the brunt of these crises of devaluation are imposed on the poor through increasing their debts, while corporations, banks, and the rich are bailed out, thus creating the conditions for new forms of investment and a continuation of the boom-and-bust cycle. Yet, nonreformist reforms could leverage crisis to the opposite effect: bailing out the poor, erasing Global South debt, letting purely financial assets devaluate, and making bailouts of companies and banks conditional on

---

57 Naomi Klein, *The Shock Doctrine: The Rise of Disaster Capitalism* (New York: Henry Holt and Company, 2010).

58 Tim Jackson, *Post Growth: Life after Capitalism* (Cambridge: Polity, 2021), 165.

59 Graham Jones, *The Shock Doctrine of the Left* (Cambridge: Polity, 2018); Tooze, *Shutdown*.

60 Patrick Bond, 'Degrowth, Devaluation and Uneven Development from North to South', in *Towards a Political Economy of Degrowth*, ed. Ekaterina Chertkovskaya, Alexander Paulsson, and Stefania Barca (London: Rowman and Littlefield, 2019), 157–76.

public ownership, democratic control, and strict criteria for social-ecological well-being.

This can be further illustrated with one example from the COVID-19 crisis. In the early days of the pandemic, the idea gained traction in the US that effectively addressing climate change would involve taking fossil fuels out of the market by nationalizing fuel industries and their oil, gas, and coal reserves – and that this crisis was a good opportunity to do so. A group of scholars in economics and energy studies argued in a 2020 white paper, 'Out of Time: The Case for Nationalizing the Fossil Fuel Industry', that this was the only way 'to overcome many of the systemic hurdles that prevent meaningful action, allowing us to move towards decarbonization in a way that is planned, provides for workers, and supports communities'. In their convincing case, the authors refer to hundreds of historical examples in which the US government had nationalized key industries and critical resources during wars and financial crises. To achieve this, they argued no expropriations or compulsory acquistions were necessary – the easiest would be if the Federal Reserve simply bought majority shares of every fossil fuel company, whose value was at that time of crisis estimated to be no more than $700 billion (and thus much less than the corporate bailouts provided during the pandemic).[61] This example shows how non-reformist reforms could potentially play critical roles in times of crisis. However, as this also makes clear, such an effective response to capitalist crises would need to go beyond traditional leftist or ecological Keynesian approaches by demanding a wholesale restructuring of finance and economy and by fundamentally shifting the balance of power between private capital and the democratic public – a response that certainly needs to be prepared beforehand and requires effective popular pressure.

Third, it is in moments of crisis that *counter-hegemony* can become especially powerful. Crises can shape a counter-hegemonic common sense, in that they are moments when the unfairness and irrationality

---

61 Mark Paul, Carla Santos Skandier, and Rory Renzy, 'Out of Time: The Case for Nationalizing the Fossil Fuel Industry', Democracy Collaborative, June 2020, thenextsystem.org; Stan Cox, *The Path to a Livable Future: A New Politics to Fight Climate Change, Racism, and the Next Pandemic* (San Francisco: City Lights Books, 2021), 83.

of the economic system crystallizes in people's mind – such as, when, during the coronavirus pandemic, many governments prioritized economic growth over people's lives, resulting in a terrible calculus in which the elderly who do not contribute to the economy are considered disposable. Patrick Bond, in an article on the role of crisis for degrowth, points to two key ways that degrowth-oriented movements can organize in response to crises. First, an effective response to crisis involves building links with workers and communities in the Global South, as they are the most affected by the unequal imposition of debt following global economic meltdowns. Second, in the face of post-crisis devaluation of social reproduction (for example, cuts to medicine, housing, or increasing rates of energy costs), organized social movements may campaign for expansion of the requirements for survival, demanding access to basic goods and therefore expanding the desire for a care-based economy.[62] We would add that, more generally, organizational structures that build towards dual power can be activated and strengthened during moments of crisis as people turn to mutual aid organizations, alternative forms of democracy, and nowtopian experiments. What is imperative, however, is that these networks embed international solidarity in their organizing, as moments of crisis are precisely also moments when the losses of the rich tend to be socialized and shifted on to the poorest.

Yet crises are also charged with extreme risk. They can and often do strengthen the right and tend to reinforce the growth paradigm, capitalist hegemony and the logic of law and order that supports it.[63] Today, political coordinates have shifted significantly with the rise of the New Right in the US, Europe, India, and Latin America. These populist movements see success by and large through promising to retain the status quo for the privileged middle class while breeding resentment among downwardly mobile working and middle classes against

---

62 Bond, 'Degrowth, Devaluation and Uneven Development'; Stefania Barca, *Forces of Reproduction: Notes for a Counter-Hegemonic Anthropocene* (Cambridge: Cambridge University Press, 2020).

63 Matthias Schmelzer, *The Hegemony of Growth. The OECD and the Making of the Economic Growth Paradigm* (Cambridge: Cambridge University Press, 2016).

migrants or other 'outsiders' – taking advantage of declining rates of growth and migrant crises to further their agenda of maintaining a hierarchical status quo by any means necessary. This aggressive defence of the fossil fuel–dependent imperial mode of living has so far hardly been taken into account in the strategic discussion on degrowth and in the ecological left more broadly, even though this has a considerable influence on the windows of opportunity for communication and the implementation of degrowth.[64]

In times of crisis, the voter bloc of the nationalist right can expand rapidly, when many people favour stability and order over transition and the insecurity that comes with it. In times such as these, it is imperative that degrowth appears, not as destabilizing and inspiring fear, but as the necessary transformation that both expands people's freedoms and gets to the root of the crisis itself. It is for this reason that a formation of a counter-hegemonic common sense – one that is internationalist, antiracist, queer-feminist, and inclusive, and stands for global ecological justice – is one of our greatest tools in preventing a fascist resurgence today.

6.5. Is degrowth achievable?

Degrowth is not a blueprint that needs to be followed. Rather, it is an invitation, a broad set of principles and ideas, a path whose twists and turns have yet to be taken. We hope that we have convinced you that degrowth is not just a good, timely, and necessary idea, but one that could, in fact, really work. Yet whether a degrowth society can and will become reality cannot be answered theoretically; it depends on the practices, relationships, and organizing of all of us. To make this vision real requires a massive, concerted effort from every corner of society – let alone those who consider themselves to be on the left. We have made some proposals for how to think about the strategies for systemic change, combining nowtopias, non-reformist reforms, and the building of counter-hegemony and transformative power. But to start this

---

64 See, however, Malm and the Zetkin Collective, *White Skin, Black Fuel*.

journey, we need a broad but unified 'movement of movements' for life and against capitalist growth to confidently take the first steps along this path of transformation. You don't have to call this 'degrowth', but we hope that the core concerns of both the critique and the proposal of degrowth will be integrated into more and more struggles and trans-formative practices. There are endless ways to follow this path – from starting a workers' cooperative to setting up a mutual aid centre or pushing for non-reformist reforms in your municipality. Whatever you choose to do, know that our trajectories are aligned.

7

The future of degrowth

When the coronavirus pandemic hit in the spring of 2020, a debate began in almost every country about whether we should shut down the economy to preserve lives, or whether we should keep it going to protect the economy and economic growth. Some countries, such as the United States, Brazil, and Sweden, initially chose to keep the economy largely open, leading to many avoidable deaths. The economy and growth, many said, was much more important. Other countries, however, deliberately shut down parts of the economy to save lives. Here – in a process of crisis and under capitalist, hierarchical, and largely undemocratic circumstances – we could see something resembling degrowth more than anything hitherto experienced. For the sake of argument, the politics to fight the pandemic can be interpreted as a deliberate and planned shutdown of large parts of the economy, with the goal of furthering the common good (flattening the curve and thus saving lives), thereby differentiating between sectors that were essential for the provisioning of basic goods and services and those that were less so. To achieve this shutdown and cushion its effects, governments introduced policies that had long been deemed impossible – furloughing workers, protecting livelihoods, ordering planes to stay grounded, securing employment through short-term work allowances, investing in care, or intervening directly in the production process by nationalizing crisis-ridden companies and health facilities or planning the production of health equipment – all by using the government's sovereign power of money creation. These and many other far-reaching interventions were initially backed by large majorities, and they led to (temporary) significant reductions in emissions and material throughput.[1]

Of course, this is a highly idealized account that only reflects certain aspects of the policies of some governments in the first half of 2020, neglecting that, even then, it was mainly the rich who were bailed out, and that this came with austerity measures, vaccine apartheid colonialism, increasing global inequality, authoritarian tendencies, or public support for and fast rebounding of carbon-intensive industries and emissions. Governments' reactions to the pandemic were *not* degrowth. As we argued in chapter 6, recessions are not degrowth because the economy is still dependent on growth. Similarly, the responses to COVID-19 are not degrowth because, ultimately, they are designed to get the economy back on track towards growth. Nonetheless, initial reactions of some governments to the threat of the pandemic did inspire hope and spark debates about a future that did not go back to 'normal'.

With this debate, and with the unfolding of the various crises related to growth – the chronic emergency of climate catastrophe, mass extinction, and the increasing threat of pandemics – interest in degrowth has grown. The degrowth manifesto that provoked a debate in mainstream Dutch media, which we discussed in the beginning of the book, is symptomatic of this opening of a window of opportunities. Many no longer accept that we must choose economic growth over people's lives

---

1 However, these reductions were later offset by an increase in carbon emissions, as economic crises are often followed with more harmful economic activity, encouraged by governments to rally growth. See Pierre Friedlingstein et al., 'Global Carbon Budget 2021', *Earth System Science Data Discussions* (2021): 1–191. See also Amitav Ghosh, *The Nutmeg's Curse: Parables for a Planet in Crisis* (Chicago: University of Chicago Press, 2021); Adam Tooze, *Shutdown: How Covid Shook the World's Economy* (London: Penguin UK, 2021); Andreas Malm, *Corona, Climate, Chronic Emergency: War Communism in the Twenty-First Century* (London: Verso, 2020); Tim Jackson, *Post Growth: Life after Capitalism* (Cambridge: Polity, 2021).

– the dichotomy is rejected as wrong in its very basic assumptions. In the time since, people's emotional approach towards radical ideas such as those of degrowth have shifted, and, for many, it now seems to be a more realistic proposal than that of keeping the current system intact. Today, a critique of economic growth is common among many who do not want a society that sacrifices human lives for the sake of protecting the annual GDP growth rate.

Fundamentally, questioning economic growth means asking: What kind of society do we want to live in, and how do we get there? These debates have been immensely productive: they have triggered discussions on what a post-capitalist future could look like and have (re-) politicized 'the economy'. And they are an important and timely contribution to understanding and tackling the social, economic, and ecological challenges of the twenty-first century. Today, the multiple limits and crises of the growth society, the hegemonic growth paradigm, and the dynamics of growth and expansion fundamental to modern societies are topics that can no longer be ignored in socio-political discussions and scientific research.

In this book, we have attempted to systematize these fields of research and discussion on degrowth – both as a criticism of growth and as a proposal for transformation. We wanted to make clear that diversity is a central characteristic of degrowth, the strength of which lies precisely in the interplay of different strands of growth criticism, policy proposals, and visions for transformation. Systematizing these various approaches, we think, is necessary to advance the discussion within degrowth and to overcome incomplete or simplified approaches. We have also sought to define the core of the degrowth perspective. Our argument is that degrowth is a political project and a research paradigm that illuminates pathways for comprehensive global justice beyond capitalism: for a convivial way of life in solidarity with others. Degrowth aims to achieve global ecological justice by fundamentally restructuring and radically reducing the energy and material throughput in the Global North through policies, institutions, and everyday norms that promote social justice, self-determination, and a good life for all without being structurally dependent on social dynamics of expansion, acceleration, and accumulation.

Degrowth as a scientific research paradigm has indeed developed rapidly. Nevertheless, there is still a long way to go before the degrowth hypothesis – that it is possible to live well without growth – is even discussed in the mainstream of various disciplines, especially economics. We are also not yet at a point where degrowth is well established and studied, with all the consequences and questions that follow from it.[2] The political path towards a degrowth society seems yet more distant even if everyday common sense – the increasing awareness of ecological catastrophes caused by heatwaves and storms; cyclical crises leading many to feel a sense of frustration with the promises of economic growth; the unease with life in the professional hamster wheel; the everyday crisis of not having enough time to care properly for the young, the old, and the sick; the desire for fairer conditions, meaningful activities, and a more joyful everyday life – encourages more interest in degrowth.

Given the scale of the challenges, there is much more to discuss. Certainly, aspects of the degrowth literature are robust and well developed: in particular, analyses of the capitalist growth economy and the hegemony of the growth paradigm (chapter 2), as well as the different strands of the growth critique, some of which have been discussed for decades (chapter 3). Yet the vision, contours, and central policies of a degrowth society (chapters 4 and 5) and, in particular, the question of transformation (chapter 6) call for deeper analyses yet. There are still many open questions, research gaps, and unresolved controversies. We argue that some key issues are often ignored within the degrowth discussion and require critical engagement. We have already discussed some of them in the chapters of the book – such as the ambivalent and unresolved relationship to the state, the significance of the feminist growth critique for degrowth, or the question of how degrowth should respond to the rise of authoritarian, racist, and populist parties and movements.

In order to advance this discussion, we would like to conclude by taking a look at some other important challenges that have been only

2 Giorgos Kallis et al., 'Research on Degrowth', *Annual Review of Environment and Resources* 43 (2018): 291–316.

partially addressed in the book. The goal is to stimulate a deeper discussion. We focus on four areas.

7.1. Class and race

In parts of the degrowth discussion, there is a tendency to mainly focus on ecological issues and to do so from a class-blind and consumer-focused perspective that downplays social issues and fundamentally depoliticizes degrowth. This may be due to the fact that in the degrowth spectrum, a majority of participants are white, come from privileged social contexts in the Global North, and have academic backgrounds.[3] However, the focus on individual consumer renunciation – on consuming eco-consciously and less – ignores the perspectives of people who can't afford to do so, and it stands in the way of a broader growth critique and the development of majorities who would support degrowth positions. Not only is this analytically false and politically foolish, but it also does not have to be this way. As we have shown, degrowth has the tools to address class in all its complexities. Degrowth, we argue, should speak directly to the question of class inequality, acknowledge and address the existing structural growth dependencies and their repercussions, analyse the role of consumption and the critique of consumerism through the lens of class, and emphasize distributive justice, public abundance, and social security in the vision of a degrowth society. In order to place degrowth on a broader social footing, the focus could be further strengthened by centring the improvements of a degrowth transition – from radical redistribution through wealth and inheritance taxes, to shortened working hours and an 'alternative hedonism', to a re-evaluation and more gender-equal redistribution of care work and to the expansion of public and democratically controlled services – in the areas of housing, energy, water,

---

3 Dennis Eversberg and Matthias Schmelzer, 'The Degrowth Spectrum: Convergence and Divergence within a Diverse and Conflictual Alliance', *Environmental Values* 27, no. 3 (2018): 245–67. For a critique see Matthew T. Huber, 'Ecological Politics for the Working Class', *Catalyst* 3, no. 1 (2019), catalyst-journal.com.

and mobility – that are accessible to all. Degrowth needs to link these policy proposals more strongly with ongoing struggles such as those around rent and housing, the phasing out of fossil fuels and a just energy transition, feminist struggles around care work, trade union struggles, and the movement for economic democracy – such as efforts to democratize the workplace.[4] Beyond this, and more practically, those who advocate degrowth must also move beyond academic confines and discourses to engage organically with movements and society at large. In the end, degrowth is in great part about overcoming class society – not only within capitalist centres where the advantages of the imperial mode of living accumulate, but globally.

Race is also under-explored within degrowth. There is an urgent need to incorporate into degrowth an understanding of how racial capitalism drives class relations within and between countries, and is intrinsic to capitalist growth. Much could be learned from how social movements are bringing together concerns for racial, migrant, and environmental justice, as well as aligning with Indigenous land struggles and support-ing refugees' right to freedom of movement. Further, the connections between prison systems, policing and criminalization of marginalized populations, and segregation can also be understood in a degrowth context. For example, gentrification and urban development often occur for the sake of growth and increasingly operate through a sheen of 'green growth', but depends on the exclusion of minorities – such as migrants, homeless, Indigenous, and Black people. Overcoming a growth econ-omy thus means tackling these dynamics of exclusion that actually drive the growth machine. Ultimately, the development of a degrowth society is a question of decolonization – as it concerns who owns the land, who takes care of the land, and how we can build a world of abundance that does not exclude whole groups of people.[5]

4 Corinna Burkhart, Matthias Schmelzer, and Nina Treu, eds., *Degrowth in Movement(s): Exploring Pathways for Transformation* (Winchester: Zer0, 2020); Stefania Barca, 'The Labour(s) of Degrowth', *Capitalism Nature Socialism* 30, no. 2 (2019): 207–16; Leigh Brownhill, Terisa E. Turner, and Wahu Kaara, 'Degrowth? How about Some "De-alienation"?', *Capitalism Nature Socialism* 23, no. 1 (2012): 93–104.

5 Jamie Tyberg and Erica Jung, *Degrowth and Revolutionary Organizing*

7.2. Geopolitics and imperialism

Degrowth advocates have not adequately tackled the geopolitical ramifications of the transition that they envision. This includes the relationship between growth, the state, imperialism, and militarization, and the
political-economic effects degrowth would have on international relations and on communities in the Global South in particular. Although
the focus on ecology, social metabolism with nature, and structural
growth constraints of the economy has strengthened our understanding of the material dimension of current crises, many parts of the
degrowth spectrum focus primarily on cultural critiques of or normative discussions about consumer society and the prospects of bottom-
up alternatives, side-lining world-systemic relations or a materialist
perspective on global power dynamics. The role of the state in disrupting necessary transformations, its monopoly on violence, the racist
incarceration system, the borders it maintains, and the power of the
global military-industrial complex are often not confronted in the
degrowth literature.[6] For example, it is not at all clear under which
conditions and based on what balance of social forces elites would give
up their privileges, which are built on uneven development and global
injustice and backed up by military might. The degrowth vision can
hence sometimes come across as naïve and unrealistic, constricted to a

---

(New York: Rosa Luxemburg Foundation, 2021); Erica Jung, 'Rethinking Our
Relationship to Land: Degrowth, Abolition, and the United States', degrowth.org,
September 28, 2020; Jamie Tyberg, *Unlearning: From Degrowth to Decolonization*
(New York: Rosa Luxemburg Foundation, 2020); Walter Rodney, *How Europe
Underdeveloped Africa* (London: Bogle-L'Ouverture Publications, 1972); Cedric J.
Robinson, *On Racial Capitalism, Black Internationalism, and Cultures of
Resistance* (London: Pluto Press, 2019); Keeanga-Yamahtta Taylor, *Race for Profit:
How Banks and the Real Estate Industry Undermined Black Homeownership*
(Chapel Hill, NC: University of North Carolina Press, 2019); Harsha Walia,
Border and Rule: Global Migration, Capitalism, and the Rise of Racist Nationalism
(Chicago: Haymarket Books, 2021).

6 See, however, Giacomo D'Alisa and Giorgos Kallis, 'Degrowth and the
State', *Ecological Economics* 169 (2020): 106486; Max Koch, 'The State in the
Transformation to a Sustainable Postgrowth Economy', *Environmental Politics* 29,
no. 1 (2020): 115–33. See also Walia, *Border and Rule*.

vision of cultural change. Further, while it seems obvious that the transition towards a degrowth society would, even if confined to early industrialized countries, have serious consequences within the current world system, these questions have not been much discussed thus far. The geopolitical dimensions of degrowth could be further advanced by creating closer links with fields that study geopolitical, world-system, and securitization dynamics, as well as by building alliances with anti-militarist, anti-imperialist, and decolonial movements.[7] As we have argued, the repercussions of degrowth in industrialized countries on communities in the Global South should be an integral part of the degrowth agenda, from export markets or tourism to the questions of reparations – another key issue that requires more sustained exploration.[8] How could degrowth be managed in a way that overcomes global inequalities and does not deepen dependency, while also addressing centuries of colonial and ecological debt on the part of industrialized countries? We also need to better analyse how the rise of emerging markets like China, which account for an increasing share of global growth, emissions, and consumption, complicates the degrowth agenda.[9] Furthermore, we know little about the possibilities for degrowth at a transnational level, on the related transformations and role of institutions such as the European Union or the United Nations – key questions, since the transition to a degrowth society is hardly conceivable in

---

7 Arturo Escobar, 'Degrowth, Postdevelopment, and Transitions: A Preliminary Conversation', *Sustainability Science* 10, no. 3 (2015): 451–62; Padini Nirmal and Dianne Rocheleau, 'Decolonizing Degrowth in the Post-development Convergence: Questions, Experiences, and Proposals from Two Indigenous Territories', *Environment and Planning E: Nature and Space* 2, no. 3 (2019): 465–92; Corinna Dengler and Lisa Marie Seebacher, 'What about the Global South? Towards a Feminist Decolonial Degrowth Approach', *Ecological Economics* 157 (2019): 246–52.

8 See Max Ajl, *A People's Green New Deal* (London: Pluto Press, 2021).

9 Jin Xue, Finn Arler, and Petter Næss, 'Is the Degrowth Debate Relevant to China?', *Environment, Development and Sustainability* 14, no. 1 (2012): 85–109; Rowan Alcock, 'The New Rural Reconstruction Movement: A Chinese Degrowth Style Movement?', *Ecological Economics* 161 (2019): 261–9; Tyler Harlan, 'Green Development or Greenwashing? A Political Ecology Perspective on China's Green Belt and Road', *Eurasian Geography and Economics* 62, no. 2 (2021): 202–26.

a single country. Finally, degrowth needs to engage with and support demands for demilitarization, a strengthening of democratic world politics, a globally just trade and monetary order, and freedom of movement – in particular for climate refugees. All these are key levers for a degrowth transition that furthers global ecological justice.[10]

7.3. Information technology

A third void in the degrowth debate is the relationship between degrowth and digitalization, and the question of how the transition to information capitalism will transform the degrowth agenda. On the analytical side, degrowth literature rarely engages with the literature on the political economy of digitalization, which has produced analyses on, among other things, how digitalization affects growth in its various dimensions (resource and energy consumption, well-being, alienation, accumulation dynamics, care work, South–North relations, and so on).[11] More generally, degrowth's relationship to technology, and especially to information technology, must be clarified. There are certain streams of degrowth that sweepingly reject most forms of industrial-scale technologies. With regard to digital technologies, in parts of the degrowth discussion a scepticism and a practical rejection of digital technology such as smartphones prevails. This is unfortunate, because, at the very least, degrowth actually has a lot to offer contemporary discussions about information technology. Degrowth suggests ways to go beyond the absurdities of Silicon Valley's endless pursuit of growth, which – given the tendencies of

---

10 Kenta Tsuda, 'Naive Questions on Degrowth', *New Left Review* 128 (2021): 111–30, 122. Here, of fundamental importance is, of course, building alliances with Global South movements as well as further pushing the mainstream discussion on the continuing legacy of colonialism, while also developing policies and political platforms that centre climate debt and demilitarization.

11 Steffen Lange and Tilman Santarius, *Smart Green World? Making Digitalization Work for Sustainability* (Abingdon: Routledge, 2020); Paul Mason, *Postcapitalism: A Guide to Our Future* (London: Macmillan, 2016); Nick Dyer-Witheford, *Inhuman Power: Artificial Intelligence and the Future of Capitalism* (London: Pluto Press, 2019).

saturation in consumer markets – has to create products such as the metaverse, or non-fungible tokens, as yet again new areas for appropriation, speculation, and accumulation. Instead of an economic system that depends on continuous accumulation and creates the technologies to enable this, and instead of spending endless time and resources on these farcical ventures, we could just stop the growth machine and create technologies that actually benefit us and allow convivial relationships to flourish. There are those within degrowth and allied to it who do refer to the objective possibilities arising from a prospective digital commons.[12] In our book, and building on this perspective, we argue for a nuanced approach that democratically weighs the benefits and costs of technologies based on social, ecological, and participatory criteria and accordingly for a society that autonomously sets limits, also for specific technologies (see chapter 5). Degrowth, we argue, should actively engage in these debates and fathom the possibilities that might arise, while critically highlighting the democratic challenges and the often flatly ignored resource and energy requirements and their global justice implications. Beyond critique alone, degrowth needs to analyse how platform cooperativism – which refers to efforts to build new, cooperatively owned platforms to replace for-profit social media and entrepreneurial platforms – could be integrated into the degrowth vision.[13] Closer cooperation with the peer-to-peer movement and the innovations in new currencies and value production, manufacturing, and knowledge-sharing is another potential avenue.[14] There is a need to build links between degrowth and labour movements in the information technology and logistics industries, for example with Amazon and Uber workers – and to connect those struggles with an analysis of the material impacts of smart technologies.

---

12 Michael Bauwens, Vasilis Kostakis, and Alex Pazaitis, *Peer-to-Peer: The Commons Manifesto* (London: Westminster University Press, 2018); Eversberg and Schmelzer, 'The Degrowth Spectrum'; Silke Helfrich and David Bollier, *Free, Fair, and Alive: The Insurgent Power of the Commons* (Gabriola Island, BC: New Society Publishers, 2019); Lange and Santarius, *Smart Green World?*

13 Trebor Scholz and Nathan Schneider, eds., *Ours to Hack and to Own: The Rise of Platform Cooperativism, a New Vision for the Future of Work and a Fairer Internet* (New York: OR Books, 2017).

14 See P2P Lab, 'About', p2plab.gr/en.

And, ultimately, links must be made with the communities living and working in rare earth and lithium mines, as well as with those living in the sacrifice zones of toxic waste generated by information technology.[15]

7.4. Democratic planning

Finally, degrowth should engage more explicitly with the question of planning. Curiously, while 'planning', 'design', or 'coordination' are often mentioned in degrowth discussions, the reality of planning itself – its primary actors, whether it is centralized or decentralized, participatory or imposed – is rarely engaged with. For example, a recent paper defined degrowth as 'a planned reduction of energy and resource use designed to bring the economy back into balance with the living world in a way that reduces inequality and improves human well-being'.[16] However, there is strikingly little explicit engagement with or research into what exactly 'planning for degrowth' could look like, given the fact that degrowth favours decentralized structures over hierarchical and bureaucratic centralized ones. In view of the ambition and challenge of a transition beyond growth, this is a gap that urgently needs to be addressed. If degrowth requires transforming our infrastructure (for example, away from automobile-dominated mobility), our energy systems (for example, away from a centralized fossil fuel industry), and basically our entire economy (away from profit-oriented private businesses), then, as we have argued, this must involve various forms of short-term and long-term democratic planning. Economic planning has long been an important question in both economics and socialist literature and is today seeing a revival with the rise of new left parties and visionary proposals such as the Green New Deal.[17] Proponents of

---

15 Nick Srnicek, *Platform Capitalism* (Cambridge: Polity, 2016); Martín Arboleda, *Planetary Mine: Territories of Extraction under Late Capitalism* (London: Verso, 2020).

16 Jason Hickel, 'What Does Degrowth Mean? A Few Points of Clarification', *Globalizations* 18, no. 7 (2021): 1105–11, 1.

17 Leigh Phillips and Michal Rozworski, *The People's Republic of Wal-Mart: How the World's Biggest Corporations Are Laying the Foundation for Socialism*

degrowth are in a position to engage more actively in this debate and further investigate which kinds of planning degrowth could involve, but also, how the discussions about planning would have to be adapted for the specific questions, requirements, and challenges that arise in the context of degrowth. These include, for instance, the management of absolute caps in resource use and emissions, their harmonization with social targets such as universal access to essential goods and services, planning just transitions in the phase-out of dirty sectors, or questions regarding the participatory planning of investment and divestment decisions, including technological innovation and what has been discussed as collective *dépense*.[18] Practically, questions need to be asked regarding how degrowth would relate to, for example, the logistics industry, existing infrastructure projects, and the democratic management of planning. We do not know enough about how new digital tools can help in supporting democratic planning and decentralized decision-making – and thus how they can help to democratize economic activities, a project central to degrowth. How would democratic, decentralized planning take nature, and ecological boundaries, into account? And what kind of economic indicators would degrowth economies use to inform planning if GDP were abandoned, keeping in mind that a universal indicator that breaks the entire world down into one number will not suffice to understand the multiplicity of dimensions relevant to democratic decision-making from below?

(London: Verso, 2019); Jasper Bernes, 'Planning and Anarchy', *South Atlantic Quarterly* 119, no. 1 (2020): 53–73; Marta Harnecker and José Bartolomé, *Planning from Below: A Decentralized Participatory Planning Proposal* (New York: Monthly Review Press, 2019).

18 See, however, Martín Arboleda, *Gobernar la utopía: sobre la planificación y el poder popular* (Buenos Aires: Caja Negra Editora, 2020), chapter 4; Fikret Adaman and Pat Devine, 'Democracy, Participation and Social Planning', in *Routledge Handbook of Ecological Economics* (London: Routledge, 2017): 517–26; Simon Tremblay-Pepin, 'De la décroissance à la planification démocratique: Un programme de recherche', *Nouveaux Cahiers du Socialisme* 14 (fall): 118–25 (thanks to Bengi Akbulut for this reference); Jin Xue, 'Urban Planning and Degrowth: A Missing Dialogue', *Local Environment* (2021): 1–19.

7.5. Degrowth: A visionary pathway to post-capitalism

Despite new interest in degrowth, many – from conservatives to social democrats, eco-modernists, and productivist leftists – disregard it as a romantic idea that need not be taken seriously, an idea which is regressive and anti-consumerist, or one that is either too radical or not radical enough. But, even if there is room for debate on some of the gaps and biases in the degrowth literature, degrowth should not be rejected outright. In this book, our goal has been to show that degrowth poses a set of key questions that all emancipatory alternatives need to address, which are often ignored. Degrowth offers answers to them as well. If people want to know how to address the challenges of ecological destruction, the ideology of capitalism, or the industrial, hierarchical, and imperial mode of production, degrowth is much more advanced than many other realms of debate – and this includes many of the debates on the left.

Degrowth, we argue, is one important guide to a world beyond capitalism. We will need others on its side. Throughout the book, we have sought to draw out some of the best approaches from the degrowth literature in order to offer a diverse, yet visionary, critique of capitalism – including proposals for how to move beyond it. We have not shied away from some internal debates and contradictions and have presented them honestly in order to enable people to make up their own minds. We hope that this introduction contributes to a wider interest and understanding of degrowth – both as an emerging scientific research paradigm and as a political project. We do not think degrowth itself will develop into *the* social movement bringing about the urgently needed social-ecological transformations. But we hope, in the next counter-hegemonic cycle, that larger blocs of social movements and political forces opposing both capitalist globalism and authoritarian nationalism will integrate key critiques, perspectives, and proposals from degrowth. Theoretically and practically, there are many open questions, conceptual opportunities, and political challenges. It is our conviction that these can be addressed through critical debate and political engagement. Because one thing is certain: we need to break free from the capitalist economy. Degrowth gives us the tools to bend its bars.

Index

Red Nation, the 272
redistribution 2, 33, 46, 192
reforestation 208
refugees 290
relational freedom 204
relationality 209
relative income effect 99–100
re-municipalization 220–1
renewable economy, transition to 8
renewable energy 62
reparations 33, 200–1, 244, 245, 247, 292
reproduction, forces of 232–3
reproductive justice 185
reproductive work 133, 137–9, 232
research 15
Research & Degrowth network 192, 213,
    263
Resilient Puerto Rico 278–9
resistant practices 32
resonance 205, 209
resource prices 71
retail therapy 23
revolutionary change 33
revolutionary Realpolitik 214, 253, 263
richest 1 per cent 227
richest 10 per cent 227
Riesman, David 97
rights 22, 57, 226–7
right-sizing 199–200
Robinson, Kim Stanley 179
Rockström, Johan 68
Rojava, Syria 259
Roosevelt, Franklin D. 8
Rosa, Hartmut 112, 115, 205n
Rousseau, Jean-Jacques 106
ruptural strategies 254, 255

Salleh, Ariel 139–41
Santarius, Tilman 88
savings 80
scarcity 127–8, 128–30, 131
scarcity economics 184
Schachtschneider, Ulrich 263
schooling systems 207
Schumacher, E. F. 115, 145
Schumpeter, Joseph 238
scientific research paradigm 17
secular stagnation 26, 71
securitization 292
self-determination 32, 105, 143, 195, 202,
    203–4, 205, 213, 287

self-limitation 203, 238
self-optimization 115
self-organization 7
self-sacrifice 258
self-sufficiency 183n
self-transformation 260–1
semantic frame 27–9
sharing economy, the 187
simplicity 105
Situationist International 107, 108–9, 109
slaves and slavery 50
Silence (magazine) 12–13
slow economy 184
Smil, Vaclav 82–3
Smith, 39
snail, as symbol of degrowth 151–2
social alternatives, evaluation 211
social conflicts 55
social decline, societies of 27
social ecology 152–3
social hierarchy 98
social imaginary, the 180
social improvement 58
social institutions 208–9
social justice 4, 195, 202, 203, 213, 225,
    287
social media 108–9, 294
social metabolism 84–6, 152–3, 193, 213
social metabolism democratization 33,
    237–44
social mobility 100
social organization 102–3
social participation 102
social returns 59
social rights 202
social security 33, 225–6, 242
social transformation 34, 180, 182–3,
    251–2
society–nature relations 153
socio-ecological interactions, prioritizing
    93
socio-economic growth critique 76, **78**,
    94–104
    consumer criticism 97–8
    and degrowth debate 102–4
    early 94–7
    happiness and income paradox 98–101
socio-technical systems 151–2
solar energy 81–2
solidarity 264
solidarity economy 186, 216–17, 219–20